WITHDRAWN
UTSA LIBRARIES

(E X) T E N S I O N S

(EX)TENSIONS

Re-Figuring Feminist Criticism

Elizabeth A. Meese

UNIVERSITY OF ILLINOIS PRESS
Urbana and Chicago

Library of Congress Cataloging-in-Publication Data

Meese, Elizabeth A., 1943–
    (Ex)tensions : re-figuring feminist criticism / Elizabeth A. Meese.
    p.   cm.
Includes bibliographical references.
    ISBN 0-252-01682-3 (cloth : alk. paper). — ISBN 0-252-06105-5
    (paper : alk. paper)
    1. Feminist literary criticism.   2. Women in literature.   3. Women
    and literature.   I. Title.
PN98.W64M44   1990
809′.89287—dc20
                                                        89-20176
                                                        CIP

"[T]his problem of dealing with difference without constituting an opposition may just be what feminism is all about."

—Jane Gallop, *The Daughter's Seduction*

"Right now, I think the fundamental challenge of feminist criticism is to 'break set'—to reground our figures—of both sexes—and to refigure our grounds."

—Judith Kegan Gardiner, *The Challenge of Feminist Criticism*

"The subject of revolution is ourselves, is our lives."

—Audre Lorde, *A Burst of Light*

Contents

Preface

This project grows directly out of my previous work, *Crossing the Double-Cross: The Practice of Feminist Criticism* and represents what I see as an (ex)tension of that work. My interest now is to clarify and to focus some of the concerns first explored there: feminism's desire to be inclusive, critical theory's refusal of the monolithic or illusory whole, the metalogical conflict between theoretical discourses on "woman" and politically committed feminist action in the world. As a literary critic approaching these issues, I continue in the conviction that criticism is best written in the dialectic of theory and practice, moving back and forth between the theoretical and the practical. But now I choose to work within the context of specific texts which present reading lessons concerning the theoretical and the practical since I find such separations impossible to hold with confidence, as they regard both critical practice and practical struggle. Thus, it is my hope to explore the dimensions of the one as it finds itself expressed in the other.

The specific focus of *(Ex)Tensions: (Re)Figuring Feminist Criticism* is the ways in which women's writing helps us to figure the relationship between the consolidation of identity (individual or personal and collective/feminist) and the politics of inclusion which threatens the notion of singular identity but appears to be politically necessary for a socially effective and responsible feminism. I am not concerned with specifying a way or a place for feminist critical writing, but with discovering spaces between, creating gaps and wedges to problematize the oppositional terms that compel our allegiances and keep us apart in structured antagonism. These dis/continuities, breaks, and contra/dictions are constructed in the interest of formulating a new economy of relationships that wants to trans/form institutional structures (cultural, social, educational, political, and economic). Such changes require the impossible: that we rewrite the dominant and dominating logic of bipolar oppositions—masculine/feminine, self/other, center/margin—which characterize Western thought and structure its discourse in an economy of the Same. While the "going beyond" is metaphysically and perhaps discursively impossible, it is a desire necessarily engaged and articulated in language's figurative capacity, or at least suggested in its excesses.

I propose a kaleidoscopic approach to this crucial question of the relationship between art, politics, language, and identity. Because this entrapping self/other dichotomy inhabits the language and logic of Western white analytic discourse, I resist the geographical imperialism of "English Studies" to consider texts by women from other cultures for ways of staging breaks in this system (Rigoberta Menchu, a Guatemalan Quiché Indian; Leslie Silko, a Laguna Pueblo Indian; and Sherley Anne Williams, an African-American). Similarly, I examine writings by women exploring the parameters of received identity, scrutinizing their "place" in the topography of the controlling logos (in chapters on the white South African writer Nadine Gordimer; on the lesbian/feminist poet Adrienne Rich; and on an assortment of American feminist critics). In a number of chapters (those on Nadine Gordimer and a white "French" woman, Marguerite Duras), I hope to approach the question of relationships through the way in which the author represents the struggle of white women characters confronting racial and political difference; I later read this narrative of relationship as told by the African-American writer Sherley Anne Williams. The overall project is conceived in the interest of formulating different ways of "figuring" (out)—that is, being able to determine or at least to represent determinations through the figures of language—these relationships in the hope of re(dis)covering newly powerful discursive and political understandings, if not articulations, for feminist critical theory and practice.

Acknowledgments

I am particularly grateful to Claudia Johnson and David Miller for long-standing collegial support and friendship, to Richard Rand, who first taught me the idea of reading lessons, and most of all to Alice Parker for the inspiration of her example. For years of consultation and advice, I thank the members of the Language and Social Theory Group, particularly Stephen Karatheodoris, Harold Weber, Rhoda Johnson, and Lynn Adrian. Unflagging assistance which made my research possible was contributed by English graduate students: Terrie Byrne, Andrea Cumpston, Chapman Greer, Alicia Griswold, Catherine Jones, Jackie Duffey, and Michelle Hippler.

I am especially in the debt of the University of Alabama Research Grants Committee, which provided summer grant support in 1987 and 1988 so that I could complete Chapters 2, 3, 4, and 6, and, finally, to Sara DeSaussure Davis, in the office of the dean of Arts and Sciences, who provided support for typing at a crucial time.

Chapter 3 appeared in a slightly shorter version in *Feminism and Institutions*, edited by Linda Kauffman, and an abbreviated version of Chapter 7 appeared in the *Dictionary of Literary Biography: Modern Criticism since 1955*, edited by Gregory Jay. I wish to thank the publishers for permission to reprint. Finally, I want to express my appreciation to Ann Weir and Patricia Hollahan for their assistance and support throughout the editorial process.

(Ex)Tensions: Feminist Criticism
and Deconstruction

Schema, figura: a shape, a form, as well as that particular form that one can give to language in order to move away from the common or the banal. It should be noted that the term *figura* bears etymological connotations with a representational construct. *Figura* was formed by adding the suffix *-ura* to the root *fig-*, from which *fingere*, to mold or to model soft clay and in the broader sense to imagine or to invent, derives.

—Marie-Rose Logan,
"Introduction" to Gérard
Genette, *Figures of Literary
Discourse*

Is it the inevitable conclusion to the formation of an interpretive community that its constituency, its specialized language, and its concerns tend to get tighter, more airtight, more self-enclosed as its own self-confirming authority acquires more power, the solid status of orthodoxy, and a stable constituency?

—Edward Said, "Opponents,
Audiences, Constituencies, and
Community"

At this complex and exciting moment, so vexing it has been termed an "identity crisis" (Alcoff), it is difficult to "see" a direction for feminist literary criticism. Some critics claim that it has no theory, and others (usually female) want feminist criticism to stay away from theory, or at least deconstruction and psychoanalysis (and sometimes Marxism), which have become theory's synonyms. Some critics (usually male) attack feminist criticism for staging a hegemonic role reversal whenever it strays from enumerating structures of "female experience" to criticize past critical practice ("theirs"); others protect their own positions as radical intellectuals by noting the wonders of feminist criticism, but then neglect to mention any feminist critics or writers (a

1

charge some feminist critics also level against feminist deconstructors). A number of these moves strike me as attempts to mark off a territory preliminary to defending it against trespassers or to charting the terrain in one's own interest—enterprises perhaps inseparable from "doing" literary criticism. So, in a sense, they represent rather commonplace critical problems. The complaints on which I wish to focus, because they trouble me most, are those made by feminist critics, and especially by black, Marxist, and lesbian feminists, including those women outside the academy. Theirs are claims already advanced in the name of "feminist literary criticism" and, as such, signal the need for feminist criticism to reconsider questions of the differences within what we take for that rather unproblematic identity, Feminist Literary Criticism. These complaints suggest, as well, that issues of identity always entail and complicate matters of relationship, and vice versa; that, indeed, an intricate choreography of simultaneous attention and articulation must be performed if feminist criticism wants to represent itself, which indeed I believe it does and should, as a polyvocal and polylocal (perhaps even polysexual) discourse.

Since deconstruction made its entrance on the critical scene, feminists within the academy have diversified their approaches and allegiances. Feminist Literary Criticism—to the extent that the term functions as the expression of a consolidated identity, type, or recognizable form—has always represented itself as having a substantial cast in the "margins," but perhaps if this identity is to persist, we should consider how it might designate a space figured as "all margin" in the interest of disseminating the center and transforming the place of knowledge into a free space. Recent conventions as well as much current literary critical work, however, can be read as a challenge to the differences between "our" feminist papers and those presented in "other" sessions on the program, and, specifically, to the meaning of the term Feminist Criticism. Feminist psychoanalytic critics, Marxist feminists, and feminist deconstructors (and combinations of these) like Shoshana Felman, Peggy Kamuf, Jane Gallop, Gayatri Spivak, and Barbara Johnson are speaking at least in part to different audiences, and always in rooms too small to contain those interested in explorations of feminist criticism in relation to deconstructions of sexual difference. While the causes and implications of this development are perplexing and somewhat obscure, it is clear that a remarkable shift has been taking place.

Although my assertion of such categories of presumed difference is itself an arbitrary construction, an effect of an already consolidated feminist critical identity, the exploration of this provisional opposition

2

promises to be instructive. If a shift is occurring in the position of feminist criticism, the explanations for it might be several: (1) the multiple approaches which have marked feminist criticism from its beginnings; (2) the refusal to define feminist criticism and politics explicitly; and (3) the ensuing inability to identify or to accept the "feminists" among psychoanalytic, Marxist, and deconstructive critics. Alice Jardine, in her provocative study *Gynesis: Configurations of Woman and Modernity*, presents the problem of self-definition in a somewhat different light, through a rewriting of Freud's (in)famous question on women, by offering a series of questions which demonstrate that feminist critics have not addressed the problem of what feminist literary critics want: "That is, to and for whom are feminist critics writing? Is there a desire for men to start writing 'about' woman in a 'feminist style'? For them to stop writing about women altogether? Do feminist critics want the male critics to read them? Or do they want just women to do so? It is essential to ask these banal and yet unanswerable questions because feminist scholarship has reached something of a double bind, raising numerous strategical and political problems" (56–57).[1] These internal problems (of concern to self-defined women's studies scholars/feminists) are further complicated by the current revolution in critical discourse—a phenomenon which tends to separate literary critics, including feminists, by age, training, institutional affiliation, and inclination, and doubtless further exacerbates differences of race and class as well.

As interesting as the construction of new explanatory possibilities, an effort of suspect strategic value, is the projection of potential effects. It is easy to imagine some ways in which feminism's critical diversity, signaled in the historically unanswered (unanswerable) question of what "woman" wants, can be construed as positive, a fluidity worth defending against fixity, but we can just as easily cite instances where Feminism's avowed pluralism masks the repression of differences.[2] These are the problems I want to consider here by extrapolating from the critical moment that I have composed as a tension between and within feminist criticism and deconstruction.

The danger inherent in the tensions inhabiting feminist literary criticism (particularly when it is figured as a path or direction) is that the work of self-identified feminists (what we might call academic or women's studies feminists like Showalter, Baym, Auerbach, and Kolodny) will languish somewhere along the wayside, losing its revolutionary potential, while criticism undergoes a revolution in theory and practice which many refuse to acknowledge or engage, or that the force of this feminist opposition, coupled with our presumed

3

loyalties, will carry feminist criticism along with it and out of all relationship to contemporary practice or some useful forms of it. Is it important or even possible to know, for example, if it makes a critical and/or political difference to locate one's work in the tradition of writers like Woolf, Beauvoir, Lorde, and Rich as compared with Lacan, Barthes, Foucault, and Derrida? Or, is this choice not a choice, a "both/ and" rather than the suspect "either/or"? In other words, do those feminist literary critics who claim one lineage rather than another hold their path without interference, the two being so separate and distinct? Can these competing and ostensibly conflicting paths be represented as alternative figurations (among many) through a space which is feminism?

While this dilemma is not unique to feminism, feminist criticism, like other aspects of contemporary theory and philosophy, is facing a figurative crisis of its own.[3] In 1971, J. Hillis Miller cautioned (and I think this speaks to other current tensions within the profession, for example, those between some creative writers and critics, in addition to differences between critical schools), "A critic must choose either a tradition of presence or the tradition of 'difference,' for their assumptions about language, about literature, about history, and about the mind cannot be made compatible" (216). (Another suspicious either/ or?) Some of us have already begun to experience the effects of differences within feminist criticism. In the absence of conscious, careful efforts to identify similarities and differences among the practitioners of feminist and other modes of criticism, we run some perilous risks, the most worrisome being persistent fragmentation and alienation, which undermine feminism's ability to form the political coalitions needed to bring about change (even on the level of the academic institution). Of at least equal concern is the threat of a feminism which, figuring itself in its own voice from the site of the academy, fails to engage the political conditions of women who speak and write from other locations in other voices.

Perhaps most troublesome at this moment is the way in which Feminist Literary Criticism (with a proper name) seems to be staging its own internal power plays—maneuvers not unfamiliar to black, lesbian, nonacademic, and socialist feminists—as reigning Feminist scholars, in the interest of a particular though perhaps unexamined Feminist ideology, reenact patricentric gestures of exclusion that have historically characterized "phallic" authority's production of orthodoxy or dogma. A double issue of *Tulsa Studies in Women's Literature*, released later in revised form as *Feminist Issues in Literary Scholarship*, edited by Shari Benstock, allows us to witness how Said's question in my epigraph pertains to Feminist Literary Criticism. While some collections attempt to represent other stories—*Making a Difference*, edited by Gayle Greene and Coppélia Kahn; *Feminist Studies/Critical Studies*, edited by Teresa de Lauretis; *Conjuring*, edited by Marjorie Pryse and Hortense Spillers; *Feminist Criticism and Social Change: Sex, Class, Race in Literature and Culture*, edited by Judith Newton and Deborah Rosenfelt; and a recent issue of *Feminist Studies* (Spring 1988) come to mind—any number of anthologies and current journal articles rewrite, that is, write again and again, the narrative of Feminist Literary Criticism's impulse to homogeneity that can be read in the *Tulsa Studies* issue and the Benstock collection. The collection, to which I will return later, demonstrates some of the ways in which feminist critics are aligning themselves, figuring oppositions, and shaping feminist discourse for the years ahead: how the soft clay of the emerging field is being molded and formed, "bodied" forth. The recent impulse to write the history of feminist literary criticism and to en-tome women's writing as *The Tradition in English* (the subtitle of the *Norton Anthology of Literature by Women*) reflects similar efforts to refine, tidy up, and codify the field of inquiry. The institutionalization of Feminism or Feminist Literary Criticism, as doctrine or proper name (which I want to differentiate from "feminism(s)" or the lowercase "feminist literary criticism"), involves the constitution of a doctrinal group with, as Foucault puts it, "the political means of maintaining or of modifying the appropriation of discourse, with the knowledge and the powers it carries with it" (*Archaeology* 227). Thus, the means of exclusion are suggested whereby the autodidact, the "self-taught" or "other-styled" critic, is relegated to the margins, having refused subjection to the discourse of the group through proper subordination to the perspectives of today's Feminist luminaries, having resisted appropriate "disciplining." Said elaborates this point: "Licensed members of the field, which has all the trappings of a social institution, are identifiable as belonging to a guild. . . . To acquire a position of authority within the field is, however, to be involved internally in the formation of a canon, which usually turns out to be a blocking device for methodological and disciplinary self-questioning" (16). Another way of putting this, and Marcelle Marini does it eloquently in her essay "Feminism and Literary Criticism: Reflections on the Disciplinary Approach," is to say that Feminist Literary Criticism has become "a field" and is therefore endangered by, just as it profits from, having a proper discourse legislated by a body of experts. Both the potential risks and prospective gains should compel the attention of all of us engaged in "disciplining" roles, as teachers and scholars, in the positions of students being "disciplined," and in our roles as members of diverse communities who have a stake in the production and operation of "power/knowledge" within academic and community-based feminism.

If, for example, we consider Feminism from the point of view of the African-American woman, the Indian woman, the Japanese woman, the term may appear imperialistic, an extension of the socio-economic and politically hegemonic practices of white middle-class U.S. women over others, since the former make up the majority of "equal rights" and academic feminists. In most cases, Feminism as it is written and debated, as we receive it and produce it, is of necessity a movement and a discourse inhabited by the limitations of those women with the luxury, the privilege, to speak, to write, to study, and to be heard. Gayatri Spivak amplifies this view with her reminder that "the structure or means of production of explanations is, of course, a very important part of the ideology of cultural explanations that cannot be clearly distinguished, in fact, from the explanations themselves" (*IOW* 105), a point she supplements elsewhere with her statement that, when we try to address the question of who this "other" woman is, to encompass her within a feminist inclusivity or universality, in India alone we discover a woman's labor force that is 84 percent illiterate, primarily composed of unorganized peasant labor, speaking eighteen or twenty different languages ("Asked" 10). Thus, the white U.S. feminist's desire for identity, inclusion, and speaking difference, as fundamental tenets, involves a task of awesome and forbidding magnitude, if not hopelessly reprehensible arrogance, recalling Deleuze's lesson from Foucault on "the indignity of speaking for others" ("Intellectuals" 209).

Feminism has as many definitions as it has advocates and challengers. The inadequacy of the definition appears in the very surface structure of the word: it is singular ("Feminism")—a feature reiterated in simple dictionary definitions—a doctrine (that is, dogma, "A principle, belief, or statement of idea or opinion, especially one formally or authoritatively considered to be absolute truth") and a movement ("The activities of a group of people to achieve a specific goal").

In this singular, totalizing form (and the consolidation of identity into/through definition is unavoidably this), Feminism, as proper name, as "dogma," "absolute truth," and "specific goal," is a term we cannot afford to keep. As Audre Lorde observes in "The Master's Tools Will Never Dismantle the Master's House": "If white American feminist theory need not deal with the differences between us, and the resulting difference in our oppressions, then how do you deal with the fact that the women who clean your houses and tend your children while you attend conferences on feminist theory are, for the most part, poor women and women of Color? What is the theory behind racist feminism?" (*Sister* 112). In its unexamined form, Feminism presents itself as monolithic ("massive, solid, and uniform"): Identity. It speaks the institutionalization of Feminism and the attendant constitution of feminist critics as a group in the service of doctrine. Feminism, like an(y) institutionalized discourse, functions to enforce homogeneity, Sameness, through the figuration of its identity and at the expense or through the control of how differences are represented.

In addition to the complexities entailed in the material specificity of the lives of individual women throughout the world, which Feminism, as the singular, proper name has to engage if it is to represent all women (which it wants to do), feminism confronts within the more homogeneous nation of white, middle-class U.S. feminists other troubling diversities and tensions. In *Feminist Politics and Human Nature*, Alison Jaggar remarks that "the term *feminism* carries a potent emotional charge. For some, it is a pejorative term; for others, it is honorific. Consequently, some people deny the title 'feminist' to some who would claim it, and some seek to bestow it on those who would reject it" (5). We see this more clearly if we move away from apparently simple definitions of feminism to the more complex considerations of feminist critical discourse.

Feminist criticism, in some quarters, is spoken of as having staged a break with the Fathers. The production of such a self-representation is not viewed problematically—that is, in terms of how it seeks to impose itself through certain forms of order or limitation, through a rhetoric which is ideologically and "ethically" charged. This impulse is evident as early as 1979. In "Toward a Feminist Poetics," Elaine Showalter offers the following analysis:

> We are moving towards a two-tiered system of "higher" and "lower" criticism, the higher concerned with the "scientific" problems of form and structure, the "lower" concerned with the "humanistic" problems of content and interpretation. And these levels, it seems to me, are now taking on subtle gender identities, and assuming a sexual polarity—hermeneutics and hismeneutics. Ironically, the existence of a new criticism practiced by women has made it even more possible for structuralism and Marxism to strive . . . for systems of formal obligation and determination. Feminists writing in these modes, such as Hélène Cixous and the women contributors to *Diacritics*, risk being allotted the symbolic ghettos of the special issue or the back of the book for their essay (38).

7

Showalter attributes this "theoretical impasse in feminist criticism" to the fact that feminist critics "are both the daughters of the male tradition, of our teachers, our professors, our dissertation advisers," etcetera, "and the sisters in a new women's movement which engenders another kind of awareness and commitment, which demands that we renounce the pseudo-success of token womanhood" (39). This particular construal of woman's divided consciousness, about which I will comment later, proves to be a convenient (interested) fiction which validates a particular kind of criticism ("matrilinear" or "gynocritical"), although it pretends not to judge, not "to betray the other," while Showalter has already spoken against the ("patrilinear") feminist deconstructors. Her final call for a "new language, a new way of reading" precludes the possibility that this work might issue from a feminist deconstructive practice. Neither does Feminist Literary Criticism acknowledge its own counter-discourses or contra/dictions—the ways in which language never says only (or even) what we want it to mean, that as meaning is produced, it carries along with it the shadowy traces of the exclusions according to which a letter, a word, a position asserts itself as "itself." Her Feminist Criticism associates itself with a "humanistic field," the terrain of "*her*meneutics," and feminist writing in a post-structuralist mode stands for or mimics the more "scientific . . . *his*meneutics."

It is only fair to note that this piece was published at a time when many feminist critics' suspicions were first aroused by the strange new work produced in the wake of structuralism. In her 1981 article, "Feminist Criticism in the Wilderness," Showalter reiterates her earlier refrain of woman's "dual parentage," maintaining that "a woman's text is not only mothered but parented; it confronts both paternal and maternal precursors and must deal with the problems and advantages of both lines of inheritance. . . . a woman writing unavoidably thinks back through her fathers as well" (203). Still, her position remains virtually unchanged, although the fathers of these feminist daughters gain increased specificity: "So long as we look to androcentric models for our most basic principles—even if we revise them by adding the feminist frame of reference—we are learning nothing new. And when the process is so one-sided, when male critics boast of their ignorance of feminist criticism, it is disheartening to find feminist critics still anxious for approval from the 'white fathers' who will not listen or reply." (Showalter has already noted that feminists are speaking to this "male-stream" through *PMLA*, *Diacritics*, *Glyph*, *Tel Quel*, *New Literary History*, and *Critical Inquiry*.) She continues, "Some feminist critics have taken upon themselves a revisionism which becomes a kind of homage; they have made Lacan the ladies' man of *Diacritics* and have forced Pierre Macherey into those dark alleys of the psyche where Engels feared to tread" (183–84). Despite her protest to the contrary—that she does not want "to replace psychoanalysis with cultural anthropology as the answer to all our theoretical problems or to enthrone Ardener and Geertz as the new white fathers in place of Freud, Lacan and Bloom" (205)—Showalter fails to explain just how feminist revisions of Freud, Lacan, Marx, and Derrida (at best a reductive characterization of post-structuralist feminist criticism) might prove inferior to the male-derived eclectic criticism of the seventies and her own importation of Edwin Ardener's and Clifford Geertz's models as theoretical components of feminist criticism. It is difficult to see that she hasn't done what she claims she hasn't done. How, in fact, is the parentage of Showalter's text to be understood any differently from the lineage of Gallop's or Kamuf's texts? How does any instance of feminist criticism escape being another "dress-up" game, or "Annie Hall" *reprise?*[4]

I do not want to give the impression that Showalter is alone in her resistance to feminist deconstruction. Indeed, even practitioners like Kamuf, Gallop, and Spivak figure this relationship with judicious caution. The essays in *Feminist Issues in Literary Scholarship*, notably those by Showalter, Baym, Marcus, Robinson, and Auerbach, which appeared in both the journal and the anthology, display a variety of figures for post-structuralist feminism; the reviews by Duyfhuizen and Spillers in the journal issue complicate the discussion of what feminists are saying feminist literary criticism is and who may practice it. But as a "pioneering feminist critic," a role Showalter claims for herself, she is instrumental in shaping a dichotomy which, despite her continuing claims to openness, urges feminist critics to stick with theory received "via the women's movement and women's studies" ("Towards a Feminist Poetics" 35)—that is, theory which ostensibly has been "mothered" but only obscurely fathered. Over the years, Showalter has tempered her views on deconstruction, but traces of her disapproval can still be read through the more subtle rhetorical scene of her recent essay, "Women's Time, Women's Space: Writing the History of Feminist Criticism," included in *Tulsa Studies* and the Benstock collection.

Here Showalter presents a disclaimer in the form of a topographical decentering—"our Women of Letters are scattered all over the map rather than concentrated in major universities"—instead of a quarrel with the notion itself of these or any "Women of Letters" who "dictate what will henceforth be 'normal' [in this case, 'Feminist'] criticism." In her role as Woman of Letters, Showalter wields the power to establish direction and fears the inevitably impending obsolescence or displacement that necessarily occurs when one is a "pioneering practitioner"; rather than engage these and other issues of difference (among the truly pressing "Feminist Issues in Literary Scholarship"), she masks them through an unquestioned insistence that Feminist Literary Criticism does not derive "from a single authority or a body of sacred theoretical texts. There is no Mother of Feminist Criticism, no fundamental work against which one can measure other feminisms" (29). She fails to apply the designation Woman of Letters to all women who write (or perhaps read and speak), missing the opportunity to create the rhetorical leverage needed to operate a dispersal rather than a consolidation of identity.

Although Showalter professes a desire to avoid "a hostile polarization of French and American feminist discourse," I find it hard to overlook her alignment with those feminist pioneers (Atalantas) whom she describes in the following passage:

> For some pioneering feminist critics . . . the glittering critical theories of Derrida, Althusser, and Lacan seem like golden apples thrown in Atalanta's path to keep her from winning the race. In the adaptation of continental theory to feminist practice they see the dictatorship of the dominant, the surrender of hard-won critical autonomy to a reigning language and style. The post-structuralist feminist, some would argue, is a rhetorical double agent, a little drummer girl who plays go-between in male critical quarrels. (35)

By figuring the post-structuralist feminist critic as a vacuously sinister go-between acting in the service of men, Showalter perpetuates the opposition she professes to abandon in favor of work "on both fronts . . . enriched by dialectical possibilities" (36). Cautioning practitioners to engage theory suspiciously, she reinscribes the opposition in the way she "figures" deconstruction and Feminist Criticism's necessary resistance to it: "Insofar as the production of theory is not the business of modern criticism, there will be increased pressure on feminist criticism to accommodate itself more and more to the prevailing terminologies and systems, abandoning in the process the political priorities and the concerns for the personal that have made it so effective in the past" (41). The problem with Showalter's critiques, as Janet Todd explains in some detail, is that they advance positions which are never clearly elaborated: "with these images, Showalter often escapes from the difficult implications of her genuine arguments against deconstruction and theory" (45). Among the powerful, unexamined assumptions

10

reinforcing this opposition are the notions that socio-historical feminist literary criticism has no theoretical or practical relation to past and present criticism written by men, and that deconstruction ("modern criticism") is neither political nor feminist. These latter features Showalter is correct in demanding of deconstructive criticism in its negotiation with feminism if one is to be of use to the other. Nonetheless, there can be no interplay (an unexplored potential of the "double agent" or "go-between" as shuttle) between feminist literary criticism and deconstruction, a motive relating this book to my previous work, if feminist criticism refuses to be as accommodating as it asks deconstruction to be or if feminist criticism installs itself in a position of denial, refusing to explore the repression it works in the interest of securing its difference as (socio-historical) identity through its own insistence on "a reigning language and style."

In what appears to be a persistent Feminist narrative, Nina Baym similarly characterizes feminist Marxist and deconstructive practice as against feminism, speaking to and for men while ignoring the tradition of feminist literary criticism. In "The Madwoman and Her Languages: Why I Don't Do Feminist Literary Theory" she writes: "feminist theory addresses an audience of prestigious male academics and attempts to win its respect. It succeeds, so far as I can see, only when it ignores and dismisses the earlier paths of feminist literary study as 'naive' and grounds its own theories in those currently in vogue with the men who make theory: deconstruction, for example, or Marxism. These grounding theories manifest more than indifference to women's writing; issuing from a patriarchal discourse, they exude misogyny. Mainly, feminist theorists excoriate their deviating sisters" (45). And this recourse to the path of feminist pioneers represents a refrain which persists today, for example, in Annette Kolodny's call in the *Chronicle* for a history of feminists and feminist activity, "commencing with the first women who dared to introduce feminism in the classroom or who organized on behalf of women's studies programs" ("Respectability" A52) as an *antidote* (my word, recalling the *pharmakon*[5] as poison and remedy) for the institutional respectability that is eroding feminism's revolutionary force, an antidote for what she calls the "pedantry and moral abdication" of "theory devoid of activist politics" (A52).

The parallel threat of the notion that politics or discourse can be devoid of theory presents itself in Nina Baym's contribution to the Benstock collection. Of all the critics represented here, Baym, out of her desire to defend critical pluralism, is the most hostile to literary theory. When viewed from a post-structuralist perspective, her characterizations of both pluralists (not theorist?) and theorists, if we are to hold theory and deconstruction as somehow conveniently synonymous, are most surprising:

> Pluralists [feminist practitioners like herself] anticipate the unexpected, encourage diversity; while legalists [theorists who center their words on the Word] locate the correct position and marshal women within the ranks. Theory is, by nature, legalistic; infractions—the wrong theory, theoretical errors, or insouciant disregard for theoretical implications—are crimes; theory is a form of policing. Pluralists "dance"; theorists "storm" or "march." Theorists constrain what may be allowably discovered; their totalizing, in the name of feminism, reproduces *to the letter* the appropriation of women's experience by men, substituting only the appropriation and naming of all women's experience by a subset of women: themselves. This repetition of authoritarian structure betrays an infatuation with male forms and deconstructs the feminist project (45).

In this uncanny passage, Baym attributes to pluralists the terms that deconstructive critics have used to describe themselves, in their opposition to the hegemonic force of centrism masked by pluralism. The passage produces a vertiginous disorientation where Baym's inclusive, diverse pluralism excludes deconstruction and Marxism, and I am no longer sure of who does what to whom or how I am contributing to the problem and the solution.

According to Baym, theory is an effort to imitate or seduce men. Proceeding without proper acknowledgment of feminist work, it discredits or slights the pioneers, and must therefore be the work of nonfeminists—men or women who act like men, who are uncannily out to seduce other men. Theory, which Baym believes she speaks without (or outside of), becomes the scapegoat for all discursive and institutional crimes against women, the antithesis of feminism: "Deconstruction . . . is a procedure whose vocabulary, shared by nonfeminists and men, yields identical results no matter whose texts it analyzes . . . to me it [theory] seems a guarantee of continued oppression" (49). Blind to the contentious, repressive exclusions established by her own analytics, Baym mocks Jane Marcus's "Storming the Toolshed" (especially p. 626): " 'She must . . . she must . . . she must.' If that *she* is *me*, somebody (once again) is telling me what I 'must' do, asserting (not incidentally) her own monopoly on truth as she does so. I've been here before" (59, n. 32). Baym shares the antitheoretical bias of numerous other feminists writing today. Certainly the admonitory rhetoric that marks feminists' desires to transform society and its institutions, including the institutions of literature, tests the bonds of sisterhood. While we can each be shown in our most uncomplimentary moments—and I am undeniably guilty, by taking people at (as) their word, of seizing these moments so frequently indistinct from the instances of our greatest passions—"theorists," it would seem, have no corner on fractious or contentious discourse. Or as Laurie Finke notes in "The Rhetorics of Marginality: Why I Do Feminist Theory," an astute reading of the journal issue (which, to their credit and in the interest of negotiating positions, *Tulsa Studies* published), the angriest essayists "direct their anger not at patriarchal ideology, or men, or even women who self-consciously reject feminism, but at other feminists whom they perceive as practitioners of 'phallic' feminism" (258).

Not all feminist figures shape up the same way or add up to the same sum. Nina Auerbach's "Why Communities of Women Aren't Enough" represents feminist criticism as "playing a deadly serious game of pluralism" (153). Her defense of pluralism as an identity for Feminist Literary Criticism takes shape in opposition to Showalter's gynocritics. Auerbach claims that she wants to refuse the temptation "to legislate the future direction of feminist criticism" which its institutionalization seems to invite. Her goal in opposing gynocriticism is to protect her right to engage texts signed by male writers ("writers I love")—a project which the following unfortunate figuration might lead one to sum up as "eating the father" or "critical cannibalism": "Writing about something is my way of claiming power over it: its magic is dispelled by being understood; it loses its frightening otherness as it takes on the shape of my consciousness and my language. Probably I share the primitive superstition that by writing about the patriarchy, as by eating it, I engorge its power" (156). Auerbach reluctantly prefers "the lure of assimilation" ("the lesser of two evils") over "the lure of separatism" because "we live in one world . . . with men" (155). These pluralistic gestures of inclusion or assimilation do not, however, encompass critical works by men, though her professed goal is the "transmutation [of their work] . . . through a female prism" (155). Lumping together male "critics" Jonathan Culler, Jerome Mc-Gann, Wayne Booth, Lawrence Lipking, Terry Eagleton, and J. Hillis Miller (all of whom ostensibly occupy a different status from that held by male "writers"), Auerbach erroneously notes: "Lauding their own enlightenment, they fail to cite the names of any actual, female feminist critics" (154). She fears women's continued anonymity through absorption by male theorists who, in her view, perform one kind of writing while women write another.

The "engorgement" of patriarchy, as figure and strategy for feminist assimilation, is Auerbach's liberal feminist response to what appears to be an essentialist belief in all women's marginality. She explains, "I think that it is important for us as women to make the ways
of men and the patriarchy part of our imaginative map. It is not enough
to know each other. . . . Understanding the power that subordinated
us is the first step toward demystifying, diminishing, and finally
engorging that power" (156). The men in Auerbach's world exist in a
singular and undifferentiatedly oppressive relationship to women.
Gender is the only distinction operating here, and it takes the form of
a non-relation which women bridge through "engorgement." She
sustains and shores up her point with the familiar topographical (con)-
figuration: men at the "center" depend on women at the "margin,"
and vice versa. In the "real" world out there, Auerbach maintains,
"communities of women are a mere whisper on the margins of fallen
society" (157). These (non)relationships between men and women in
society, between feminist (read "female"?) literary critics and "others,"
between theorists ("male" ?) and feminist practitioners are admittedly
tricky ones to figure (out). Indeed, it is unlikely that we will ever write
or speak our way out of them since our subject positions, which are
multiple and varied, direct our words, and our words and those who
receive them designate who we are as fully as we do in our wish to
control how we are perceived and how our words are heard and read.

Jane Marcus's socialist feminist analysis in "Still Practice, A/
Wrested Alphabet: Toward a Feminist Aesthetic" gives a new twist to
Showalter, Baym, and Auerbach, complicating the crisis in critical
figuration. Marcus also resists "current theories based in psychology
or in formalism" (79) in favor of a model for feminist criticism based
on " 'read'[ing] the body of the text of the oppressed and silenced . . .
a frustrating and selfless activity that must include . . . a recognition
of one's own complicity in the silencing of the subject" (80). Her
insistence on the examination of privilege—based on sex, race, class,
heterosexism—directs us toward a deeper understanding of differences within. Her attention to "the other" or the other-in-one's-self
(as complicit in repression) allows me to locate her in a position which
might break open Feminist Literary Criticism as institutional discourse
and begin negotiations between feminisms and other criticisms, particularly deconstruction.

This is surely not a function Marcus claims for herself. She denies
what I regard as deconstruction's usefulness in figuring the space
between the utopic lives of feminist Amazons and the historically
repressed and silenced woman—how it helps us to read difference as

absence or the relationship between what is and is not there, to speculate about what is and is not represented, and why. Marcus's image
of deconstructive reading echoes the objections of others considered
thus far. Rewriting Virginia Woolf's figure of Alan and Phoebe from
A Room of One's Own (103–4), she describes deconstructive criticism as
an assertion of ego, a violation or rape of the text (ego, penis, and pen
being indistinguishable). Again, deconstructive reading is presented
as a male activity, or at least a nonfeminist act. She groups all "American formalist deconstructive critics" together as theorists who write
"the hieroglyphics of a self-appointed priesthood" (86), à la Geoffrey
Hartman. Theory assumes what appears to be a male body: "Theory
is necessary and useful but is not superior to other literary practice or
immune to historical forces. In fact, despite its birth in the left-wing
beds of Europe, it has grown in practice to be an arrogant apolitical
American adolescent with too much muscle and a big mouth" (87). It
is a territory reserved for men or for women who forget what it is to
be feminists. Placing the "female critic" as theorist within the family
drama, Marcus describes her in terms that bring to mind Jane Gallop's
The Daughter's Seduction. Marcus characterizes the feminist literary
critic as playing the "daughter to the father, not daughter to the mother
. . . she must provide herself with a male medium through whom to
approach the text" (89). Noting that it is possible to be a feminist critic
"without insisting on the role of daughter of Derrida or *femme de
Foucault,*" she calls on Spivak and Kamuf, for example, whose insights
she values, to abandon "male formalist models for criticism" (90). The
question remains, however, by what means those valuable insights
are produced.

The preferred figure for the feminist critic in Marcus's work is a
separatist female. Women should cultivate loyalties to one another (in
the form of acknowledging the scholarship of feminist sisters) and
abandon relationships with men (a model derived from fathers and
brothers). The sexualization of Marcus's proposed model for feminist
criticism grows more complicated as she presents the "ego-less"
reader/critic being seduced by the writer: "Woolf's critical 'still practice'
as the enraptured reader, ego-less and open to the text rather than
aggressively attacking it, is consistent with the goals of feminist philosophy. The reader's desire to be enraptured by the writer, which Woolf
celebrates, is very different from contemporary criticism's assertion of
intellectual superiority over ["domination" of] writers and books"(86).
This image of feminist criticism as a response to textual seduction,
rather than as an initiator or coproducer of intercourse, suggests various theoretical and philosophical problems. Does Marcus have in

mind only certain texts? Women's texts? And certain critics (female?)? I would suggest that Marcus's plot for feminist criticism requires a woman reader and writer, and that it is easier to write this particular narrative in terms of Marcus's relationship to Virginia Woolf than, say, to Norman Mailer or Ernest Hemingway. If, as it seems, the critic in this scheme is sexed female, can we say that Marcus is urging the adoption of a lesbian separatist reading practice? If she is, she should certainly make explicit such a potentially revolutionary case. Marcus's description of feminist criticism resembles a reversed reinscription of traditional criticism's homosocial (men speaking to men about men) or misogynistic heterosexist structure. Still, Marcus's resistance to deconstruction leads her to proscribe collaboration between feminist women and men practicing feminist criticism: "One is as reluctant to lend them [male theorists practicing feminist criticism] the materiality of our reading practice as ballast as one is to see good feminist critics throw that materiality overboard to soar in the high ether of theory with the men" (87). But what is the "materiality" of a feminist reading practice? Certainly not the letter or the figure through/in which our practice spells itself out. Is it rather in this working out, a matter of our *bodies*, the material ground for separatist feminism, identity in remove rather than in relation? Further, it is somewhat curious that Marcus should figure feminist criticism in terms that amount to a (lesbian) seduction theory—the controversial strategy enacted most memorably in a "heterotextual" form by Jane Gallop, that feminist psychoanalytic deconstructor who has in her texts so outrageously and wittily negotiated with the "forbidden" male authorities.

As is the case in various ways with other critics discussed thus far, the value of Marcus's analysis—specifically, her desire as a socialist-feminist "to expand and elasticize" (87) the world of writers, readers, and subjects of study—goes beyond these moments that I have isolated here and which Finke elaborates in detail (258–60). In this context, I should add, however, that Marcus's impulse to speak "for her sisters" (79), a compulsion many of us who are committed to global feminism share, deserves thoroughgoing scrutiny and self-suspicion. At the same time, the contrast between Marcus's comments on deconstructive feminism and her long-standing effort to form alliances with others suggests the extent to which our figures write us. As a critic of certain exclusions, Marcus offers us a keen sense of some of the institutionalizing forces at work within Feminist Literary Criticism. Questioning Shari Benstock's conviction that feminist critics are willing to change, Marcus introduces what might be read as the subtext of the feminist critical drama—loyalty and betrayal: "I assure her that several of my feminist colleagues, who agree with my analysis, have nevertheless urged me to delete some of the following remarks. Standing on tiptoe, under an umbrella, in the margin of the margin, can we really engage in dialogue with each other?" (88). I have experienced similar effects of feminist criticism's institutionalization, having been asked five minutes before giving a short version of this chapter at an MLA session, to modify my remarks about "pioneering feminist critics"; further, I have been asked to intervene with university presses on behalf of feminists whose writing was slated for exclusion in part because feminist readers deemed their critiques inappropriate. Feminist deconstructive critics report being judged unsuitable by virtue of their scholarship, for positions in Women's Studies—a complaint advanced historically by lesbians, blacks, and Marxists.

Some feminist critics, acting as though they know the limits of the margin, legislating acts of propriety, believe they know what that elusive term "Feminist Literary Criticism" means and who can practice it. An anonymous reviewer, for example, made the following objection to my last book manuscript (and similar complaints have been made of this one):

> This manuscript derives from an apologetic stance shared in many books and essays (Jane Gallop's *The Daughter's Seduction* is cited) by self-styled feminist critics and theorists. They call for a reconciliation between feminism and some other critical or theoretical mode—feminism and Lacan, feminism and Freud, feminism and Marx, feminism and Derrida, feminism and whoever; but the questions of why there 'should' be such a reconciliation, why it is always the feminists rather than the Marxists or deconstructionists who seem to feel the need for it, and above all why the reconciliation *always requires compromise from the feminist side* (that is, feminism is always the side that is asked to incorporate the methods or assumptions of the other) are scarcely posed and never dealt with at any length. I want Meese to say: why is she doing this? what good is it going to do feminism? (One can hardly argue that deconstruction needs the feminists' help, so it can only be the good it does *us* that is a concern here.)

The language of this passage discloses some important though unexamined assumptions concerning the reviewer's sense of feminist identity politics and the limits of relationship they entail. There are "self-styled feminist critics and theorists" and then there is this reviewer and, presumably, her community of reference (one she perhaps shares with feminist "pioneers" and/or socio-historical feminist critics). Who or what is she? An "other"-styled feminist critic, produced by a sanc-

17

tioned, disciplinarizing agency or some requisite set of experiences—not an "other" at all? One who does not write or rewrite Freud, Marx, Lacan, and Derrida? And what can these "self-styled" (disloyal and improperly apprenticed or unauthorized) theorists argue? Only that deconstruction or Marxism needs feminism, not that negotiations might be mutually beneficial. Recalling Jardine's earlier queries, this review veils a peculiarly circular assumption—that "self-styled" feminists write to persuade feminists not deconstructive critics (whereas "other"-trained feminists, those non-Marxist, nonpsychoanalytic, nondeconstructive critics, write only to persuade or to confirm one another). And isn't this "other-styled" though proper Feminist Literary Criticism rewriting, or being written by, the criticisms of Abrams, Empson, Frye, Crane—the unacknowledged fathers who parented the criticism of the sixties and seventies? Similarly, Finke observes, "While feminist new critical readings of literary texts can provide a 'turn of the screw' to male readings, they remain indebted to the aesthetic values and ideological fictions of New Critical doctrine—the autonomous, unified, experiencing self, the superiority of 'poetic' experience to the mundane concerns of economics and politics, and the holistic coherence of the literary text as a reflection of experience—a doctrine articulated by a male intellectual elite" (262). In short, we might ask: what are the rules of/for Feminist Criticism?

But why am I doing this? Why am I saying these terrible things about Feminist Criticism? Not in order to attack or deride, not because I know how to figure feminist or deconstructive criticism "correctly," but because I read another story in Feminism's phobic representation of deconstruction[6] and am searching for a strategy to open Feminist Criticism to feminisms, to create a space within which proper and improper questions and assertions may take place. The threat of deconstruction, borrowing for a moment Hillis Miller's simple opposition, is that it speaks a "different" language, a language of difference which cannot be controlled by a language of presence, the language of nondeconstructive feminism, which wants to exclude what it sees as other than "itself." The issues underlying the fears feminism and deconstruction have of one another can be described very briefly in a simple, totalizing scheme useful only as the continuation of another discussion. American academic feminism fears deconstruction because (1) the latter denies critical pluralism its mask of inclusion, seeing pluralism instead as a capitulation to the center, both forcing and denying choice; (2) further, deconstruction denies certainty to Feminism's ethical vision, demanding that it reveal the exclusions, the traces that are covered over in order to make any such unicentered, coherent narrative of identity possible (the reason I argue that Feminism is more nearly feminist when we speak of it as "feminisms"); and (3), deconstruction would force feminism to (dis)articulate itself in terms of an as-yet-unimaginable end, an unending drama with a changeable cast. Deconstruction likewise fears feminism because (1) the latter wants to write female desire in nonoppositional, nonmasculine, or nonheterosexist terms; (2) further, feminism wants male deconstructive critics to refuse their power over women, to read and respond to texts written by women, and to apply the practices of deconstruction to their own phallogocentrism in the interest of unsettling male heterosexual and homosocial privilege (matters carefully written out of most male deconstructors' works in the U.S.); and (3) finally, feminism challenges male deconstructors to review the knowledge of centuries, constructed through (among other things) the repression or absence of women to permit the production of the particular androcentric, heterosexist, racist narrative we call Western Civilization.

Approaching the assumptions underlying these fears, Lillian Robinson's article "Feminist Criticism: How Do We Know When We've Won?" focuses on some of criticism's most serious exclusions. She asks questions which prepare the way for coalition politics by attempting to identify differences within as they relate to feminist women critics, and by extension to the emerging issue of what Peggy Kamuf calls "femmeninism" and what others discuss as men in/and feminism.[7] Robinson asks, "*Is* there a place for research—criticism and scholarship—on women's literature that, while not being explicitly anti-feminist, nonetheless is not explicitly feminist either? What sort of place? And what work (or whose, as we might more candidly express our uneasiness) may properly be characterized as 'merely work on women' but not feminist work?" (143). Robinson wishes "to define the limits" (146), to articulate the rules for identifying and conducting feminist criticism. This strategy of articulation necessitates the exposure or unveiling of the phallus, making public Feminist Literary Criticism's normative assumptions and rendering them open to challenge or invasion.

Robinson's goal is to foster plenitude, unlike the "repressive tolerance" of pluralism, in the interest of ameliorating the negative effects resulting from the invisibility of "writers of color, working-class writers, writers of popular 'women's fiction' " (144). She describes her position as an informed empiricism, "not vulgar empiricism, increasing the Body-of-Knowledge stuff, but, if you will, an enlightened empiricism, originating in and sustained by the conviction that every piece of something that is provided is better than nothing" (144). Robinson focuses on the socially constructed and historically materialized differences (race, class, ethnicity, and sexual orientation) which separate women from one another. On this point, Robinson offers a challenge: "what bothers me even more is the implication that only women of color possess a racial identity that has to be understood by the critic, that only working-class women possess a class identity whose consequences need to be studied. In fact, in a society divided not only by racial differences but by racism, all writers have a significant racial identity. In a society wracked by class tensions—acknowledged or not—all have a class identity" (149). Finally, this blindness to one's own position, as it inhabits the discourse of reader-response and deconstructive criticism (as well as Feminist Criticism), deserves Robinson's attention, although her claims on behalf of "class identity" and "racial identity" return us to the problematic relation of any "identity"-based politics and its post-structuralist critique.

Robinson, nonetheless, turns the tables on us, arguing that, if deconstructive criticism is going to be practiced, if there is interest to be gained from it, it should be practiced on everything. Pointing to what she calls "a curious double standard," Robinson observes that critics apply the full range of analytical procedures primarily to the literature of middle-class white women: "Literature by women of color and, perhaps, even by working-class white women may be granted some modicum of critical and (even likelier) pedagogical attention, but it is rarely, if ever included in general discussions of the female tradition, and it is almost never read according to the modish new ways of reading [linguistic and psychoanalytic]. Instead it is read as social document" (149). As usual, Robinson makes hard judgments. She speaks as though she knows what feminism and feminist literary criticism are, but her "enlightened empiricism" leads her to occupy the self-consciously duplicitous position of knowing and not knowing, judging but insisting on inclusion (the "illusive imperative"). Reviewing the ideological bias of her past work, she comments: "Thirteen years ago, I was saying that feminist critics must not remain 'bourgeois critics in drag.' Seven years ago, I was saying that working-class women needed no outside apologists to make and justify their literature for them. Four years ago, I was applauding Jane Marcus's trenchant aphorism (wishing I had said it first) about how it is far more important to be Shakespeare's sisters than Bloom's daughters" (145). But now Robinson's pragmatism leads her to modify her positions in the interest of the notion that something, more work, is better, although she still insists that some work is better than other work.

Robinson raises a race- and class-based, antiexclusionary variant of the current critical conundrum: who's wearing whose clothes? This question needs to be pursued with respect to the review section of the particular *Tulsa Studies* issue I have been discussing. Benstock's introductory essay, which opens the volume from Paris, occupies a tense relation to the essays between it and the reviews, as though she is attempting to place, without "placing," the essays at the volume's center in the contexts of diverse feminist critical approaches, including post-structuralist feminist analysis. Otherwise, Feminist Literary Criticism's studied acknowledgment of deconstructive work is found at the back of the book in Bernard Duyfhuizen's review of work by Culler, Norris, Ryan, and Spivak. Duyfhuizen is one of the few men admitted to the margin of the margins, and ironically his task is to speak of/for a gathering of three men and a woman theorist as representative of the relationship between deconstruction and feminist criticism. In authorship and placement this review essay verifies, perhaps in an unwittingly stereotypical fashion, Feminist Literary Criticism's insistence on the "masculine" allegiance of deconstruction and its marginal relationship to feminist criticism. It remains easy not to "take in" his arguments concerning the relatedness of the two terms.

Duyfhuizen suggests why deconstruction and feminist criticism should attend to one another. He misleads us with his contention that "Feminists have turned to deconstruction . . . more often than deconstructionists have turned to feminism" (159), since we quickly discover how the works of Ryan, Culler, and Derrida (as well as those of Booth, Heath, and Scholes and the gestures of Lentricchia and Eagleton) complicate this simple claim. Benstock's introduction and the names of Kamuf and Spivak, whose writings are often contested by feminist critics but are not included in the volume, stand as the few representatives in this collection of those many feminists who have "turned to deconstruction."

At the back of the journal issue (the review section is sacrificed in the book and the essays are curiously supplemented) with comforting self-confirmation because it is signed by a man, feminism is formally introduced to deconstruction. Michael Ryan's *Marxism and Deconstruction* earns deserved praise for his discussion of deconstruction's role in creating the possibility of social change and promoting "progress in socially reconstructive action" (162). Some men admiringly observe (even if they cannot always practice) this possibility of "a political struggle to open restrictive and repressive critical ideologies to the play of sexual difference" (163). Duyfhuizen admits himself as suspect:

a man adding feminism to his "critical bag of tricks," afraid that he exemplifies Showalter's complaint about "critical cross-dressing." This concern among some feminists about "dressing up" or "passing" has assumed contradictory forms. Showalter, for example, complained first about feminist critics wearing men's clothes, the "Annie Hall" game, and then more recently about men in drag as feminists. These regulations for feminist practice, which figure the figurative crisis within feminist criticism today, tell their own story of an outmoded dress code where men wear the pants and women the skirts. (Perhaps this offers a clue to the materiality which Marcus did not want to loan.) We should question whether or not it makes a great difference in terms of sexual economy to talk about women passing as men and its reverse. We know the presumed benefits for women in a phallogocentric economy, but what's in it for men who want to "pass themselves off" as feminist critics? Not much, Showalter notes after some irritating though witty jibes at the male critics she finally designates as friends. Refocusing Culler's interest in "reading as a woman," she astutely suggests that the way to avoid female impersonation is to read as a feminist, which requires "a willingness to explore the masculinist bias of their own [men practicing feminist criticism] reading system" ("Critical Cross-Dressing" 143). Yet the figurations of feminist criticism and critical theory I have already discussed would seem to preclude the male practice of feminist criticism and to restrict men's attention to theory (that supposed male domain of nonfeminist practice)—sexualizations of the critical text and practitioner by striking a relationship of literal equivalence between the sex of the practitioner and the form of practice, the signature and the text, rather than assuming, as Peggy Kamuf puts it, a "necessary detachment of the signature from the signatory, of the signs from any singular, historical referent" (*Signature* 4). To my mind, the most important story is not so much who's wearing whose clothes; rather it is the narrative covered over by the figures, who has clothes to wear, who made them, and how the sociopolitico-economics of choice is operating in a given text and context. Further, there is the story of how figures put on a life story of their own.

The identity feminist criticism wants for itself it can't successfully construct because the nature of the whole suppresses the parts. Peggy Kamuf's questions in "Femmeninism," reflecting concepts elaborated in *Signature Pieces*, point out some of the parameters of the problem: "Has feminist theory figured out how to stand the signature up as a ruler against which to measure a new hierarchy of values or to lay it out on the ground like a tape measure that will point exactly to the limit beyond which out is out and in is in? Has feminism learned to absorb its 'own' difference, the unreliability of its signature, so that it can sign for everything else?" (83). The singular, single-sexed identity, where everyone wears his or her own clothes according to some theory of "true sex," and things are unambiguously what they seem to be, is a vexing illusion, inhabited of necessity by contradictions. The task of feminist criticism as a rewriting of the social text requires a collective critique proceeding along coincidental axes of identities with a problematic capacity to identify anything in particular, simultaneous and irreducible differentials, not just of sex, but of race, class, and sexual orientation. Feminist criticism and deconstruction, like identity and relationship, are at an impasse until they engage these differences, the irreducible and/or illusory, in newly figured forms. In her "Critical Response" to the reprinted version of the special issue of *Critical Inquiry* on writing and sexual difference, Gallop rewrites the romantic figures of parentage and identity: "In our culture, we have a singular identity, one name, the name of the father. For the purpose of consolidating an identity, one-half of our parentage is denied. That one is the child of two parents is another way of formulating the difference within. The feminist critic in her inheritance from both feminism and criticism lives the at once enabling and disabling tension of a difference within. We write in sexual difference. That is the critical difference in feminist inquiry" (290). It is the tension of the double cross, of identity, parentage, property, and language that feminist criticism is always attempting to cross(over) and uncross. In this sense too feminisms can never be written and will always be written as identity and the relationships between identities are negotiated and re-figured.

Another important essay at the back of the *Tulsa Studies* issue deserves remark. Hortense Spillers, writing " 'Turning the Century': Notes on Women and Difference," joins Duyfhuizen there. This time, since it is not the first time, this speaking from the place at the back renews painful historic and current reverberations; the subject is black women writers, black feminist criticism—other complicating differences within, obscured and occluded by consolidating Feminist identity in any single figure. Spillers observes the tensions inhabiting "difference":

> "Difference" emerges as the single most troublesome theme along
> a range of stress points, both in the life experiences of American
> women and within feminist discourse. Precisely segmented por-
> tions of cultural content—race, sexual preference, and gender [as
> well as class] among them—have assumed such rigidity of status
> that cultural and critical inquiry itself fractures into exclusionary

and isolated symbolic practice: as we seek the long view, wishing to stand solidly within the conditions of our own private and collective history, we are hindered by the very same symbolic modes that allow us to determine and choose the "good" over the "bad." In other words, the division of social and cultural phenomena into categories of simple binary oppositions appears to be a root cause of the abuse of power relationships. (182)

Spillers, like Robinson, points to feminist criticism's need to cultivate a multivoiced critique of ideology which the formulation of identity as definitional universality and institutional centrism will never permit. She offers a tricky caution concerning the "purism of conviction" which marks ethical discourses and conceals as much as it reveals, threatening from within the very integrity of position which many feminists, socialists, and lesbians, among others, wish to secure. She warns, "To conflate 'feminism' and female intrasexual or heterosexual expression is to render a false economy of identities that allows no freedom of the play of meanings" (182). Such simple reifications set the stage for the drama of the dress-up game in only slightly altered forms. Tensions foreclose extensions and lead to exclusion, like occlusion—"To prevent the passage of; shut in, out, or off." The project ends. The subject dies.

The questions feminist criticism and deconstruction need to ask implicate everyone's past practices as they pose the need to rethink what we are saying; not so much, as Nancy Miller contends, because the subject of our tensions is boring and needs to be changed, but because, as Miller also recognizes, some of our best efforts have revolved around tired binary oppositions and, I would add, diversionary jibes and jabs. Instead of attempting to silence deconstruction through wholesale rejection—a strategy which has already failed—feminist literary critics need to be reading and writing with care, considering one another's work with the kind of conscious respect one gives to "the other." (It is worth noting that very rarely are specific references made to the texts or even the arguments of feminist deconstructors by their detractors.) We need to continue debating tough questions concerning the power of language, one's own as well as that of others, to say more and less than it intends, the capacity of feminism to represent the materiality of women's lives, as they are figured through language in the daily paper, popular fiction, and traditional literature and criticism by women and men, the imbrication of theory and praxis in the political role of feminist intellectuals. Do sexism, racism, homophobia, poverty, and class differences have "reality" other than the forms they assume as language constructs? What does it mean to say that power is always mediated in/through language—the oppressor, master, slave owner, and slumlord turned linguist? What are the implications for feminism and Marxism of Derrida's comment: "when it is said about the deconstructive perspective that there is nothing outside the text, then I say to myself: If deconstruction *really* consisted in saying that everything happens in books, it wouldn't deserve *five* minutes of anybody's attention" ("Deconstruction in America" 15). The challenge to re-figure the politically and intellectually powerful relationships between language and life, as they are played out in the identity struggles of race, gender, ethnicity, class, and sexual orientation, could easily encompass the future work of both feminism and deconstruction.

What, then, I also need to ask, is the *one* deconstruction, Deconstruction as a proper name, that Feminist Literary Criticism figures as male and/or in order to oppose to itself? Whose practice stands for this deconstruction? And what is this *one* Feminism? Whose practice embodies it? Derrida and some deconstructive critics tend to see Feminism only as monolith, exemplified in the most inflammatory terms in *Spurs:* "Feminism is nothing but the operation of a woman who aspires to be like a man. And in order to resemble the masculine dogmatic philosopher this woman lays claim—just as much claim as he—to truth, science, and objectivity in all their castrated delusions of virility. Feminism too seeks to castrate. It wants a castrated woman. Gone the style" (65). Derrida's outrageous figure, which it is tempting to dismiss as an all-too-familiar repetition, nonetheless recalls the difference that constitutes iterability, or that iterability displays,[8] a feature conveying a particular lesson for Feminist Criticism with respect to the need to see difference. The "masculine dogmatic philosopher," guardian of truth and objectivity, offers a fit model neither for the feminist nor for the Derridean philosopher, hence the force of Christie McDonald's unsettling question to Derrida in "Choreographies"—what about Emma Goldman, that "other" kind of feminist woman whose maverick dance traces steps requiring feminism to consider new choreographies. In "Deconstruction in America," Derrida clarifies his position as follows: "certain feminists—certain women struggling in the name of feminism—may see in deconstruction only what will not allow itself to be feminist. That's why they try to constitute a sort of target, a silhouette, a shooting gallery almost, where they spot phallocentrism and beat up on it [tappe dessus]" (30). But Derrida also proposes a redirection, a resistance to discursive institutionalization, for deconstruction which parallels the one that feminism might rework as a strategy in order to escape a dogmatic adherence to truth. This resistance requires the recognition that, instead of *one* Deconstruction or *one* Feminism, "There are very diverse, heterogeneous phenomena which resemble each other, which in a way come together under that name, but only to a certain point. So we also have to take this great diversity into account" (4), and further, "it's difficult to define the *one* deconstruction [*la* deconstruction, like *la femme*], and not only because it is finally, I believe, a rather heterogeneous movement. Personally I would even say that its best interests are served by keeping that heterogeneity—although I don't know whose interests or what interests these are. But if deconstruction has an interest then this heterogeneity has to persist, otherwise it would be precisely the end of deconstruction" (6). Like feminism (a point Derrida will not make, indeed, cannot make as long as we insist on a unitary Feminism), "Deconstruction," he maintains, "is also difficult to define because it is neither a system nor a unified discourse. It's as you say a multiplicity of gestures, of movements, of operations. And what's more, multiplicity is essential for each of these gestures" (6). Deconstruction, in other words, has as much to fear as feminism does from its institutionalization as discourse.

Furthermore, "feminism(s)," especially in its plural form, rather like Derrida's notion of a heterogeneous deconstruction, is a term we can't afford to do without. Despite the fact that deconstruction requires a deconstruction of feminism (30), I will insist on the need for feminism(s) to be spoken because it is politically, that is, strategically, necessary, because the word itself offends people, because some women and men do not want to associate themselves with the word *feminism* or with people who do (part of the strategic ingenuity of Showalter's refocusing of "reading like a woman" to "reading like a feminist"), because employment is *still* lost as often as it is gained (*pace* Kolodny) through public alliance with lesbian feminism if not feminism in general. One can read the power that the word has. So as long as it is a pejorative term, exercising power over and against people, it remains a strategically necessary utterance for all of us committed to ideological criticism and social change. As much as it works against us, it constitutes us, returning us to another meaning for the word "movement": "A change in the location . . . for tactical or strategic purposes." In other words, feminism (or better, feminisms, the plural) still has the power to coalesce groups of people, to be and be part of a coalition: "1. An alliance, especially a temporary one, of factions, parties, or nations. 2. A combination or fusion into one body; union." It is this power of feminism(s) to see itself as containing differences as well as being differences within other (con)figurations that gives it the potential for momentary, nonillusory but *strategic* wholeness—one body, unified through coalition. Feminism might represent or re-figure itself as strategy, of which Derrida remarks, "There is no single strategy. Since a strategy is dictated by places really, and therefore by forces and individuals who are inscribed in these places, what may be strategically opportune here at one moment, is no longer opportune there at another moment" ("Deconstruction in America" 21). Thus, I picture feminisms as strategies, which, to remain "strategic," adopt the clever, chameleonlike hue of the guerrilla fighter—here and then gone again. A term with no entry in the dictionary; a meaning, that is, identity and/as relationship, that all of us, despite what we say about one another, are committed to figuring out.

How then might we re-figure this difficult arena of feminist speculation? A major problem in feminist writing, indeed all writing, is that figures lack (mathematical) precision. They lie, betray, mislead, escape. While this troublesome, even painful, fact about figures is inescapable, it is precisely in this slippage that an excess, something unaccountable, accrues. As Derrida asserts in *The Post Card*, "progress can be made only within metaphoric transference. *To borrow* is the law. Within every language, since a figure is always a borrowed language, but also from one science to another. Without borrowing, nothing begins, there is no proper fund/foundation [*fonds*]. Everything begins with the transference of funds, and *there is interest in borrowing*, this is even its initial interest" (384). My purpose here is neither to produce a nonfigural writing nor to claim a preferred figure for feminist literary criticism; rather, it is to call attention to the (con)figurations of the feminist problematic, along theoretical and cultural lines, to attend to how feminist criticism is figured and re-figured in this text and others.

The ideological critique practiced for so long with respect to the masculinist, oppositional logic of "phallic criticism" needs to be turned on the construction of knowledge within Feminist Literary Criticism, exposing its own "dark sides," the repression of which permits mono- and ethnocentric assertions of authority and domination, read in the marginalization of African-American and Native American literatures and the continued deferral of lesbian feminism. Certainly I do not trust myself to (re)write/right the problematics of difference and the effects of (mis)naming and cultural (positional) distortion. Spivak's warning in "French Feminism in an International Frame" suggests a way of proceeding out of the present stalemate: "I see no way to avoid insisting that there has to be a simultaneous other focus: not merely

27

who am I? But who is the other woman? How am I naming her? How does she name me? Is this part of the problematic I discuss?" (*IOW* 150). I need another woman to tell me who she is and who I am. In this local instance, whenever we speak of Feminism and Deconstruction, we can begin by asking ourselves what or whose feminisms, what or whose deconstructions? What is the copula that is powerful enough to conjoin these antagonistic images and to preserve their political force? Is there any escaping the "metalogic"? Do we want to? Don't we have to? I want feminism(s) to be a space from which difference can speak and be spoken with respect, a space where we can write and/or speak *with* one another rather than for or against each other. From this unfeasible but critical figuration issues a call for many voices and perspectives, choreographed into (con)figurations at some future moment; otherwise, we risk double-crossing one another, believing that "we" (me and those most like me) are writing the discourse of liberation.

For feminism(s) to be a contra/dictory space for polyphonous forms requires that respect be granted and that positions be negotiated rather than consolidated and insisted upon. Respect is a matter of engaging deferral, suspending judgment from the first word forward, until the structure of analysis fundamental to making sense, even provisionally, closes in on us again; or "the end" comes. In the interest of creating space for other views that complicate the simple pair of woman and man, feminist and nonfeminist, I have chosen to read texts which display strategies for re-figuring "woman," as the repressed term of linguistic and psychoanalytic projects, "the other," as the exclusionary structure of political domination, and the "feminist theorist" as the suspect "other/woman" of American feminist criticism. I hope to complicate the definitional and relational tasks of Feminist Literary Criticism as it is practiced in the United States by selecting texts, such as *Ceremony*, *Dessa Rose*, and Adrienne Rich's poetry in which an economy of the same confronts an economy of difference, or *Burger's Daughter* and *The Lover* in which white women grapple with their positions as subjects, or *I . . . Rigoberta Menchu* in which a Guatemalan Indian activist figures her relationship to feminism. By interrogating relationships between identities in feminist writing, I am hoping for the production of excess, the discovery of different registers and locations through/in which we have already been written, counting on some shadowy, incalculable, but splendid return which might suggest other productive past and future dimensions for the feminist critical project.

28

CHAPTER TWO

Crossing Cultures: Narratives of Exclusion and Leslie Silko's *Ceremony*

A half-breed (for such is what each of us is best characterized as) is not in a position to accept either-or viewpoints.

—Paula Gunn Allen, "This
Wilderness in My Blood"

The gift, effacing all determination, sexual or otherwise, produces the destination. Supposing that a gift has been given; that supposes that before it took place, the giver is not determined, and the receiver is not determined. But the gift determines; it is the determination, it produces the identity of the giver and the receiver. The gift is not simply floating in a definitive determination. It gives itself the right to determine.

—Jacques Derrida, "Women in the
Beehive"

One of the institutional tensions addressed by feminist literary criticism, but one it cannot remain outside of, involves the literary canon as it articulates itself in the form of a gender-biased standard of value for the study of literature and as it claims to express the coherent identity narrative of our "common heritage" (Kolodny, "Integrity" 306). This question of the politics of interpretation invites us to engage another form of the question—the interpretation of politics, as it shows itself in teaching and writing. Adopting this focus for the moment, I want to disengage our concentration on the "literary canon" as a monolithic institution, or Identity in its own right, that controls (commands) our attention, and to consider its effects as a continuous narrative (one of progress, relationship between texts and homogeneity) concerning what is valued. Further, I want to sidestep the two alternatives (as well as the pluralistic third—the simultaneous pursuit of both) commonly offered to and by feminist criticism, the either/or that the half-breed "is not in a position to accept": to work within the concept of the canon through exposé and argument (to integrate and accommodate, realizing that we are "in" it or at least "in relation" to it, like it or not) or to establish another tradition, a counter-canon (to segregate and to separate).

The debates among feminist critics concerning the publication of the *Norton Anthology of Literature by Women*, edited by Susan Gubar and Sandra Gilbert, suggest that even a feminist revision of the literary canon, ostensibly sensitive to race, class, and sexual orientations as well as gender, is fully as problematic as the codification it set out to revise.[1] Lillian Robinson's "Is There Class in This Text?" illustrates my point. To engage the question of the canon or the counter-canon is already to have decided that *it is* in order then to consider its (con)figuration. These moves, as Lillian Robinson points out, "fail to call the notion of the canon itself into question" ("Treason" 87); neither do they succeed in "radically redefining literary quality itself" (89). The canon, in other words, functions as a codification of national literary identity and (as) value, striking relationships among those texts which can be integrated without rupture into its schema.

Kolodny encounters precisely this difficulty in her essay "The Integrity of Memory: Creating a New Literary History of the United States." She states that recent scholarship demonstrates both the need for a new literary history which will take account of black, gay and lesbian, Hispanic, Chinese-American, Native American, and women's literature, and yet it suggests at the same time the inadequacy of all such totalizing narratives. On balance, however, the project of constructing the new feminist narrative compels Kolodny's loyalties. Her complaint, for example, against the relegation of works by blacks and women to tangential chapters so that they can be "represented" in the grand narrative of literary history is that "the bracketing-off defeats any possibility of telling a coherent, integrated story about our literary past" (297). She writes as though the "heroic rereading" (302), the "new decipherings," hold out "the possibility of genuinely new, wholly reconceptualized literary histories" (303). Her provocative notion of the canon as a literature of memory (which I would read as function and effect of writing) is also compromised in the context of her question: "how we might compose a literary history that recovers the integrity of memory" (300). The subjection of memory to history and to its own "integrity" serves to focus and delimit its trajectory from the start. Following Jane Tompkins's lead of considering the relation of texts to power, Kolodny finds a particularly engaging prospect: "To understand how a text works out 'problems inherent in the culture at the moment of composition' [quoting Tompkins] or how a text is reconstituted by some later cultural elite so as to work out the problems of another period—and thus how it achieves power at any given time" (304). This articulation affords an opportunity to move away from the notion of a canon to some new "mechanics" as a basis for collections of works according to what they did or do now ("an anthology of texts which do x," "a course on texts which do y"), where we choose to include what we do because it is or was somehow useful or valuable to us or others. At issue then is the way in which a text writes itself, *how* it gives itself (away), like a gift, and *what* it gives.

In the failure to question the very notion of literary history as an Identity with its constituent relationships, even the breaks, discontinuities, and dangers Kolodny recognizes find themselves subsumed under and glossed over in the project of rehistoricization. This rather single-minded interest leads her to pass up the unsettling story of the limits of representation as they are played out in the experience of reading the figure of Jacob and the angel that she chooses to illustrate her project. She writes, "Like Jacob wrestling with the angel, the creators of a new literary history will have to wrestle with the antecedent power of established canons and inherited historical designs" (301). In 1971 Roland Barthes struggled to read the narrative(s) of Jacob's struggle with the angel, only to assert its irreducibility in the face of contradictory reading pressures, its insistence on being more than one story. Barthes offers a more open conclusion to the figure of the struggle which might lead us to a different beginning: "The problem, the problem at least posed for me, is exactly to manage *not* to reduce the Text to a signified, whatever it may be . . . but to hold its *significance* fully open" (*Image* 141).

Leaving in reserve for the moment the question of the canon as canon and the difficulty posed by holding significance open in a system which presses us to resolve the struggle, to settle the story of reading, I want to return to the question of an/other selection process, one that neither seeks to establish an alternative story of "women's culture" nor purports to give us an expanded story of a "whole" culture, or of culture "as it *really* is or was." In exploring the prospects of a different process of selection and another kind of reading project, I am not so much interested in what is chosen, suggestive of identity and intrinsic value, as I am in the terms according to which selections might be made and, even better, continuously (re)made; that is, in a process of selection which speaks of relationships between texts and readers that are never finished, that cannot serve as the foundation for a new literary history (except perhaps in the form of how, why, and by whom choices are made), a new canon, a new identity narrative

31

for specified texts in determinate relationship to one another. But in any writing, one feels the force of the literary/linguistic institution's assimilative, neutralizing capacity to accommodate and to de-fuse (diffuse) any contra-dictory narratives, to keep them from "going off." Even as I write against identity narratives for literary history and feminist criticism, words choose other words, insisting on a representation that somehow becomes what it resists and speaks against.

Though she stops short of putting her argument or explanation to use, Barbara Herrnstein Smith, in "Contingencies of Value," an article to which too little attention has been paid (and now the title essay for her book from which I cite), makes some provocative claims concerning the production of literary value and its consolidation in the form of a canon. She notes early in her essay that "Recent moves in the direction of opening the question of value and evaluation in the literary academy have come primarily from those who have sought to subject its canon to dramatic revaluation, notably feminist critics. Although their efforts have been significant to that end, they have not amounted as yet to the articulation of a well-developed noncanonical theory of value and evaluation" (24). In this chapter I would like to make a gesture in response to Robinson and Smith and in the direction of a radical redefinition of "literary value" which might serve as the beginning for an articulation of a "non-canonical theory of value and evaluation" that can be read and complicated through readings of the texts which follow in later chapters.

As I have argued in the first chapter, feminism as a political force has an investment in identity, in being able to stand for or behind a consolidated definition or understanding of itself, and, as such then, the ideas of a revised canon/literary history and a counter-canon are attractive. Arnold Krupat articulates this as Law: "Canon formation . . . always involves partisanship" ("Criticism" 13, n. 17). Through the efforts principally of those critics writing in the interest of blacks, lesbians, and Native Americans, we also know, at this juncture, that Feminist Criticism's past efforts to speak from a consolidated identity have been flawed and inadequate, even dangerously so since such an identity depends upon the repression of identities which differ from the One of interest to the one writing. But if we abandon the canon as canon, replacing or blending "their" partisanship with "our" partisanship (just as hard to specify as it is to keep these differences apart), it seems as though we must also have to abandon the idea that feminist criticism has something "of value" to offer the academy which has historically codified value in the form of a literary canon and a literary history, or that without a canon, perhaps value will simply be masked rather than absent. This need not be the case if, within the certain limitations of our capability, we foreground rather than disguise the question of value and if we specify the kind of value we are talking about in a new economy which compels our interest.

When works of art are discussed, we typically think and argue in terms of "intrinsic" value, but as Barbara Herrnstein Smith observes, "All value is radically contingent, being neither a fixed attribute, an inherent quality, or an objective property of things but, rather, an effect of multiple, continuously interacting variables or, to put this another way, the product of the dynamics of a system, specifically an *economic* system" (*Contingencies of Value* 30). If value does not inhere in things (texts), but is produced through the interaction of or relationships struck between texts and reading/writing subjects, both produced by and producing a system which has socioeconomic, psychosexual, racial, and political dimensions, perhaps what matters most is what I can do with or to a given text and what it does to or with me. Its value, in the case of Leslie Silko's *Ceremony*, which I have chosen as my example here, may reside in its usefulness of the moment (rather than in its durability, permanence, universality—those terms from the lexicon of "intrinsic value" typically used to characterize canonical texts and the subject as representative "identity speaking for culture"). And *the* history of literature, if it seems necessary to create such a thing, might then be a description of the uses to which texts have been put, the purposes they have served for various people at different moments, the ways in which these interests have been and are being written. Even so, in the case of the "noncanonical," the "Third World," or what Guattari and Deleuze call "minor literature," interpretation (too often the speaking about the minority by the majority—the very words, concepts, and structures of the discourse) and recuperation (adding to the canon in terms of "use" or value) are unavoidably imperialist gestures, the motive suspect, since these acts are always conducted in the "terms" of what the First World can see or wants to see, what it values according to its own partisanship. Interpretive activities, like other language(d) acts, inevitably install us in a matrix of difference or differential relations, an (ex)tended field of tensions which are reduced to or contained only with limited success as "pure" Identity.

Because the individual reader, the "I" standing (in) for the critic, teacher, and student, has the capacity to occupy contradictory and multiple sites, and these sites re-present or stand (in) for a body historically, materially, experientially, and linguistically situated, the record of interaction will necessarily be an account of local and specific engagements reflecting the positionality of readers, writers, and texts. As Smith explains, "Like its price in the marketplace, the value of an entity to an individual subject is *also* the product of the dynamics of an economic system: specifically, the personal economy constituted by the subject's needs, interests, and resources. . . . Like any other economy, moreover, this too is a continuously fluctuating or shifting system, for our individual needs, interests, and resources are themselves functions of our continuously changing states in relation to an environment that may be relatively stable but is never absolutely fixed" (30–31). Surely too, a distinct separation cannot be articulated between the economic system, its objects and subjects, or the subject's sense of need, her perception of an object's ability to meet the need, and the economic system's inscription of values (what its subjects should need). Rather than replicating the institutional mode of canon production—a process Smith describes as making "texts timeless by suppressing their temporality" (50)—I am interested in an economy of differences (rather than sameness, an economy of abundance rather than scarcity) through a process of selection that presents texts as "timely" by suppressing considerations of their "universality," so that, in an important sense, the "same text" can never be selected twice, or even once since its self-identical nature and that of its interpreter are both assumed to be problematic.

Smith's aim, as elaborated in her book-length work, and suggested in its subtitle, is to explore alternative perspectives for critical theory.[2] In her critique of value (intrinsic, exchange, and use), feminist critics might discover productive ways to shift the order of literary debate if we were to make our critical interventions in terms of the "use value" of texts rather than through arguments concerning their alleged "intrinsic value." This is no remedy for critical disagreement (a heterogeneity we might wish to cultivate), since, as Smith is quick to point out, a judgment we make about value, like the value itself, is also contingent: not a matter of a work's absolute or "truth-value" but of how well it "may perform certain desired/able functions quite well for some set of subjects" (47). Nonetheless, we could foreground in disagreements of this kind what we variously, individually and collectively, expect a text to do for us, under what conditions, and who "we" are (or think "we" are) in order to judge it useful—a position in which we attempt to speak our own needs and desires as readers, and to articulate or at least to expose our subject positions, rather than to make "truth claims" concerning the undying, universal, and intrinsic value of a given text, masking in rather transparent ways the belief that it is (or should be) useful, does or says something, for all time and for all people. A focus on the question of "use value" might, in other words, change the kinds of arguments feminists and other critics make about texts.

Before I go too far with this, however, I want to acknowledge Baudrillard's discussion of "use value" in *For a Critique of the Political Economy of the Sign*, where he argues that the system of labor and production constructs our understanding of "use" just as it does the "needs" to which we believe use responds; thus, use value is no pure, untainted alternative to either exchange or surplus value, but is instead, to some indeterminate degree, their product or effect. Use value bears the marks of our romantic, idealized forgetting, in a masquerade of "naturalness." Baudrillard exposes this idealism at work, a project he shares with Nietzsche in "On Truth and Falsity in an Ultramoral Sense," through the analogy of the sign where transcendental idealism manifests itself "in the attempt to rescue the Sd(Rft) from the terrorism of the Sr" (160). Omitted from and forbidden in these "humanistic" signifying schema is the very human space of "response and reciprocity": "The generalized order of consumption is nothing other than that sphere where it is no longer permitted to give, to reimburse or to exchange, but only to take and to make use of (appropriation, individualized use value)" (171). As Baudrillard explains in *The Mirror of Production*, use value inheres, not in the thing itself but in *the relation of the thing to the user*, a relation articulated as symbolic exchange through an unending, self-consuming process "of continuous *unlimited* reciprocity between *persons*" (70), a trajectory which resembles the unending circulation of gifts. The narrative desire I hold for feminist criticism, and for literary criticism in general, is to create a space for the gifts of respect and reciprocity which have no place in the present economic/political/linguistic systems as they prohibit liberating, egalitarian relationships in favor of a closed system of narcissistic individualism and cultural imperialism. The gift takes us by surprise, (con)structs unsuspected connections between us; it announces itself by disclosing and connecting giver and receiver. Then it is up to me, the recipient, to acknowledge it and to find its use. Thus we might begin by saying that this other woman and her text(s) are gifts, and, in a rewriting of Spivak's query, ask ourselves "Who am I in relation to these gifts?"

Perhaps as a function of my age and time, I find myself "between" things—between ages, centuries, critical modes, nuclear holocaust and disarmament, imperialism and self-determination, ecological annihilation and conservation, black separatism and white pro-activism, antifeminism, feminism and "post-feminism." My position in between makes me interested most of all in finding my "place," in settling the question of identity with respect to my relationship to others and my desire to take positions that facilitate the circulation of respect. In "Coalition Politics: Turning the Century," Bernice Johnson Reagon advises women to learn from and to protect the individuals in their midst who have survived multiple struggles (civil rights, Native American rights, gay rights, the antinuclear movement): "Anytime you find a person showing up at all of those struggles, and they have some sense of sanity by your definition, not theirs (cause almost everybody thinks they're sane), one, study with them, and two, protect them. They're gonna be in trouble shortly because they are the most visible ones. They hold the key to turning the century with our principles and ideals intact. They can teach you how to cross cultures and not kill yourself" (363). Out of this interest I turn to Silko's *Ceremony*, whose value rests for me in the fact that *today*, right now even, I can read it (in my position as white feminist scholar and teacher in the U.S.) as a lesson in crossing cultures, another set of (canonical) boundaries. I can read, by negotiating between my analogies and Silko's, lessons about my subject position and about crossing cultures, which might equip me for moving in the "between," for participating in the affirming gestures of reciprocal exchange, a fragile, genuinely anxious participation in giving and receiving, in this precariously constituted global village.

I want to choose this trickiest of examples and to put Smith's comments, which lead me to the comforting notion of use value, up against those concerning "minor" literature, the desire of the other not to be interpreted or produced in someone else's terms, particularly when the agent and code of production represents a dominant culture—objections which provide the focus for my reading of *I . . . Rigoberta Menchu* in Chapter 5. This gesture of "territorialization" is the Law of the Same at work, appropriating for its own use the property (the "proper," the body even) of the Other. Deleuze and Guattari suggest a contrary desire to "deterritorialize," to escape interpretation in the register of the "major," "to create a becoming minor" (27). It becomes necessary then, returning to the idea of use value, to stipulate the proper use of use, the way in which feminist literary critics make texts useful to us in order to avoid the oppressive dimension of an inevitable reterritorialization, what we can say about others without appropriating (interpreting?) and canonizing them. In a certain sense everything is at stake in these representations and negotiations—our systems of meaning, identity politics, and theoretical investments (Kaplan 191). My dilemma then poses itself as a question of how to elude, even momentarily, what Guattari calls in an interview the "powerful signs which massacre desire" (Seem 41). As writer and critic, I cannot control the uses to which this writing will be put, for example, by those wanting to reinvent new literary canons, to interrupt the circulation of gifts, and to formalize or codify positions.

Ceremony, like the ritual invoked by the title, straddles boundaries. Silko like me is "between": she is white, Laguna Indian, Mexican. Her people are Marmons and lived in the governor's house: "My family are the Marmons at Old Laguna on the Laguna Pueblo reservation where I grew up. We are mixed bloods—Laguna, Mexican, white— but the way we live is like Marmons, and if you are from Laguna Pueblo you will understand what I mean. All those languages, all those ways of living are combined, and we live somewhere on the fringes of all three. But I don't apologize for this any more—not to whites, not to full bloods—our origin is unlike any other. My poetry, my storytelling rise out of this source" (Velie 106–7). Though I have only a stranger's experience of Laguna Pueblo, and therefore don't "understand" what she means about the Marmons' position there, I can imagine some ways in which she is neither this nor that, and lives in the "place" of the whiteman (a matter of structural and other relations of class and race, perhaps also sex in both our cases) in the midst of another whom he rules. Through her character Tayo, caught (not so much by blood but by a symbolic system) in the space of convergence between the whiteman, the Native American, and the Mexican as a curious supplement, Silko creates a space, as described by Wendy Rose, of "complex relations . . . that include conquest, colonialism, paternalism, racism, and guilt" (47).

Ceremony provides an occasion to examine the violence required to construct the continuous narrative of literary (or other forms of) history and of singular identity, to homogenize the wild diversity of peoples (Indians, Africans, Spaniards, Jews, Asiatics, immigrants and exiles) in this country. "American literature" historically performs exclusions of its native peoples, repeating the gestures of colonialism and imperialism, another staking out of the territory. *Ceremony* takes two silences—a personal one and a political one—the half-breed in relation to "pure" racial and cultural Identity and World War II, in which Indianness is repressed in the service of "American Identity" and "national interests," and turns them into account, that is, turns them into (produces) "value" in an/other (kind of) history lesson.

For me, in this moment, the value of a work of art depends upon its revolutionary function, its usefulness in a very specific sense. As Benjamin summarizes it, "*An author who teaches writers nothing, teaches*

no one. What matters, therefore, is the exemplary character of production, which is able first to induce other producers to produce, and
second to put an improved apparatus at their disposal. And this
apparatus is better the more consumers it is able to turn into producers—that is, readers or spectators into collaborators" (233). Thus, the
most useful text becomes a revolutionized version of what Barthes
later offers in his (non)distinction between the readerly and the writ-
erly text—how a text like *Ceremony* turns me into a writer who produces political and personal value through what I choose to read,
teach, and write, as I negotiate the tricky crossings in my life as a
feminist critic.

*   *   *   *

To begin again with feminist criticism in the interest of an/other representation.

To begin again with *Ceremony,* which performs its revolution in
the letter as it comes to us in the form of a gift, inscribing us in
ceremony, as it circulates in this text of feminist literary criticism with
its desire for a (dis)integration of the distinction between giver and
receiver.

Ceremony opens within the envelope of a dual creation myth. The
text begins with Ts'its'tsi'nako, Thought-Woman, the Grandmother
Spider, who with her sisters created the Universe. Her special power
links ideas and things through a language art: she names things and
they appear. Speaking makes them "real" (puts them before us) if not
"true" (universal and enduring). Everyone is enlisted in the speaking;
the word circulates. In the narrative present, in the (con)text of this
creative power and the novel, she thinks of a story which some undes-
ignated other ("I") tells us now. In this gesture, Silko (con)fuses the
oral tradition of Native American storytellers which offers stories that
are traditionally conserving, on the side of life rather than death, and
the Western book, formerly (that is, before Silko, Momaday, Allen,
and other Native American artists) a site of confusion, destruction,
and forgetting with respect to America's indigenous peoples. *Ceremony*
is this space of (con)fusion, itself a "cure," the effectiveness of which
is to transform both the oral and the written through the displacement
of this and other oppositions. By (ex)tension, the text offers strategies
according to which we can re-figure feminism's narrative of woman's
identity and her relationship to others.

The main character, Tayo, suffers from "battle fatigue" and "ma-
larial hallucinations," words that classify an axiological disorder in

terms of illness (the abnormal, the unnatural), and in doing so, attempt to contain the range of their disruption, to obscure the relation of sense (masculine/Anglo) and non-sense (feminine/Indian). Tayo's symptoms manifest themselves in conflicting voices—the sounds of the jukebox, Japanese soldiers, the Laguna words of his mother— swirl cacophonously, thwarting meaning: "when he was about to make out the meaning of [his mother's] words, the voice suddenly broke into a language he could not understand" (6), and everything is overtaken by the loud flashing jukebox, a legacy of Western technology, a black hole ("pulling the darkness closer") into which an/other sense disappears. Like the spidery tangled threads from his grandmother's sewing basket, the strings of words and thoughts refuse separation: "He could feel it inside his skull—the tension of little threads being pulled and how it was with tangled things, things tied together, and as he tried to pull them apart and rewind them into their places, they snagged and tangled even more" (7). Similarly, he is unable to keep the races straight; the white men and the Indian soldiers are the same color in the bloated darkness of death, and the murdered Japanese enemy looks like his uncle Josiah. No amount of "reasoning," of "facts and logic" (8) on his brother Rocky's part, can set the record straight. The complex knot of intricated identities and (de)nominations replaces the tidy binary oppositions of a linear logic.

Tayo's (con)fusion offers interpretive choices as to what is at stake here. Seeing Silko in relation to Tayo, her mixed-breed character, critics want to read the novel as a return to "Indian values" and "Indian identity." Velie comments, for example, "Silko can teach at a state university, drive a car to work, eat spaghetti, and take aspirin for headaches without compromising her integrity. In *Ceremony*, however, Tayo must find his cure and salvation within an Indian context. His cure must come from a medicine man rather than from a white doctor. The medicine man uses some paraphernalia from white civilization, but, however eclectic his medicine bundle, his cure is fundamentally Indian. There is integrity in this too" (Velie 114). In a move resembling those of some feminist critics discussed in the previous chapter, Velie elaborates a traditionalist and separatist interpretation that is designed to keep the Indian in his "place" through his insistence on the integrity of "fundamentally Indian" identity. While he acknowledges the blurring of categories, that Silko may take certain liberties with respect to moving between the white and Native American worlds, he insists that her character demonstrates a regressive notion of loyalty to "pure" Native American tradition: "The values in *Ceremony* are Indian, and the message is that Indians are best off when they remain within their traditional culture (even though that is constantly changing) and that the old gods still have power. The book was written, however, by a woman who is white as well as Indian, and whose profession is writing poems and novels and teaching in a predominantly white university" (Velie 114). Velie's argument, reducing Silko's Anglo, Indian, and Mexican heritage to the simpler Anglo/Indian pair, obscures the sense in which Tayo's cure depends upon figures between several worlds—the Mexican woman Night Swan, the eclectic medicine bundle, and the half-breed healer Betonie, no longer "purely" reflective of traditional culture—as well as upon the mountain spirit Ts'eh who, as Patricia Clark Smith and Paula Gunn Allen point out, is Tse-pi'na, "in Keres, 'Woman Veiled in Clouds'— the Laguna name for Mount Taylor" (192). Silko's representation of practice as ceremony or ceremony as practice may affirm the traditional values Velie wants to assert, but sometimes the agents of destruction, like Emo and Leroy, are "pure" Indian and the agents of affirmation are "mixed," exceeding codification in a dualistic either/or schema. Certainly the form and content of "ceremony," like the book of that name, are (con)fused and (ex)tended, marking as it does, before witnesses, the passages between states of being, themselves indeterminate.

The value of Silko's text resides in the imbricated figuration of writing and ceremony. Like critics, readers, and writers, Tayo is a teller of stories. Carrying his wounded "brother" Rocky out on a stretcher through the monsoon rains in the Philippine jungle, Tayo fabricates "a story for all of them, a story to give them strength": "The words of the story poured out of his mouth as if they had substance, pebbles and stone extending to hold the corporal up, to keep his knees from buckling, to keep his hands from letting go of the blanket" (12). Cursing the rain to make it stop, to find "the words to make a cloudless blue sky, pale with a summer sun pressing across wide and empty horizons" (12), Tayo tries to exercise the creative capacity of story to make things happen, to take us through one moment to the next, to negotiate differences through (in) writing relationships between terms. He occupies the "place," that is, assumes the capacity, of Iktoa'ak'o'ya, Reed Woman, and of Nau'ts'ity'i in the poems following this episode, where they steal the rain and drought ensues to convey the lesson that there is no magic powerful enough, no substitute for respecting the mother corn altar. While Tayo believes in the power of his curse, that his words make substance, constructing a reality which corresponds to the story he is creating, his words are without power or effect in the material world he seeks to change.

As a half-breed, Tayo is a person doubly out of "place." Nothing has or at least stays in (its) place: "so he cried at how the world had come undone, how thousands of miles, high ocean waves and green jungles could not hold people in their place. Years and months had become weak, and people could push against them and wander back and forth in time. Maybe it had always been this way and he was only seeing it for the first time" (18). This (ex)tension of people, places, things, and time beyond the boundaries, the outlines of their identities, so that the "identifiable" substance, the substance of identity, comes in and out, is as diffuse as the wind, calls into question the security of bounded identity and place as represented both in traditional Native American metaphysics and in the identity politics of presence in Western metaphysics, including U.S. Feminism to the extent that it occupies this terrain. The story poses this tension, and through the ceremony it performs, offers to instruct us as to its resolution, or reconciliation, or at least as to its effects.

Rubinstein presents another interpretive fiction in her description of Tayo's situation as a "struggle for wholeness" (197): "In recovering Josiah's legacy, he finds a partial antidote to his own sense of homelessness. In a larger sense, however, Tayo's placelessness can never be ameliorated. His people's historical loss of their land is a deep and terrible injury that challenges their collective identity" (Rubinstein 198). To a degree the text bears this out, as Betonie explains to Tayo that "there were transitions that had to be made in order to become whole again, in order to be the people our Mother would remember" (170). But if, as readers, we abandon the fiction of "wholeness" that our desire produces, a more discomforting field emerges in which there is no purely Indian or purely Anglo, just as there is no absolute separation of good and evil, no "true sex" for woman and man, no politically correct position (practice, place, or identity) that differentiates absolutely the feminist from the nonfeminist. Smith and Allen extend this point, claiming that "Witchery, not white people, has set a loveless, fearful, mechanistic, death-bent force loose in the world" (191). These words offer us consolation at the same moment that they implicate all of us, "Anglo," "Indian," and half-breed, in the web of words, agency, responsibility, and alliances. Thus, Tayo engages a "wholeness" redefined, re-figured as a "mixed-breed": how "it all depended" (11). Speaking from this "no-place," Tayo tells his Indian "buddies," "I'm a half-breed. I'll be the first to say it. I'll speak for both sides" (42). He bears the shame of and for the Native American, in that space between cultures. Emo's insult articulates the confusion of absolute categories: "You drink like an Indian, and you're crazy like one too—but you aren't shit, white trash. You love Japs the way your mother loved to screw white men" (63). What is certain here is that blood or identity politics settles nothing in the ever-circulating fields of desire, choice, and change.

Tayo's aunt represents this limit in a way that is similar to Baym's effort to distance herself from "feminist" theorists. Out of loyalty to traditional values and purity, she creates a secret distance between herself and Tayo, and between Tayo and her pride Rocky, the Indian all-American. Her cruelty requires him to be "close enough to feel excluded, to be aware of the distance between them" (67). Overlooking the betrayals of her Catholicism and her lies in Grandmother's name, Aunt Thelma pretends to live in an unchanged world of traditional Indian values: "An old sensitivity had descended in her, surviving thousands of years from the oldest times, when the people shared a single clan name and they told each other who they were; they recounted the actions and words each of their clan had taken, and would take; from before they were born and long after they died, the people shared the same consciousness. The people had known, with the simple certainty of the world they saw, how everything should be" (68). This certainty of belief Tayo had lost, if he had ever had it: "he wasn't sure any more what to believe or whom he could trust. He wasn't sure" (63). Auntie doesn't see the splitting that has taken place in this "fifth world" where names were no longer pure, their meanings now uncertain, having become "entangled with European names: the names of the rivers, the hills, the names of the animals and plants— all of creation suddenly had two names: an Indian name and a white name" (68). Identities are entangled, meanings ensnared in the conflict of cultures that results from change. Auntie thinks she knows what is needed, but her idea of it is to invest in the "pure Indian" and to secret the half-breed in shame, as she followed the old way: "to gather the feelings and opinions that were scattered through the village, to gather them like willow twigs and tie them into a single prayer bundle that would bring peace to all of them. But now the feelings were twisted, tangled roots, and all the names for the source of this growth were buried under English words, out of reach. And there would be no peace and the people would have no rest until the entanglement had been unwound to the source" (69). Auntie says the right words— those of reconciliation and peace—but she hides her desire in a "pure Indian" analysis of its cause (the nontraditional, the "im"-pure in an already impure and imperfect world) and of its cure (the right cere- mony to restore an originary harmony). Her behavior, however, belies her words as she accords Rocky privilege and support for his success in "passing" into Anglo culture.

The traditional Indian medicine man, old Ku'oosh, who comes to work a cure on Tayo, at least realizes the limits of his power in the face of change. Serving as a limit text for the futile task of significatory control, old Ku'oosh's speech issues from a world of certainty where in war, before the dehumanizing distance of technology as a death machine, one had to know when one killed another. But despite certainty, balance is "fragile":

> The word he chose to express "fragile" was filled with the intricacies of a continuing process, and with a strength inherent in spider webs woven across paths through sand hills where early in the morning the sun becomes entangled in each filament of web . . . . no one word exists alone, and the reason for choosing each word had to be explained with a story about why it must be said this certain way. That was the responsibility that went with being human, old Ku'oosh said, the story behind each word must be told so there could be no mistake in the meaning of what had been said; and this demanded great patience and love. (35–36)[3]

But Laguna has changed, as have the relatedness and the origins of words—sacred lands, Los Alamos, Trinity Site occupy this space, giving rise to the terrifying metonymic slide of signification. Without question, "great patience and love" are demanded of us, but in the service of negotiated relationships rather than in a quest for origins and totalizing figures.

An important use of Silko's novel rests in the half-breed, a figure in which the self and others are represented in a re-figured consolidation. Wendy Rose's explanation of her use of the term serves well in this context also: "By 'Half-breed,' I'm meaning something that transcends genetics. It's a condition of history, of society, of something larger" (55). The dilemma of existing in the between is not new with Tayo. His mother created him there: "The feelings of shame, at her own people and at the white people, grew inside her, side by side like monstrous twins that would have to be left in the hills to die" (69). Tayo and Rocky reenact these twin positions, the irony of which is that Rocky, the "pure" Indian, distances himself from his culture in the interest of winning and success in the white culture. By contrast, Tayo, the unwanted half-breed, observes ceremonies of love and respect in "the ritual of the deer" and assists with the raising of the spotted and resilient Mexican half-breed cattle. As Lincoln explains, "Twins personify an image of unified dualism, just as Pueblo moieties synchronize tribal life in complementary divisions. In *Ceremony* the blood 'cousin-brother,' Rocky, killed in the war, and the returning mixed-breed, Tayo, reenact a contemporary variant of old twin myths, reasserting the need for idiosyncratic pairing: a full-blood who imitates and dies for whites, a half-breed who gaps the two, accepted in neither, surviving" (235–36). Tayo figures the (con)fusion in the signifying system, how he is and is not his twin—a point which can be made theoretically if not materially with respect to an/other, and, as such, threatens the security (or "purity") of identity politics and the comfort of tradition (or literary history) which give us "place" or relation with respect to an origin that, by securing the fixed relation between signifier and signified, guarantees meaning and value.

On the one hand, to cultivate a view of fragmentation and rupture, as Duane Niatum points out, is "cultural suicide" (27) for Native American and tribal people. On the other hand, Anna Lee Walters cautions in the same volume,

> The terms "American Indian thought" and "American Indian identity" are themselves social and political reflections of the time and government policy upon us. There is no such thing as a united, single tribe of one million plus members, the American Indian Tribe. What we are, are some one hundred plus tribes with distinct (sometimes related, sometimes separate) identities who are individually recognized by the United States government, and by virtue of these tribes' status as the original inhabitants of their country, have negotiated special relationships with that government. . . . If an "American Indian identity" does exist, it was created subsequent to the establishment of American government. So "American Indian thought" then is an extension of this so-called "American Indian identity." (36)

Taken, then, to the level of the tribe, we are by analogy questioning the notion of "Laguna identity," a matter made further difficult by Tayo's position as a mixed blood, "half-(of a)-breed."

How to read Feminism's dilemma of Identity as political-cultural necessity versus Identity as reductive, exclusionary construction gains elucidation through the reading lessons *Ceremony* offers. Just as the half-breed represents for Silko, Rose, and Allen a "space" that is culturally rather than racially or genetically constructed, the "pure" terms of the opposition—American Indian versus Anglo or "European"—can be similarly described. Thus, Russell Means articulates difference as a social construction: "When I use the term 'European,' I'm not referring to a skin color or a particular genetic structure. What I'm referring to is a mind-set, a world view which is a product of the development of European culture. People are not genetically encoded to hold this outlook, they are *acculturated* to hold it. The same holds true for American Indians or for the members of any other culture" (30). He continues, "Caucasian is the white term for the white race; *European* is an outlook I oppose" (30). Betonie echoes this view, commenting "Nothing is that simple . . . you don't write off all the white people, just like you don't trust all the Indians" (128). The conflict, in fact, is irresolvable, requiring that we live in the borderlands, on the frontier (Anzaldua 194–95) where "illness" threatens the body and the spirit, language and ceremony, in a perpetually circulating tension between the text of desire for health, wholeness, and Identity, and the text of dis-ease, pain, and heterogeneity. These tensions between competing categories require a particular ceremony that takes (its) place in the place of struggle and negotiates a way.

Betonie, the healer, also provides for the (con)fusion in difference in the novel. The medicine man occasions the reenactment of the fear of the other that Night Swan explains to Tayo: "They are afraid, Tayo. They feel something happening, they can see something happening around them, and it scares them. Indians or Mexicans or whites— most people are afraid of change. They think that if their children have the same color of skin, the same color of eyes, that nothing is changing. . . . They are fools. They blame us, the ones who look different. That way they don't have to think about what has happened inside themselves" (99–100). Betonie, in his difference from the traditional healer, instills fear in Tayo who must, himself, explore the tensions that construct conflict. The encounter begins with the question "What kind of medicine man lives in a place like that, in the foothills north of the Ceremonial Grounds?" (116). The question splits: what kind of medicine man, what kind of place? Another economy is introduced as Betonie explains location in terms of comfort: " 'We know these hills, and we are comfortable here.' There was something about the way the old man said the word 'comfortable.' It had a different meaning—not the comfort of big houses or rich food or even clean streets, but the comfort of belonging with the land, and the peace of being with these hills" (117). Responding to questions which structurally parallel the one I asked in the first chapter—what kind of feminism?—Silko's text enacts the process of redefining a geopolitical economy in other words. Betonie, who doesn't talk or act like a medicine man, who doesn't live in the "place" of the traditional medicine man, suggests that "in place" is where he is, and the "out of place" is the white town butting up against the Indian hills and the settlement under the bridge of derelict outcasts like the young Tayo and his mother, perhaps even the reservation as the "Indian place" assigned by the white government.

The world of the narrative is pried loose from static oppositions and is figured in terms of a "continuing process" in which the old and new challenge one another, event (as story) tests story for its adequacy, and vice versa: "Dragonflies came and hovered over the pool. They were all colors of blue—powdery sky blue, dark night blue, shimmering with almost black iridescent light, and mountain blue. There were stories about the dragonflies too. He turned. Everywhere he looked, he saw a world made of stories, the long ago, time immemorial stories, as old Grandma called them. It was a world alive, always changing and moving; and if you knew where to look, you could see it, sometimes almost imperceptible, like the motion of the stars across the sky" (95). Stories not only shift and change but are polysemic (of many hues) as compared with Ku'oosh's explanation of webs of determinate meaning in which each word "has its place" and its origin. In this encounter, language circulates like a gift in a virtually infinite, unchartable field; as it circulates, an excess is produced—more gifts and relationships result. This world of stories to be apprehended, pulled out, and put forth, is constitutive of and constituted by the community's vision, thus my investment in the narratives feminists advance about themselves and others. Stories are co-(ex)tensive, encompassing the range of what we call the visible because they are (in) us. They (in)form what we "see" as our "vision," just as they conceal the equally powerful figures that we are unable to read. Our stories make what we see (as) ours. These narratives offer the illusory promise that through them we can take possession of the world, but on reflection, they (only) describe a pool on the surface of which our own image hovers—there and not there. *Ceremony* enacts this process at work.

Ceremonies in a world alive cannot be static, cannot reside for the mixed-breed (and with respect to the question of difference we are each one) in "pure" traditional ritual. According to Betonie, whose people for generations have responded to change, such a simple purity has not existed since the white man arrived, and one suspects things might never have been so. While we may long for this "sense" of ease (an ease of "sense"), the obscure indeterminacy of the lost originary scene requires, as I shall show more specifically in my discussion of Duras's *The Lover,* that we write what is always a story of our desire, our longing. Betonie speaks against our capacity to construct the literal reenactment/repetition of ceremony: "long ago when the people were given these ceremonies, the changing began, if only in the aging of the yellow gourd rattle or the shrinking of the skin around the eagle's claw, if only in the different voices from generation to generation, singing the chants . . . . in many ways, the ceremonies have always been changing" (126). He sums up his lesson, from his grandmother, another Mexican with green eyes: "things which don't shift and grow are dead things" (126).

In a gift of discursive generosity, Silko explores the effects of exclusion (an analogue of feminists without theory/theorists without feminism) in the interest of narrative simplification. Whites as well as Indians are victims of a great lie—that dark-skinned people steal and whites have the money to buy, that whites own the stolen land upon which the American empire is founded and from which native peoples are excluded, stolen, and confined like Josiah's Mexican cattle: "the lies devoured white hearts, and for more than two hundred years white people had worked to fill their emptiness; they tried to glut the hollowness with patriotic wars and with great technology and the wealth it brought. And always they had been fooling themselves, and they knew it" (191). The economy of competition and scarcity produces scarcity, impoverishment rather than wealth: "It was the white people who had nothing; it was the white people who were suffering as thieves do, never able to forget that their pride was wrapped in something stolen, something that had never been, and could never be, theirs. . . . And what little still remained to white people was shriveled like a seed hoarded too long, shrunken past its time, and split open now, to expose a fragile, pale leaf stem, perfectly formed and dead" (204). In this other world of the "out of place," things are valued for their ability to produce use value—food, regeneration, function, replenishment. The hunter's old rifle " 'works good . . . it works real good. That's the main thing' "(207). This is the antithesis of the logic of scarcity where the destroyers work to see how much can be lost and forgotten (229), where land, "place," and language are owned by one group or individual with the power to keep them from another.

When Tayo, having ceremonially reclaimed Josiah's missing cattle, observes the offspring of the Mexican animals and the yellow bull, he sees the power of "mixed-blood" in both its figurative and narrative dimensions. The young animals participate in an older, longer story: "he could see Josiah's vision emerging, he could see the story taking form in bone and muscle" (226). As the traditional narrative of combating drought requires the son to intervene, Grandma sends Tayo to be the actor in Betonie's ceremony. Story, as it alternatively takes place through the mixed blood, materializes our negotiations with one another. It comes like a gift: you put yourself in another person's hands (Hyde 15).

With the conclusion of the ceremonial narrative and Tayo's cure, we can return to the notions of "wholeness" and "identity" as instances never concluded, requiring continued negotiations in the field of difference. The words seem "right" as a way of accounting for Tayo's restoration to health, but they are limited if we think we mean by them anything like their conventional meanings in Western metaphysics. Tayo's alienation is of a different order. As Lewis Hyde explains, "gifts carry an identity with them, and to accept the gift amounts to incorporating the new identity" (45). To accept the mixed-blood poses a challenge to the One. Story provides a connective network between conflicting but interconnected forces. Tayo suffers not from fragmented self-identity but from the separation of the "self" (however whole or fragmentary that may be) from other complex identities—ceremony, people, and land. Because stories circulate, ceremony as a negotiation of identities, a network of relations, never ends and the figure it traces remains, at any given moment, provisional.

It is difficult to find words in English, in this format, for such an intricate and absolute coalescence—an integration of one in the other, so that there is only one (a state of being before the "other"), and a language function in which story, event, earth, and people (re)present this one only in a moment, on the way to becoming something other. Thus, as Allen notes, "only a cosmic ceremony can simultaneously heal a wounded man, a stricken landscape, and a disorganized, discouraged society" (123). Larson makes a related claim for the interconnectedness of image, scene, and text, an Indian harmonics: "Because of a core of recurring images, such as the spider web . . . in one sense *Ceremony* has no conventional beginning and end. It would be possible to begin reading the novel at almost any page and continue from there since the images are circular, related to one another by imaginative association. Like these interwoven images, the subject of *Ceremony* is the 'continuing process' " (152). But these observations too are easily mis-taken and romanticized if they are separated from the ever-returning need for ceremony, the circulation of the gift, as both the constructive and deconstructive capacity of language. The power of the destroyers, which is an ancient one, is only kept in abeyance, and that by the function of abundance: "as long as you remember what you have seen, then nothing is gone. As long as you remember, it is part of this story we have together" (231). The counter-narrative catches us up, unites us in a struggle against death as one clan of human beings (Indian and Anglo, American and Japanese) against the powers of destruction in which we too are agents, another story begun long ago and unfolding still. The destroyers' narrative is not nullified or defeated. It has been displaced—Emo, the most evil one of all, having killed the others, is said to be in California. He is a deferred "agency," until another telling or writing begins.

Beginning again, I want to ask what use can be made of texts which disrupt conventional narratives of literary value and canonicity. Are they merely occasions for an/other narrative of intrinsic value, a feminist version of canonicity? Must we read Silko's story "Yellow Woman" or interpret *Ceremony* only in terms of a female spirit world, recalling Robinson's challenge, if we want to find a use for it within feminist literary criticism? The text of *Ceremony* opens the question of literary value and feminist criticism to other negotiations. In a sense, the novel stages its own counter(categorical)-insurgency as it contests the differences in male and female power, the identities of the Indian, Mexican, and Anglo subject, the separation between written and oral genres, and the conventions of "American literature." Silko points us in the direction of new and constantly shifting, woven and rewoven conceptions of identity—textual, personal, and cultural. Her book obliges us, as feminist recipients of the gift, to work. The following comment by Hyde suggests our task: "we cannot receive the gift until we can meet it as an equal. We therefore submit ourselves to the labor of becoming like the gift. Giving a return gift is the final act in the labor of gratitude, and it is also, therefore, the true acceptance of the original gift" (51). But this is an incalculable matter, full of surprises. The value of the book is the economy of the book: the complexity of crossing cultures, given the more and less of language and identity. The value of a gift always exceeds the personal and the interpersonal because it installs (as it designates) giver and receiver in a sociopolitical network of exchange. *Ceremony* interrupts the canonical debates— feminist and other, feminist and feminist—(ex)tending them as it disrupts its own narrative from within through other stories and voices that, in important and useful ways, are and are not its story and still, while distinguishable, are inseparable from it. In the ever-circulating confluence of narrativity, it arrives, like a gift, announcing itself, con- structing giver and receiver in relation to certain insoluble questions: What is this gift? How can I use it? Am I worthy? In relation to this gift, who am I and who is this other person? Is this a gift? Will I accept it? The gift, however, goes on.

The Political Is the Personal: The Construction of a "Revolutionary Subject" in Nadine Gordimer's *Burger's Daughter*

> Your freedom and mine will not be separated. I will return.
>
> —Nelson Mandela, in Winnie
> Mandela, *Part of My Soul Went with
> Him*

> [F]or three hundred and fifty years and more, we have been not
> merely rubbing shoulders but truly in contact with one another,
> despite the laws, despite everything that has kept us apart; there is a
> whole area of life where we know each other. And I really say the
> word *know*. Yes, we know each other in ways that are not expressed.
> We know the different hypocrisies that come out of our actions and
> our speeches; indeed we know each other in the sense that we can
> read between the lines.
>
> —Nadine Gordimer, "The Clash"

That "the personal is the political" has been a caveat of the contemporary feminist movement, a maxim authorizing the private, subjective
experience of the individual woman to be read in terms of or for its
significance with respect to larger issues, or to stand as/for "the issues"
of contemporary society. Furthermore, the distinction between the
personal and the political, elided in the conflation of terms, allows
feminists to valorize one term (experience/ideas or social action/the-
ory) at the expense of another as though a separation were possible.
The microstructure of experience and the macrostructure of sociopolitical forces are made synonymous, the former dignified, given the
significance and readability presumed to belong to the political space
of "public" life, and the latter personalized, brought "home." This
was an important move at the time, the late sixties. In fact, perhaps
at any time the confounding of such oppositions is among the most
momentous events in human life, and, as Silko demonstrates in *Ceremony*, an understanding of the complex imbrication of the psychic and

50

the sociopolitical life compels the attention of all revolutionary subjects in struggle against the forces of an oppressive majority. But the valorization of the personal is a gesture which, if elevated to law-in-itself, may become an exclusionary principle inhibiting the cultivation of other political actions—outside the local sphere, in the rest of or in other parts of the world. We quickly forget the political at home, its issues domesticated in deference to our surroundings in the white middle-class, where being (at) home provides sanctuary rather than emblem of being in the world. The maxim is a curious one, since it does not rewrite an/other rule, its obverse, about the individual and political positioning, a point Terry Eagleton reminds us of in his observation "Nor is it adequate to *identify* the personal and political: that the personal is political is profoundly true, but there is an important sense in which the personal is also personal and the political political. Political struggle cannot be *reduced* to the personal, or vice versa" (*Literary Theory* 149). What then is the excess, the "more than" the personal which constitutes The Political (not as reduction) or the-political-taken-personally? And what is the "more than" or "other than" the political which constitutes The Personal in this nonidentification which Eagleton suggests? Something sounds like "truth" in his initial statement, as in that liberating maxim (or maxim of liberation) from the women's movement, but both leave unspecified the critical elaboration of this complex relationship, the site of struggle in/between the self and the world—the working-out of which might help us live in the tension.

For almost forty years, Nadine Gordimer has engaged the problem of race in South Africa from the personal, political, and artistic perspectives of the white citizen. These tensions are played out for us as readers in the sociopolitically "safe" space of fiction; this is not to say, however, that the *act* of writing cannot elicit most severe consequences in repressive regimes, but rather that the revolution in the reading subject occurs on the psychic level until such time as it finds sociopolitical form.[1] These points will, I hope, become clearer in the following chapters through the contrast between Duras's psychical exploration and the revolutionary praxis of Rigoberta Menchu. The conundrum, "Where Do Whites Fit In?" the title of an essay from 1959, has provided a structuring impulse for artistic elaboration. The question, coupled with Gordimer's method of exploration, articulates the terms of her fiction—works that offer lessons on how to negotiate that act of reading between the lines in a racially diverse society of imbricated freedoms, how to approach the question of who one is vis à vis "the other" (or better, others), and what is required in view of

51

the identity one claims and the subject positions one inhabits (chosen or not). Further, a consideration of her works elucidates the difficulty of differentiating "the personal" from "the political" and "the political" from "the artistic."

When Gordimer published this brief essay (a short note, really), she had only written some short stories and two novels. Her remarks are prefaced by a three-sentence biographical introduction which concludes with the line "*Though not involved in politics, she has many African friends*" (326). We don't know who wrote this clichéd ("some of my best friends are black") and obscure ("not involved in politics") sentiment. The essay that follows asks questions of enduring personal and political importance for white readers, as objects of future black rule, and, I would hope, to prospective black rulers of "the New Africa." Gordimer rejects "nowhere" as the answer to the title question, preferring in this "apolitical" statement to say that "if we're going to fit in at all in the new Africa, it's going to be sideways, where-we-can, wherever-they'll-shift-up-for-us. This will not be comfortable; indeed, it will be hardest of all for those of us (I am one myself) who want to belong in the new Africa as we never could in the old, where our skin-colour labelled us as oppressors to the blacks and our views labelled us as traitors to the whites" (326). In a contest between reason (rights and citizenship) and desire (for human acceptance and love), it is the "reasonable" request for legal and civil enfranchisement which may one day, in this optimistic future, be met, and that unreasonable desire of the heart which may reasonably go unfulfilled, a condition all of us struggle with, if ever black South Africa realizes this "nationalism of the heart that has been brought about by suffering" (327).

There is something embarrassing (that recalls the resonance of the French word *embarrassé* 'burdened', 'overloaded') in the encounter with this white woman's words, words that could be mine, as she tries to speak honestly about her "place" with respect to racial crime and racial capital in South Africa, her native land. As I read Audre Lorde's powerful essay "Apartheid U.S.A." and Derrida's challenge that "the problem of *apartheid* is surely an *American problem*" ("But, beyond" 170), the distance, the differences between her country and mine diminish. Gordimer foregrounds those most difficult questions which lurk in the background—how can a white person stay? Or, as Alice Parker reframes the question, "what/how can a white person s(t)ay?"[2] Gordimer asks, in the absence of ever being able to expect to be granted that intangible sense of emotional participation, of belonging, "What are we to do? Shall we go? Shall we leave Africa?" (327)— questions the characters in her fiction will continue to ask in the decades to come. She refuses to separate one set of terms from another, preferring a radical redefinition of categories: "Those of us who stay will need to have the use of our heads in order to sustain the emotional decision that home is not necessarily where you belong ethnogenically, but rather the place you were born to, the faces you first saw around you, and the elements of the situation among your fellow men in which you found yourself and with which you have been struggling politically, personally or artistically, all your life" (329). The posing of such questions involves taking responsibility, not perhaps, as Lazarus points out, *for revolution*, but *for*, that is, *against apartheid* (155). Elaborating on this point, Gordimer explains the conditions under which some radical blacks credit white writers with integrity, offer us their respect as something earned rather than ascribed, or received as a gift, the implications of which, as we have seen in Silko's *Ceremony*, will manifest themselves in some future action: "To be one of these writers is firstly to be presented with a political responsibility if not an actual orthodoxy: the white writer's task as 'cultural worker' is to raise the consciousness of white people, who, like himself, have not woken up" ("Gesture" 145). In another conversation she clarifies her point: "But what you *can* do is work among your own people to change them, because if white people are to survive in the true sense, which doesn't merely mean saving their necks, it means learning to live in a new way, then they must rethink all their values. It is on this rethinking of values that white-consciousness is founded" ("A Conversation" 30). It is a taking of responsibility in the form of "cultural conscienciza-tion" ("Art and the State" 661) for what has been made, if not actually by us as whites, certainly at least in our name. Gordimer's own retrospective self-critique, revealed in her interview with Jannika Hurwitt, makes it clear that her earlier "humanistic" or "individualistic" attitude," which might be termed the "personal approach" in light of the opening opposition, was inadequate to combat an unyielding white supremacist regime: "I felt that all I needed, in my own behavior, was to ignore and defy the color bar. In other words my own attitude toward blacks seemed to be sufficient action. I didn't see that it was pretty meaningless until much later" (Hurwitt 93). Rather, she discovers that the "essential gesture" for black and white writers alike in South Africa "is a revolutionary gesture" ("Gesture" 147), the nature of which for each, however, is marked by their different positions relative to the "bar" (as line, law, institution, and mark of subjectivity in language).

How, before the revolution (which must and will come, Gordimer and I would insist), can a white person leave, when "to leave" means leaving responsibility in the hands of those who are less responsible (in the instance of white segregationists) or politically less able to oppose it (the black majority which needs to work against the odds for revolution)? But then how, before the revolution, can one stay? Gordimer's white characters continue, obsessively, to ask and to answer this question (see Lazarus 131–34). Pauline, in *A Sport of Nature*, exclaims, "There's the world out there—There's this place. And Joe and I have to decide every day of our lives how to live here, *whites only*, no choice about that, no phalanstery without passes and black locations, white this and black that" (39). My reflections are always haunted by the idea that if you are white and alive in South Africa, you "fit in" the Old South Africa. (And what, I wonder, does it mean to be white and alive in the United States?) I do not want to conduct the kind of inquisition that Gordimer so justly resents: "When abroad, you often disappoint interviewers: you are there, and not in jail in your own country. And since you are not—why are you not? Aha . . . does this mean you have not written the book you should have written? Can you imagine this kind of self-righteous inquisition being directed against a John Updike for not having made the trauma of America's Vietnam war the theme of his work?" ("Gesture" 138–39). Out of a recognition that her cultural position is inseparable from mine, it is my own structural relations—the position of feminism and of the white middle-class intellectual—as much as Gordimer's that I wish to interrogate in order to extend my consideration of feminist identity politics and the relation of difference. Nonetheless, I believe in some other way that this matter of "taking responsibility" can involve one's life and one's death—another inseparable, inescapable pair—where and how to live and to die. As Gordimer suggests, citing Turgenev in the epigraph to her novel *A Guest of Honour* (1970): "An honourable man will end by not knowing where to live." And indeed death is the fate of this novel's white protagonist, Colonel Bray: there is nothing so intimate or "personal"; nor is there anything more "political" than murder, whether random or planned. Or, in the words of Liz Van Den Sandt in *The Late Bourgeois World*, after committing herself to interracial love and political struggle, "even the beats of my heart repeat to me, like a clock: afraid, alive, afraid, alive, afraid, alive" (95). With just such a recognition, and in the interest of taking responsibility, Gordimer writes: "You must give yourself the freedom to write as if you were dead. It is very difficult, and nobody can carry it out to the hundredth degree because you are still alive" ("The Clash" 58).

Gordimer recognizes the privilege inherent in posing the question of where and how one is to live. At the same time that the white South

African suffers the responsibility of choosing his or her "place," an "honorable," a "responsible" place in South Africa, the "other" South Africans have only restricted choices (no "choice" at all) with respect to geopolitical positioning, or as the title of Zoe Wicomb's book declares, *You Can't Get Lost in Cape Town*. In the aftermath of the 1976 Soweto uprising, Gordimer realizes that death—as (non)choice, descriptor, invocation—marks in a devastating way this particular moment in the development of Black Consciousness: "We whites do not know how to deal with the fact of this death when children, in full knowledge of what can happen to them, continue to go out to meet it at the hands of the law, for which we are solely responsible, whether we support white supremacy, or, opposing, have failed to unseat it" ("Letter" 3). In Soweto, black children who are born for life find death, that nonchoice having become life's only choice. A chastening contrast lurks in the differences between the position of the revolutionary subject and the revolutionary reader as subject.

In her seventh novel, *Burger's Daughter*, published in 1979, Nadine Gordimer explores the growth and development of a white woman as a responsible or "revolutionary subject," a position (unlike those of "white" and "black" here and in South Africa) which can only be chosen voluntarily. The writer takes her character Rosa Burger from adolescence to young womanhood, under what one might think are optimal circumstances for the production of a political consciousness capable of acting to unseat apartheid. As the novel's epigraph from Claude Lévi-Strauss suggests—"I am the place in which something has occurred"—Rosa Burger is one such place; South Africa, this novel (the discursive space of which begins by marking itself off there), the author herself, and ultimately the reader are other "places," sites for/ of production and performance. Who this subject is, where the place and what the thing that has "taken place" the reader is to discover by reading between the lines of this textual complex of interlocking relationships, just as we might learn to read the figuration of an identity for "feminism(s)" as such a complex space of multiple production and, thus, (de)nomination.

The novel opens with a description of people waiting outside a prison. Perspectives for viewing are numerous—passengers from buses that must have passed by, the warder who tries not to see, others who wait, the scene's omniscient narrator, perhaps more than one preparer of reports, constructing identities for Rosemarie Burger, Rosa Burger, Lionel Burger's daughter, schoolgirl on the first hockey team, the second swimming team, promising student, daughter of her imprisoned mother Cathy Burger. She is regarded there by all but herself. Unlike her father, whose eyes "drew together an unavoidable gaze in newspaper photographs" (10), Rosa lacks keen vision; her eyes are "transparent." She wants to see her/self, and wonders, "*When they saw me outside the prison, what did they see?*" (13)—the omnidirectional question of the subject being constituted, the illusory identity-fixing scrutiny of the mirror stage: "I shall never know [what they saw]. It's all concocted. I saw—see—that profile in a hand-held mirror directed towards another mirror" (14). Rosa sees herself "in place, outside the prison," but her attention is not focused on the public spectacle that she is and of which she is a/part. She stands in front of the prison and menstruates for the first time, becoming a woman, who, as JanMohamed puts it, is more/other than a daughter: "Thus her simultaneous yet unconnected existence as an object of public scrutiny and as a locus of private experience reflects her predicament as a bifurcated social being" (129). In her version of the story, Rosa instead focuses on her biosexual identity, the biological fact of her womanhood, turning her private, internal experience into a public one where "the internal landscape of my mysterious body turns me inside out, so that in that public place on that public occasion . . . I am within that monthly crisis of destruction, the purging, tearing, draining of my own structure. I am my womb" (15–16). She tells us in retrospect that it matters little whose identity story we read—theirs or hers—as "both would seem equally concocted" (16), a point Gordimer stays with to the end through her preoccupation with the inseparability of simultaneous personal and sociopolitical constructions of the subject.

Rosa articulates the arbitrariness of subject-construction, identity, and discursivity. How inconsequential (both everything and nothing) it is to be standing "before the law"—the prison gate of white supremacy, the periodicity of menstruation marking her womanhood, or the father's law in language. Rosa explains, "And if I were really telling, instead of talking to you in my mind the way I find I do . . . One is never talking to oneself, always one is addressed to someone. Suddenly, without knowing the reason, at different stages in one's life, one is addressing this person or that all the time, even dreams are performed before an audience. I see that" (16). The performative displaces the constative (to the extent that one ever plays a/part from the other), making evident the artifice in claiming to know either the self or the other in terms of a "subject/object" opposition, the irony of which deepens in the face of South Africa's obsession with elaborating absolute, precise calculations of racial difference (see Cooke 13). The novel becomes a space where conflicting discourses, competing ideologies, are presented for all readers to regard, where discursivity takes (its) place in the multiple discourses of subject construction and positioning.

Gordimer replays the fusions of the opening scene when Rosa's friend Conrad observes that the personal and political horrors of her family circle are indistinguishable in origin: "—Disease, drowning, arrests, imprisonments. . . . —It didn't make any difference.—" (41). Her mother died from multiple sclerosis, her father died in prison, her brother drowned in the backyard pool. To Conrad, the losses are indistinct as to cause—dead is dead: "But the Lionel Burgers of this world—personal horrors and political ones are the same to you. You live through them all. On the same level. And whatever happens—no matter what happens—" (42). The contrasting memories of Conrad and Rosa as twelve-year-old children point up a difference in the tenor of their family dramas: Rosa recalls the political memory of the Sharpeville Massacre as its aftermath works itself out in her home (the political brought home, but domesticated); Conrad remembers the consuming personal obsession of his Oedipal preoccupation with his mother and her lover. These differences continue in adulthood, as his friends plan to go to sea in a handmade boat, and hers, lacking passports to support such fantasies, go to prison (50); their uncommitted (or only personally committed) lives, like those of the people living on the French Riviera, epitomize "the bourgeois fate, alternate to Lionel's: to eat without hunger, mate without desire" (117). Trying to put herself in Conrad's "place," Rosa realizes that her family circle was characterized by nonpossession; all members existed only in relation to the political cause, the father and mother functions assumed by many and extended to numerous dependents in a revised sense of kinship.

Lionel Burger's household, with its pool, black servants, black "son" "Baasie," and steak barbecues, embodies the domestication of white revolutionary South African politics in the 1950s. The effect of Gordimer's text, however, is to demonstrate the limits of socialization and domestication as means to produce the revolutionary subject—how (de)nomination and grammatical/syntactical positioning relate to a world where subject positions are both chosen and not chosen. In response to Conrad's challenge that "Saint-Simon and Fourier and Marx and Lenin and Luxemburg whose namesake you are" (47) provide no rationale for personal existence, no raison d'être, Rosa elaborates the indistiguishability in white Communist households of the ostensible opposition of the personal and the political: "If Lionel and my mother . . . if the concepts of our life, our relationships, we children accepted from them were those of Marx and Lenin, they'd already become natural and personal by the time they reached me. D'you see? It was all on the same level at which you—I—children learn to eat with a knife and fork, go to church if their parents do" (50). The revolutionary cause, articulated in that utopic monolith The Ideal Future, its own form of immortality, stands in opposition to Conrad's elevation of "I" against "we" in the face of Rosa's question, "What do you do when something terrible happens?" (52). Rosa projects her father's reading of Conrad, another fix on the difference between the personal and the political: "Lionel Burger probably saw in you the closed circuit of self; for him, such a life must be in need of a conduit towards meaning, which posited: outside self. That's where the tension that makes it possible to live lay, for him; between self and others; between the present and creation of something called the future" (86). Thus, Gordimer makes the case for the collective identity and structural relationships revolution requires and which Rosa, while searching for personal identity in *relation* to collective purpose, must rewrite in her own name just as one reenacts the family drama in the progress of generations. How much of an assertion of the individual, the personal, how much variation such a structure of (re)writing permits is the question.

Her struggle is with the political made personal: "didn't you understand, everything that child, that girl did was out of what is between daughter and mother, daughter and brother, daughter and father. . . . I was struggling with a monstrous resentment against the claim—not of the Communist party!—of blood, shared genes, the semen from which I had issued and the body in which I had grown" (62). Rosa also struggles with the personal made political; she believes that it is Lionel Burger the man, her father, not a "God" or a "devil" of revolutionary politics (18), and Cathy Burger, her mother, with whom she must contend. Everyone concocts identities for Lionel Burger; they see him in ways that Rosa does not or cannot in her effort to see herself by seeing him: "And who are they to have decided— the law did not allow them to photograph *him*—in their descriptions of him in the dock, in the way he listened to evidence against him, in the expression with which he met the public gallery or greeted friends there, that they knew what he was, when I don't know that I do" (145). Part of what Rosa fails to see is that, because the tenets of white liberal communism have been "naturalized" in the family, they are as inseparable for her in the effort to "identify" herself as they were for her father or her mother (who, like Rosa, no one seems quite so intent on describing). Likewise, natural "identity" becomes unnatural, or is it the other way around? At seventeen, Rosa is "engaged" to an imprisoned Communist so that she can act as a go-between, carrying supplies and messages in and out of prison. She is "used" by adults to further the struggle: "it was natural" (65). But then "use," in relation to such a compelling goal, is only that, the use value someone or something has for revolutionary success.

The dichotomy is most confounded in the death of a tramp in the park where Rosa eats her lunch in anonymous pleasure. He looked alive, even in death, a lifelike statue of a man, his legs crossed "conversationally" (78). This is Rosa's first experience of death. Her family losses were somehow "obscured . . . by sorrow and explained by accident, illness, or imprisonment" (79). But this anonymous death comes unfiltered through responsibility or explanation; it eludes discursive captivity: "this death was the mystery itself. . . . we die because we live, yes, and there was no way for me to understand what I was walking away from in the park" (79). This death is the remainder, what is left after the revolution eliminates skin and class privilege, needless death (murder), and suffering. About this death the revolution has nothing to say: "Justice, equality, the brotherhood of man, human dignity—but *it will still be there*" (80). Hence the irony of Marisa Kgosana's comment when Lionel receives the life sentence: "whose life, theirs or his" (154)? In South Africa, where "life means life" (28), a life sentence is also a death sentence.

The question of where and how one should live or die encompasses the issues of choice and betrayal. Even Lionel Burger is a betrayer in the eyes of some: the man who, according to the Afrikan nationalist Brandt Vermeulen, could have been prime minister (186) turns traitor, betraying "the heritage of his people," the "white man's power" (61), in the interest of other loyalties. With Lionel Burger's death, her mother and brother already dead, Rosa is set free (the feeling of other daughters of famous men—Virginia Woolf comes to mind). She is free "to be anonymous, to be like other people" (77); to experience the loneliness of living "without social responsibility" (77)—to live as she desires (246). She must undertake the burden of Wang Yang-ming's proclamation which Gordimer places at the opening of the novel's second part, the place toward which the first is tending, as we too are moving when we as subjects admit that the subject position is a space in which something not only occurs but which also has the capacity to make something occur: "*To know and not to act is not to know*" (213). To assume this freedom is to rewrite the "death sentence" as a simultaneously existential end and a revolutionary potential. This move, like the radical figuration of "woman" and "feminism" as spaces of difference, signals the shift from a restrictive identity politics to a potentially productive polyvalence.

Despite Rosa's ultimate imprisonment carried in the verbs of the novel's opening sentences, and the inescapable answer to Claire's question of what choice (no choice) one has, Rosa is also free to act the part of the betrayer, as she escapes the demands of the Terblanches, feeling "the need to get away as from something obscene—and afraid to wound him—them—by showing it" (111). She runs from Dick's splotchy cancer-marked hands and Claire's peeling eczema, signs of the dis-ease inscribed on the white body (politic). As Rosa comments to the absent Conrad, "Even animals have the instinct to turn from suffering. The sense to run away. . . . A sickness not to be able to ignore that condition of a healthy, ordinary life: other people's suffering" (73). Thus Gordimer marks her character's turning point, the decisive moment, with another turning away in the scene with the donkey. Just as she rejects the demands of the Terblanches, Rosa fails to act on her own sense that she can and must intervene to stop the suffering.

The black man beating the donkey, a vision welding all participants into one structural form, provides a significant moment in the course of Rosa's struggle with commitment. The event holds the history of human suffering before her—from thumbscrews to solitary confinement, the ability to inflict it and the capacity to endure it. The full weight of agony presents itself in the black location, "in the 'place' that isn't on the map" (209), unnamed and un"known." Reflecting on the scene, Gordimer explains that "the image suddenly catalyses all the other forms of suffering—the suffering that man inflicts on man—into an intense awareness of the problem of suffering itself, the pure phenomenon, gathering up in her mind the atrocities committed by East and West. Her contemplation of the central human fact of suffering—and possible responses to it other than her father's chosen one—preoccupies her throughout the book" ("What Happened" 32). Rosa remotivates her need to choose, through the space of the novel as an extended meditation on suffering. She recovers suffering in all the forms in which she has experienced it, and takes a position with respect to the dilemma of self-positioning.

In a sense Gordimer's question concerning the place of whites in South Africa (given in this novel to Katya: "how will they fit in, white people?" [249]) is conflated for me as a feminist reader with that of "woman's place" in struggle, a preoccupation that motivates the readings presented in the final three chapters. In *Burger's Daughter* we can read these as correlative questions. Rosa is offered an identity—

as comrade-daughter (the Communist family), South African white (state), cultural product (language and history), corporeal subject (menstruating girl turned woman). Her problem is how to be Burger's daughter and more, other—how to be white but not the master, colonizer (problems not unlike my recurring question: how to be the feminist activist and critical theorist)—finding a representation which permits a nonhierarchical play of difference. As Radhakrishnan suggests, there is no (one) place, no "authentic constituency," for the white subject in the neither/nor of white supremacy and Black Consciousness: "The tricky task facing the 'white subject' engaged in 'self-consciencization' is one of articulation: a transformed articulation that has to divest itself from authority and privilege" ("Negotiating" 282).[3] In her address to Conrad, Rosa tries to explain the difference in her relation to identity, when, "far from poring over the navel of a single identity (yes, a dig at you, Conrad)," she, through political activity, "see[s] the necessity of many" (112). Longing to be used in the service of something outside/other than herself, to acquire "the passionate purpose, propelled by meaning other than my own" (155), she struggles with the problem of identity, another question of "place," in the midst of contra/dictions. What happens in a society like South Africa when the construction of the "truth" of your white identity (unlike the master's) is *not* formed by the reflection/recognition given you by your slave, as black servant to the white master, daughter to the father, woman to society?

In this context, the scene of the women's meeting deserves some comment. Over the years, various interviewers have asked Gordimer about her views of feminism, which she wants to keep separate from and secondary to the struggles against apartheid and for revolution. Seeing herself as fortunate, while other women are not, she resists generalizing because other women "*do* have these struggles" and regards women's situation "as part of the whole question of human rights and disaffected groups in various societies" (Hurwitt 119). Obviously Gordimer subscribes to a certain form of liberal feminism, but it is caught up in a problem of priorities: "Black women have so many terrible disabilities that they share in common with men— the oppression of racism—that the whole feminist movement means something quite different there. Unless feminism is seen as merely part of the general struggle for black liberation, and the struggle of all, white and black, against racial oppression, it has no validity in South Africa, in any view" (Hurwitt 120). This observation suggests the need to see the struggles against racism and sexism as coextensive, simultaneous rather than serial, where feminism is "part of" the struggle for liberation. This is feminism with "validity," with a value for South Africa. But what is Gordimer suggesting with this word "merely," feminism as "merely part of the general struggle"? Something makes her want to keep feminism in a secondary role, perhaps even in an insignificant role—the place of the barely mentioned or the all-too-visible "other" that discourse tries to render invisible.

Gordimer persistently represents feminism, when she allows it any place at all, through trivializing examples:

> the white man and the white woman have much more in common than the white woman and the black woman, despite their difference in sex. Similarly, the black man and the black woman have much more in common than the black man and the white man. Their attitude toward life is much more similar. The basis of color cuts right through the sisterhood or brotherhood of sex. It boils down to the old issue of prejudice and the suppression of blacks by both sexes, to the way that they are forced to live. . . . Thus, the loyalty to your sex is secondary to the loyalty to your race. That's why Women's Liberation is, I think, a farce in South Africa. It's a bit ridiculous when you see white girls at the University campaigning for Women's Liberation because they're kicked out of some fraternity-type club or because they can't get into bars the way men do. Who cares? A black woman has got things to worry about much more serious than these piffling issues. White women have the vote; *no* black, male or female, has. ("A Conversation" 19–20)

Why Gordimer characterizes feminism in this way is implicit in the circularity sustaining the hierarchy she constructs. For Gordimer, feminism is "secondary," farcical, "piffling," personal (a matter of social-club membership) not political (loyalty to the struggle against apartheid)—something for educated, middle- or upper-class whitegirls. These women share a subject position with Gordimer and her character Rosa Burger. They are like her (white women), and they also occupy the position of white privilege she wishes to denounce (to be against apartheid). In her refusal to advance a critique of the (hetero)-sex-gender system, Gordimer inscribes feminism on one side of the black/white divide that apartheid produces.

Gordimer's critique of white privilege requires her to place the black woman first, limited though her understanding may be concerning who the "black woman" is and what she wants and what that "first place" might be, matters which take on great specificity in Williams's *Dessa Rose*, for example. Gordimer also makes a gesture that saves her, however, in the endless struggle against an assigned subject position, her racial privilege—what she as a white (woman) in South Africa *has* but does not necessarily *want*. The danger in this missionary-like position is that we might only always answer for and from ourselves. Gordimer demonstrates such a limitation through the white character Hillela's meditation on her black lover in *A Sport of Nature:* "The blackness was a glove. And everywhere, all over you, the black was a cover. Something God gave you to wear. Underneath, you must be white like me.—Or pale brownish, it's my Portuguese blood.— White like me; because that's what I was told, when I was being taught not to be prejudiced: underneath, they are all just like us. Nobody said we are just like *you*" (178). In this novel, there is no such thing as "an innocent white" (162), an assertion which turns supremely ironic, encompassing Gordimer herself as she creates a white woman to be the princess for her futuristic free African state's black ruler. She seems to forget her own strategic cautions when she enters the space of the heterosexual couple. In a world where whites can't trust themselves, the test of one's political commitments under apartheid has to be addressed through the questions: What does it do for blacks? How, when, and under what conditions? Gordimer will not allow us to ask how beneficial feminism might be for blacks and whites until racial consciencization has taken place. Thus, the scene of the women's meeting in Flora Donaldson's living room, where racist white women insist on co-opting black women, urging them to "SMILE AND SAY THANKS" to promote racial understanding, or "our Bantu women must pull together with us" (202) for road safety, is captured finally in the injunction, "We don't need to bring politics into the fellowship of women" (203). The construction of a hierarchy of the oppressed and a single-focused struggle for liberation is a defeating exercise, reminiscent of Beauvoir's initial insistence that resolution of the class struggle would cure all other social dis-ease, a position she is later compelled to relinquish. The identity politics of whites and blacks prohibit interrelationship. Acting it out before us, Gordimer sums up her position, along with that of Rosa and other white Communists: "the oppression of black women [is] primarily by race and only secondarily by sex discrimination" (199).

Gordimer offers feminist readers more than an opportunity to take a critical look at our political interests. Considering Gordimer's female characters' position in the scheme of competing loyalties, Sheila Roberts provides the following summary: "I would say that the female characters in her novels are all more troubled about their moral position as citizens in a racist country than they are about their position as women relating to men. Not that these two positions do not inter-lock at times: they do. Nevertheless, in those novels with female protagonists the strongest focus is not on their status as women but on the moral validity of action as women in various circumstances in an overall political ambience" (45). There is something about Gordimer's texts that, as much as she denies it, invites us to consider this knot of interlocking oppressions and complicities. Her works are valuable to us as feminists precisely for the way in which she figures women negotiating the relationship of their subject position in the context of race and class conflict, for the repressed awareness of their interconnectedness, required in an intertwined emergence, for political effectiveness. As such, she stops short of offering texts in which revolutionary women as women—like Ruth and Dessa in Williams's text—act cooperatively to change those assignments in revolutionary ways.

There is much to be said for Gordimer's strategy of putting blacks in the lead as we resist territorialization (Gordimer claims, for example, that her novel would have had "a different ending . . . without the Soweto riots" ["Interview" 269]). They will write an/other story, as editor Ellen Kuzwayo demonstrates in her "Foreword" to the collection *Women in South Africa: From the Heart:*

> All these stories without exception, highlight the problems which confront all or the majority of black women in this country: problems of forced pregnancy from their white employers, where some of them end up killing infants from that intercourse to avoid arrest for breaking the now repealed "Immorality Act." Others are problems of lack or total absence of accommodation, whilst they have children who need a home and some comfort; or those of endless child bearing from husbands who are unsympathetic and indifferent to the health state of their wives; whilst others because of unemployment, are compelled to end up washer-women, earning very low wages; which make it impossible to react to any tragedy which befalls the family; and those deserted by their husbands who return home as corpses, the families and community expecting them to carry the cost of burying the dead man. (2)

For these black South African women, the positions of "woman" and "black," while inseparable, are not identical. They are blackwomen whose bodies are used (up) by white and black men, and whose black husbands and children return as corpses, victims of the racist state. This perspective leads Radhakrishnan to pose tentatively, as a model for constructing the revolutionary subject, an "improper *bricolage"—* "a structural *topos"* where multivalent discourses "may be said to meet, interrupt, and throw each other into crisis" ("Negotiating" 284, 285). Subjects (whites, blacks, feminists, theorists, for example) are not without positions, assigned and elected, but these Identities are subject to negotiation, intervention, and change.

Without doubt, South Africa demands unrelenting attention to apartheid/revolution, but it certainly offers itself as well for feminist intervention as a site where race and gender institutionally reinforce one another. To say, as Gordimer does, that "The feminist battle must come afterwards" ("A Story" 105) is to refuse to read the texts of feminists like Shulamith Firestone, Barbara Smith, or Virginia Woolf, who writes in *Three Guineas*, "the public and the private worlds are inseparably connected; . . . the tyrannies and servilities of the one are the tyrannies and servilities of the other" (142). The simultaneity of nonsynchronous but plural subject positions (Radhakrishnan, "Negotiating" 277) signals the need for theorizing the revolutionary subject in terms of multiple, coincident oppressions (Barbara Smith, "Introduction" xxxii), where the struggles against racism, classism, and sexism are coextensive, simultaneous rather than serial.

Gordimer's painful and misdirected segregation of feminism from political resistance occurs most often in interviews where she separates the most personal (sexual intimacy) from the political:

> there's no issue in this country—I defy anybody to bring up an issue, except perhaps the very personal one of the love relationship between men and women . . . But all other issues—can you have a bank account in your name, the ownership of property, the rights over your children, what happens when you get divorced, all these things, not to mention of course the most important of all, equal pay for equal work, and other conditions, maternity benefits and so on—as soon as you touch any of the real feminist issues you are going right into the heart of the racial problem. ("A Story" 103)

Curiously, Gordimer states my point just as she denies it. The most powerful threat of feminism, the difference she reserves for it in the passage above, would seem to be not how it might diffuse or obscure the need to subvert white supremacy but how it unsettles the very personal issue of (white?) heterosexual intimacy. Feminism presents its threat, is the most personal and the most pervasively political, when it enters the bedroom, "the love relationship between men and women." The personal becomes political in the sanctuary of the bedroom where the home (with feminism) is no longer a sanctuary. This is its excess, the personal that is more than personal, that Gordimer refuses to engage in her texts, though they perversely stage this scene nonetheless, again and again, just as they challenge the ease with which a certain kind of feminism fails to project itself into the dimension of political action that exceeds the personal.

Gordimer and her characters play out an instructive struggle with historical evolution, the making of a new future with its attendant (synchronous) relations to past and future. Just as feminists are invited to scrutinize ideological positions, political and/as discursive loyalties, Rosa reviews a history of betrayals within and issuing from the Communist party, seeking a multidimensional record of the past, as opposed to the one-dimensional political polemic. She wants to differentiate herself from her father, and other party members, who wait in prison or at home for "*The* Future" (112), as something already known and specified. Observing "I would like once and for all to match the facts with what I ought to know" (111), Rosa searches for a founding epistemology, an authorizing text upon which her present and future can be built. Like the alternative Afrikaner (and U.S.) mythos of God, family, and country, the language of revolution requires redefinition and reclamation before Rosa can act with personal/political purpose. Engaging the personally and rhetorically obscure "difference between the truth and the facts," Rosa indicts the language of struggle: "My father's biographer, respectfully coaxing me onto the stepping-stones of the official vocabulary—words, nothing but dead words, abstractions: that's not where reality is, you flung at me—national democratic revolution, ideological integration, revolutionary imperative, minority domination, liberation alliance, unity of the people, infiltration, incursion, viable agency for change, reformist option, armed tactics, mass political mobilization of the people in combination of legal, semi-legal and clandestine methods" (142). And the "reality" Rosa recalls is the alleged and unlikely suicide (a white fiction) of "Baasie's" father in prison, and the encounter where she tells her father at a prison visit that her clandestine activities had been successfully completed. Such events, while in the service of political interests, stand in contradistinction to the "propositions of the faithful" which she understands "in a way theory doesn't explain" (151).

This revision of political history is inseparable from her revision of her relationship with her parents; her analytic gesture performs the operation feminism wants in its yoking of the personal and the political: "In 1956 when the Soviet tanks came into Budapest I was his little girl, dog-paddling to him with my black brother Baasie, the two of us reaching for him as a place where no fear, hurt or pain existed. And later, when he was in jail and I began to think back, even I . . . could not have found the way to ask him—in spite of all these things: do you still believe in the future? The same Future? Just as you always did?" (115). Rosa rejects the role of waiting for the revolution, to be made. At first she refuses waiting out of a desire that the revolutionary process be over, foreclosed, or carried on independently of her: "It is complete only for Lionel Burger; he has done all he had to do and that, in his case, happened to imply a death in prison as part of the process. It does not occur to them [other CP members] that it could be complete for themselves, for me" (113). She enacts Gordimer's more complex awareness that, in this continuing political process, the moment of the Future when South Africa's black majority has been freed, enfranchised, and assumes political power, will not necessarily be the Future that revolution took as its end, that "revolution" is not a movement, the beginning and ending of which we can necessarily ascertain.

If the totalizing vision of The Future is shaken loose, diversified, the strategies required for social change of necessity change also. Thus, *Burger's Daughter* involves the translation of one generation's struggle into the terms of the next, the children educate the parents. As Rosa states, "I could have quoted General Giap's definition of the art of insurrection as knowing how to find forms of struggle appropriate to the political situation at each stage" (126). Specifically, the novel chronicles the shift from revolution as conceived by the African National Congress under the influence of white Communists to revolution designed and directed by blacks through the Black Consciousness Movement. The political "place" of the South African people against apartheid is articulated in the space between these two positions, just as I believe feminism(s) and feminist literary criticism must be re-figured as negotiation between/among positions. How ideologies are constructed and interact in Gordimer's novel are thus instructive. First, there is Rosa's reflection on what her father lived for: "*The future* he was living for until the day he died can be achieved only by black people with the involvement of the small group of white revolutionaries who have solved the contradiction between black consciousness and class consciousness, and qualify to make unconditional common cause with the struggle for full liberation, e.g., a national and social revolution" (126). Second, the extended living room debate concerning class and race struggle challenges the view of the fifties and early sixties, prevailing then and lingering still in what we might call an undecided third moment (the remainder of the discourse on apartheid) (see Derrida, "Racism's Last Word"). Here the young black man, Dhladhla, articulates the position of black solidarity: "Whites, whatever you are, it doesn't matter, It's no difference. You can tell them—Afrikaners, liberals, Communists. We don't accept anything from anybody. We take" (157); "All collaboration with whites has always ended in exploitation of blacks" (159); "He doesn't live black, what does he know what a black man needs? He's only going to *tell* him—"(the somewhat essentialist and accusatory position of the "other," rather like the one Barbara Johnson takes with respect to Derrida's standing philosophically but not politically for woman [159]). The position can be summed up as follows: "Our liberation cannot be divorced from black consciousness because we cannot be conscious of ourselves and at the same time remain slaves" (164). The rhetoric of Black Consciousness, in its capacity to ossify otherwise fluid positions, to construct opposition among those against apartheid, functions analogously to other political discourses. Rosa reflects, "I've heard all the black clichés before. I am aware that, like the ones the faithful use, they are an attempt to habituate ordinary communication to overwhelming meanings in human existence" (328). Communism schooled her in the structuring impulse embedded in destructuring (and even "deterritorializing") political discourses as revolution turns to historical finality, or as Baudrillard asserts in *The Mirror of Production*, "Positivized under the sign of progress by the bourgeoisie, or dialecticized under the sign of revolution by Marxism, it [revolution] is always the case of an imposition of a meaning, the rational projection of an objective finality opposing itself to the radicality of desire which, in its non-meaning, cuts through all finality" (155). By (ex)tension, Baudrillard offers the means to construct an/other reading of the relation between the private discourse of the bedroom that Gordimer's revolutionary social text wants to suppress, even as it presents its own critique of revolutionary struggle. But political rhetorics work; they are powerful in their capacity to provide motivating narratives. As such, we too (political activists and feminist literary critics) might agree, "They become enormous lies incarcerating enormous truths" (328).

The need to challenge the notion of difference as a politically conservative (false) pluralism, in which all positions/differences are accommodated to a controlling center, in favor of a post-structuralist play of difference which remains, though in crisis through contact and negotiation, throws a new light on the assertion of positions as political rallying points. Baym's insistence, for example, on a feminist criticism without theory offers us a firm position from and with which to negotiate. At stake, then, are the particular interests of those holding identifiable positions. In *Burger's Daughter*, Dhladhla presents an/other perspective containing a keen fix on the "no-place" of whites in the new South Africa. In his view, they work from different centers of interest. The white man "goes [to prison] for his ideas about me, I go for my ideas about myself" (159). His assessment of Lionel Burger's action is that "He knows what he was doing in jail. A white knows what he must do if he doesn't like what he is. That's his business. We only know what we must do ourselves" (160). Similarly, in response to Orde Greer's self-centered question as to what the radical young black man would do if he were white, Dhladhla responds: "I don't think about that" (167). Whites in South Africa must find their own ways of taking responsibility, just as it is of crucial political/personal importance that blacks formulate their own identity politics. Rosa is on the other side of a political dialectic, rejecting the master-slave relationship of the white colonial to the black African. What she does not realize is that once she makes this move, there is no longer a choice. In a comment which sounds the death knell to Conrad's existential isolation and which Rosa at the time cannot accept, the pitiful Claire Terblanche articulates the nonchoice position of the daughters of South African white Communists: "Yes . . . I suppose if you want to look at it like that. . . . But no! Rosa! What choice? Rosa? In this country, under this system, looking at the way blacks live—what has the choice to do with parents? What else could you choose?" (127). Perhaps Claire expresses the political-as-political: what must be chosen irrespective of the personal, the family drama and the bedroom. Rosa reflects on the difference between the position of black and white Communists of her father's generation and that of the black nationalists represented by Dhladhla and the students: "Whites, not blacks, are ultimately responsible for everything blacks suffer and hate, even at the hands of their own people; a white must accept this if he concedes any responsibility at all. If he feels guilty, he is a liberal; in that house where I grew up there was no guilt because it was believed it was as a ruling class and not a colour that whites assumed responsibility. It wasn't something bleached into the flesh" (161). In the Black Consciousness Movement's reconceptualization of revolution, the class struggle is perceived as "white nonsense," in place of which racism and capitalism will be eliminated through "a race struggle" (163)—a unity that whites, in their own self-interest, present(ed) as the interest of "humanity" (another suspicious generic rivaling "man" and "mankind") and have historically opposed. Again, the argument against a hierarchized agenda for social action is pertinent, extending as well to Gordimer's desire to defer (until when?) the struggle against sexism.

Rosa needs to rewrite the Manichean black/white: evil/good: slave/master opposition (see JanMohamed), to escape the false consciousness of romanticizing or fearing blackness. Orde Greer's embarrassing question is her question, is Gordimer's and mine too: "What would you do if you were me? *What is to be done?*" (172). The latter question echoes the title of Lenin's text, the fixed and conclusive answer he provides challenged by the insistence on revolution's open form in Gordimer and others. Without doubt, something is to be done, but the question is not enough. For the moment, Rosa, in her search for an answer to this undecidable, nagging question, settles on the idea that, for her parents, connections between people result from believing in the connections; they are a matter of faith. She reflects on her family as follows: "Lionel—my mother and father—people in that house, had a connection with blacks that was completely personal. In this way, their Communism was the antithesis of anti-individualism. . . . At last there was nothing between this skin and that . . . it was a human conspiracy, above all other kinds" (172). However, Rosa's encounter with "Baasie" concerning this comfortable theory of skin and difference demonstrates the way in which self(interested) positioning and negotiation as crisis that unsettles position advance the revolutionary project.

"Baasie's" accusing eyes followed Rosa around the room like that other BOSS, apartheid's surveillance expert, the Bureau of State Security; he has a certain moral and political if not legal undeniability, as Rosa finds herself caught between the personal indictment of her black childhood friend and the political indictment of the state apparatus. The "sibling" relationship of Rosa and Zwelinzima Vulindlela ("Baasie") proves transitory, as white "sister" and black "brother" betray one another. He rejects his Afrikaner name "Baasie" ('little master' or 'boss') and asserts his African name, Zwelinzima 'Suffering land' (318), indicting Burger as another white engaged in the "takeover" of blacks (see Clingman 183). Zwelinzima shares his complaint with the Soweto Students Representative Council: the Burgers of South Africa get accolades for their role in the liberation movement (tendencies offensively replayed in films like *Cry Freedom* and *Mississippi Burning*), while the African leaders, like Zwelinzima's father, victim (of racial murder) masked as agent (prison suicide), are discredited and erased from history. Rosa fights back, sharing in the betrayal as she accuses Zwelinzima of remaining at a safe distance from serious struggle. Cooke offers the following view of the scene:

> She shows her acceptance of a different bond between them as their taunts reach their nastiest pitch. They seem to be "poking with a stick at some creature writhing between them," an image which recalls the brutal mule beating that led Rosa to leave the

country. Her conversation with Baasie prompts her return by calling up the brutality inherent in any relationship between privileged whites and dispossessed blacks. Rosa's acceptance of hate as well as love—monstrous detachment and excessive identification—in her bond with Baasie makes the woman we see at the close of *Burger's Daughter*. (Cooke 216)

While this is without question a pivotal scene, the political resonances of which recur, it is not yet the moment of Rosa's turning back to South Africa. The Rosa of the novel's close has (re)negotiated the age-old opposition played out in the interaction between black and white, where they each take up their assigned parts: "In one night we succeeded in manoeuvring ourselves into the position their history books back home have ready for us—him bitter; me guilty" (330).

Out of her experiences, her reflection on her place with respect to the family and the state, Rosa, like all of us (even when we think we are not choosing), must make a choice. Every choice, including nonchoice, author-izes a course of action. Rosa assumes her "place," a dis-placed one, in her own name, a "place" redefined in relation both to her father and to Black Consciousness. After Black Consciousness, after the Soweto uprising, political alignments in South Africa are never quite the same again (see Mandela 118–28).

Clingman makes a good case for reading Rosa's identity as "overdetermined," that she is "the most *determinate*" of subjects with respect to socially responsible and committed life: "Certainly, her commitment has been seen to have many sides; but then all those sides accumulate towards that commitment. . . . the novel, in 'walking around' Rosa in its narrative plurality, has increased rather than decreased her final concreteness. Its procedures have set up the narrative 'space' in which Rosa has occurred, defined (if not filled) from both inside and outside, and proceeding towards her historically necessary destiny" (191). Insisting on the overdetermined in preference to the indeterminate, Clingman maintains that "for Rosa Burger in her way, and for Gordimer's novel in its own, there is the affirmation of an historical synthesis: of the inheritance of Lionel Burger in its post-Soweto form. The revolutionary 'subject' of *Burger's Daughter* has been constructed" (193). I would claim, further, that the tension between the "overly specified" and the "unspecifiable" drives the rhetoric of (re)figuration. Rosa assumes her destiny, as Lionel Burger's daughter, by accepting the responsibility to act, but her way of getting there—through a respect for Black Consciousness, the reformulation of Communist ideology, the man on the park bench, the donkey, the old woman on the Riviera, all re-figurings of the inside/outside, private/public, assigned/elected oppositions—is her own, taken in recognition that life, even the life of pleasure, is subject to that final sentence, that while existentially we all end up at the same "place," the identities we elect through action today write tomorrow in a decidedly different way.

There is a certain formalized uncertainty, the ambiguity at the heart of each individual, that Gordimer, through her mode of narration, attempts to represent, even as she leaves it in a state of mystery. It is a strategy I, as a feminist critic, find useful as a means of negotiating relationships with others. She explains in "The Art of Fiction," "I know that I've been fascinated by the kind of person Rosa is for many years. It's as if the secret of a life is there, and slowly I'm circling, coming closer and closer to it" (Hurwitt 113). So it is the mystery, the off-the- center, the expression of the not-to-be-discovered, rather than "absolute" or "determined" character, Identity-itself, which interests her and serves as a model for characterization and narrative strategy. JanMohamed aptly describes Gordimer's approach in contrast with other white colonial writers: "unlike the subjectivity in the works of Cary and Dinesen, which derives its intensity from the desire to maintain a coherent self, in Gordimer's fiction it is a product of her willingness to embrace incoherence in order to root out unconscious biases and desires" (272–73). Gordimer writes against a final interpretation—not so much to thwart the reader but to capture what the writer sees, much of which she does not understand (in the sense of being able finally to decide the proper direction and strategy for South African revolution) and can only speculate about as her characters perform alternatives. Through the novel, she poses a conflict which she regards as "central to civilized man's existence" and summarizes as follows: "what is a meaningful life? Is there a cause greater than the gift of life itself? Can one fulfil oneself simply by earning a living, falling in love, marrying and producing the next generation, with no concern for anyone outside the family circle? Conversely, can one fulfil oneself while sacrificing personal emotional preoccupations, ambitions, joys and sorrows—what is generally accepted as the pursuit of happiness—to the selflessness exacted by faith in a cause greater than oneself?" ("What Happened" 17). These are precisely the questions raised by feminism's interest in the relation of the personal to the political.

While Rosa redefines the terms of her action, the specific theory (in)forming that redefinition remains vague and her exact motive to action and future actions unspecified. In other words, the *theory* of revolution and its implementation remain "open" questions, while the *need* for revolution does not. Rosa's visit to see "The Lady and the

Unicorn" tapestry in the Musée de Cluny, an important and beautiful scene which critics rarely discuss,[4] can be read, like the unicorn tapestries, as an emblematic passage, marking the character's final turn back to South Africa upon her realization that "No one can defect" (332). In the first tapestry which, with the sixth, interests Gordimer most, the spectators gaze at the unicorn and the lady. The unicorn serves as always-illusory identity: "This is the creature that has never been" (304); "*O dieses ist das Tier das es nicht gibt*" (340). Recalling the mirror reflections constructing Rosa's identity at the novel's opening (14), we see the spectators gazing at the unicorn and the lady, and the unicorn regarding the tiny "naturalized" image of himself in the lady's hand-held mirror—a unicorn without a horn. In another closed circuit of mirroring self-(re)presentation, the lady's oval face imitates the mirror, her hair twisted up in a braid like the unicorn's horn (or his horn like her hair?), both constructed "to imitate a spiral" (340). Clearly Gordimer has studied the tapestries carefully; the visit to the Cluny is positioned near the novel's end, to (re)figure from another perspective Rosa's dilemma and ours. As Gordimer explains, the six tapestries represent the five senses, but we are left with an excess, the uncertainty of the sixth, thought by art critics to convey "a deep moral significance" concerning the renunciation of the passions (Erlande-Brandenburg 12)—what I want to call, despite my suspicion in doing so, the personal as "purely" personal—depicted in the previous panels.

The sixth tapestry is known by the legend inscribed over the lady's tent canopy, "*À mon seul désir*" (341). Here Rosa Burger turns away from being Bernard Chabalier's mistress who is "not accountable to the Future," and she meditates on the unicorn, "A mythical creature. *Un paradis inventé*" (304). The tapestry's interpreter, Erlande-Brandenburg, translates the French by analogy to the Latin inscription "Liberum arbitrium," noting, "We know what the philosophers meant by 'free will': for Socrates and Plato it was the natural disposition to behave rightly, which we lose because, through our senses, we become the slaves of our passions. . . . 'à mon seul désir,' that is, 'in accordance only with my will' " (68). While we may "know" what the philosophers meant (a point open to question), we can place alongside it the novel's second epigraph where "knowing" in this state of free will only reveals itself as knowledge when we act it (out). At the Cluny, like the earlier visit to see the paintings by Bonnard, for whom "It's as if nothing has ever happened" (287), Rosa, as "the place in which something has occurred," for whom there are prisoners in Soviet asylums and an oppressed black majority in South Africa, contemplates the juxtaposition of the utopic with the "real": "An old and lovely world, gardens and gentle beauties among gentle beasts. Such harmony and sensual peace in the age of the thumbscrew and dungeon" (341). Her identity is conflated with that of the lady, the unicorn, and South Africa (about which "there is nothing left to fear" [341]) as she "Sits gazing, this creature that has never been" (341). And, like the woman in the tapestry, Rosa renounces her life in France to (re)turn to her "place" in South Africa, itself awaiting invention as paradise. She sees in it a new way of loving: "to love you by letting you come to discover what I love" (341), a point which lends weight to Boyers's assessment that "Politics here is conceived simultaneously as a choice and a vocation, a fate and an ambitiously forbidding object of desire" (81). Leaving behind her lover Chabalier, the sensuous pleasures of food, herbs, light, love's caresses in exile, she goes home to prison, where even her prison cell is described in terms of the beauty of a spot of light, a pleasure worth relating and thus worth censoring.

Under the pretense of pursuing her "hobby," Rosa (re)draws the unicorn tapestries, the scenes from Bonnard, the boat made by Conrad's friends, and the landscape of the Riviera, in a "naive imaginary landscape that could rouse no suspicions that she might be incorporating plans of the layout of the prison etc.—it represented, in a number of versions, a village covering a hill with a castle on the apex, a wood in the foreground, the sea behind. The stone of the houses seemed to give a lot of trouble: it was tried out in pinks, greys, even brownish orange. She had been more successful with the gay flags on the battlements of the castle and the bright sails of tiny boats, although through some failure of perspective they were sailing straight for the tower" (355). Again scene and significance coalesce as past pleasures are recuperated in codes for a new political purpose, another kind of *"paradis inventé"* (287) which makes it possible "to act," her synonym for "to live" (296). Thus, Gordimer gives us, even in the end, the simultaneously necessary personal/political solution that I want to figure for feminism.

Burger's Daughter is, without question, a very political and a very personal work. In his assessment of Gordimer's achievement in the novel, Robert Boyers comments: "She has, in fact, reconceived the very idea of private experience and created a form that can accommodate microscopic details of individual behavior and sentiment without suggesting for a moment that individuals are cut off from the collective consciousness and political situations characteristic of their societies" (63). In their painful conversation, Rosa and "Baasie," once "sister" and "brother," confront each other as "other" (a position, we must acknowledge, that "Baasie" is only able to assume through the power of Black Consciousness). Revealing the "real" reason for his call and his anger, he says accusingly, "You're different so I must be different too. You aren't white and I'm not black" (321). What their names signify in the political sphere is the subject examined here; each one stands as an undeniable contradiction (which they seek to deny all the more vehemently) to the stark black/white, subject/object dichotomies that structure the political rhetoric of race (the other black/white dichotomy). In this respect JanMohamed notes that Gordimer "did not inherit the otherness of blacks as a *neutral* ontological fact, rather it was valorized for her in a manner that became profoundly problematic: 'If you are [born] white, you begin from the premise of being *white*. Are they different because they are black? Or are they black because they are different?' " (84). The narrative circles around this and other undecided problematics, the question left open in a revolutionary gesture (also the "essential gesture" for the artist) that resists the closure of the revolutionary process by refusing to "place" it, to contain it within a homogeneous narrative prescription.

Although Gordimer maintains, as she must, that "As a novelist I am not interested in 'reconciling' political ideologies" ("What Happened" 29), still, her text is subversive: it too acts out for the reader what it knows. She recuperates the excluded and the repressed, bringing together what cannot be seen, through textuality's capacity to "place" side by side what apartheid insists on keeping separate and invisible (see "Gesture" 145). She says concerning the Soweto Students Representative Council pamphlet, a historically banned publication by a banned organization, "I reproduced the document exactly as it was, in all its naivety, leaving spelling mistakes and grammatical errors uncorrected, because I felt it expressed more eloquently and honestly than any pamphlet I could have invented, the spirit of the young people who wrote it" ("What Happened" 30). This loyalty to their spirit, her respect for the materiality of their words, provides a way of guarding against the subject position she knows she occupies as a white South African. She presents us with an image of this position that she wants to resist in *A World of Strangers*, where she writes of what the white man hears when he listens to black people. The Englishman Toby Hood, in the township church at Christmas, hears the choirs of small boys and women singing "with the unearthly voices of Africans: voices that seem to have a register of their own" (194). In the interest of letting this "unnatural" voice speak as the "natural" voice of South Africa, Gordimer (re)presents the pamphlet in its unaltered form, but, as is always the case with reproduction, in a radically altered and altering context. Their words and hers share textual space, rub up against one another. Furthermore, Gordimer's strategy of using what is at hand through unattributed quotation (Marx, Lenin, Slovo), the extent of which Clingman documents well (186–88), reinforces the notion of the textual body as a *bricolage* of/ for revolution—a space of memory, re-coverer of both forgotten and forbidden words. Clingman observes, "This functionalism . . . not only introduces the actual mood of the time (in the case of the SSRC pamphlet) but from the point of view of authorship it overrides the conventions of bourgeois property relations—in this sense 'owner-ship' of the documents or phrases used. The novel opts for use-value in preference to exchange-value: what is important is that the words are reproduced, and not the exchange of ownership rights denoted by the 'purchase' of textual attribution" (187–88). Like the Burgers, Gordimer uses words as she needs them, in the interest of a larger political purpose which we are invited to "know."

Gordimer ultimately does not and cannot separate Rosa from her body; she cannot keep woman's body at home, in the realm of the personal. Instead, Rosa's "mysterious body" is turned inside out, the most personal made the most public in the political site of the prison. The body is a reading/writing place. Surely the South African land-scape inscribes itself as well in the opening description of the menstru-ating woman, an apt figure for the political body—as a "crisis of destruction, the purging, tearing, draining" (16) of the sociopolitical machinery of apartheid—without the comforting regularity, the punc-tuality of the cyclical, re-productive capacity for re/generation.

In the effort to read both history and present conflict, Rosa be-comes an analogue for the Barthesian reader: "the space on which all the quotations that make up a writing are inscribed without any of them being lost; a text's unity lies not in its origin but in its destination" (Barthes, *Image* 148); Gordimer makes of herself and us such reading spaces as well. Like Burger in the dock, and the revolutionary South African text, she redefines categories. Rosa, in the timeless, undiffer-entiated pleasure of the Riviera, feels "Like someone in prison" (222), and at the novel's close, she enjoys the fellowship of the imprisoned women. The (re)figuration also recalls Winnie Mandela's reflection that "I got more liberated in prison. The physical identification with your beliefs is far more satisfying than articulating them on a platform. . . . I am not saying it is best to be in prison. But under the circum-stances, where it is a question of which prison is better, the prison outside or inside—the whole country is a prison for the black man—

and when you are inside, you know why you are there, and the people who put you there also know" (105). My epigraph from Nelson Mandela (Mandela 148) resonates with the pronominal ambiguity of Gordimer's epigraph ("I am the space"). His freedom and mine, ours and theirs, black and white, the United States and South Africa—even though the historical context and political force of his remarks already stipulate that I read him as meaning only his freedom and that of his black brothers and sisters—coalesce in desire and politico-discursive space. Resembling Gordimer, who writes as though dead, Rosa writes from prison to a dead audience (Conrad, who if he isn't dead might as well be, her dead father, her dead mother, whose structural position she now occupies), the ones that set her free to engage this writing. Ironically, the novel's last reader, Madame Bagnelli, receives a card from Rosa, the final line of which was censored, so she "was never able to make it out" (361). This closing line of the novel suggests an interesting reversal in which Rosa, who writes from prison, has "made it out" and, in retrospect, is Gordimer's own signature anticipating the embargo, banning, and ultimate unbanning of her novel in South Africa. But who can read Rosa's censored text? Is she destined to (be)come Burger's daughter—arrested, tried, jailed for life (death) on treason charges? Did she do or will she have done what "they" (the Communist family/the South African state) say she did? How, in us as readers, the ultimate "place" of Gordimer's South African narrative, will Rosa's story be "concocted," many more times in many more versions? And how, finally, are we as feminist readers to negotiate the complex (of) identities, interests, and relationships, to theorize our actions and act (out) our theories in order to take (our) places as "revolutionary subjects"?

CHAPTER FOUR

Re:Writing "The Other" in Marguerite Duras's *The Lover*

> To know that one does not write for the other, to know that these things I am going to write will never cause me to be loved by the one I love (the other), to know that writing compensates for nothing, sublimates nothing, that it is precisely *there where you are not*—this is the beginning of writing.
>
> —Roland Barthes, *A Lover's Discourse*

> knots—entanglements among persons, characters, texts, discourses, commentaries and cross-commentaries . . . knots between desire and frustration, mastery and loss, madness and reason, illness and cure, men and women. In a word, love. Which some have called transference. Which some have called reading. Which some have called writing. Which some have called *écriture*. Which some have called displacement, slippage, gap. Which some have called the unconscious. Which some have called the discourse of the Other. Which, if it can be spoken (of), written (of) at all, produces knots.
>
> —Susan Rubin Suleiman, *Discourse in Psychoanalysis and Literature*

The question of "the Other" remains one of feminism's most pressing interests, as it seems to come to us from within—what we understand as different, but nonetheless part of "us"—and as it strikes us from without—what we understand to be something or someone else and therefore not part of or like us, the intentional and unwitting exclusions Feminism commits in the interest of consolidating and asserting its identity. The oppositions according to which the Other is figured—inside/outside, masculine/feminine, heterosexual/homosexual, white/black, subject/object, theory/practice—issue from hierarchized polarities inhabiting language and structuring philosophical thought in Western elite culture. We typically represent otherness simplistically: I am female/he is male; I am white/she is black; I am a professor/she is a carpenter; I am gay/she is straight. The fact of the matter is that we may simultaneously occupy multiple positions although, in the interest of shoring up an Identity, we write and speak as though some one-directional opposition were at issue. "Otherness" is written as a single or singular site—an opposition and a thing to be opposed, something or someone outside us, a resistance which we resist. As such, then, "the Other" (re)presents itself either as something to be destroyed, subjugated, or assimilated in the very fundamental human interest of reducing tension (in an economy of desire), that is, seeking pleasure through some perhaps only illusory but nonetheless comforting sameness; or as some mystical difference which is elevated and preserved in its status as "not me" in order to protect the fetishized singularity, the sanctity, of the subject position, "I"; or as some part of myself which I need to deny in order to "pass" in a world dominated by others who do not like the difference(s) and remind me that I am supposed to be "alien" to them; or as some essential spec(tac)ular "woman" that I want to discover and claim for "myself" and for Feminism.

Black women and radical lesbians have been most outspoken in reminding other feminists of how they have been excluded from feminist literary criticism and theory. How to engage this dilemma poses a serious threat to the interests of forging coalitional feminist politics. Todorov's study of alterity is instructive on a cultural level. He advances two options characteristic of how one views the other: to see the other as the same, in identity with the self, resulting in assimilationism, the reduction of the "object" to the values of the "subject," or to see the other as different, always leading or subject to hierarchicization—superior (self)/inferior (other). As other chapters demonstrate, with respect to the Indian (Silko and Menchu), the African black (Gordimer), the Oriental (Duras), the African-American (Williams), and the lesbian (Rich), the problem is how to see, re-mark or re-present difference without judgment, when we know that such a neutral, value-free, descriptive, and non-normative language is impossible.

A double movement is required to undo the double discourse of alterity—one including both the revelation and the rejection of alterity as it is conventionally construed. Todorov asks, "How can Columbus be associated with these two apparently contradictory myths, one whereby the Other is a 'noble savage' (when perceived at a distance) and one whereby he is a 'dirty dog,' a potential slave? It is because both rest on a common basis, which is the failure to recognize the Indians, and the refusal to admit them as a subject having the same rights as oneself, but different. Columbus has discovered America but not the Americans" (49). The question Todorov raises, in other words, is how can we see cultural alterity as alterity, not sameness, while we see human sameness as sameness, not difference? How can we speak of "woman" as neither self-presence nor lack? And, further, what does the relationship between these two problematics have to do with re-figuring feminist literary criticism?

The next two chapters throw into relief the contest between personal desire and political action we began to examine in *Burger's Daughter*. Thus far, the problem of monolithic identity has been represented in terms of the unsettling challenges posed to it through multiple subject positions, but this narrative still reads like one in which socially constructed subjects, fully present to themselves and their intentions, theorize their actions in the world or speak and act out their theories in purposeful ways. Marguerite Duras's *The Lover*, in its attention to the forces of desire, offers a limit case which, when brought back into the discussion of identity and relationships with others, suggests greater limits and larger possibilities with respect to the very personal and political problem of saying or doing what we mean and meaning what we do or say.

The project of theorizing the "Other" assumes particular import for feminist studies because it engages "woman's" conventionally assigned subject position, a negative space as compared with the positive identity that is man's and that, it is presumed, he cannot maintain without this oppositional structure. Terry Eagleton outlines the situation clearly:

> Woman is not just an other in the sense of something beyond his ken, but an other intimately related to him as the image of what he is not, and therefore as an essential reminder of what he is. Man therefore needs this other as he spurns it, is constrained to give a positive identity to what he regards as no-thing. Not only is his being parasitically dependent upon the woman, and upon the act of excluding and subordinating her, but one reason why such exclusion is necessary is because she may not be quite so other after all. Perhaps she stands as a sign of something in man himself which he needs to repress, expel beyond his own being, relegate to a securely alien region beyond his own definitive limits. Perhaps what is outside is also somehow inside, what is alien also intimate—so that man needs to police the absolute frontier between the two realms as vigilantly as he does just because it may always be transgressed, has always been transgressed already, and is much less absolute than it appears. (132–33)

The need to declare and to enforce the separation, the borderline between "self" and "other," is further underscored through the theoretical prohibition against the notion of the "Other" of the "Other," a tenet which serves as a first principle, the ground upon which an elaborate architecture of ideas is erected, the tune which a whole system of thought hums as it works, all parts ostensibly holding their places in a fine relational harmonics.

The writing system depends on otherness, as object of address or receiver, for its operation. As Todorov remarks, "any investigation of alterity is necessarily semiotic, and reciprocally, semiotics cannot be conceived outside the relation to the other" (157). Writing demands the other (in order) to work its signifying capacity, or, as Lacan puts it, the Other is "the locus in which is constituted the I who speaks to him who hears" (*Ecrits* 141). Language requires an/other to hear in order for an "I" to speak. In this sense, the other is already (in) language and (in) us as speaking subjects. Each one of us is the other, no one being purely and wholly "herself." Both the "subject" and the "Other" (the object, but more than the object) come into being through language, as one addresses another. Further, the writing system has no "itself"—no perfect selfsame systematicity without disruption.

Much has been written of late concerning the gaps, ruptures, and slippages in this grand architechtonics, the simultaneous error and insistence on the *grand récits* in which everything is put in its proper place. The site of rupture or excess is a figure expressive of the system's inability to manage, to contain (even "itself") perfectly. It points to a flaw the system needs to write (right) itself. When Lacan proclaims in *Ecrits*, for example, "there is no Other of the Other" (311), he once again, with respect to "woman," that barred subject, consigns her to the specular position she occupied in the Freudian psychosexual typography. The theoretical prohibition is exposed for what it is, a f(r)iction masquerading as Law which the One requires to maintain (his) dominance, the exclusion or repression required for signification to occur and for identity to be assumed, that is, the fiction required for the great narrative to assert its truth. To expose the scandal of "woman's place" is to ask for a new writing practice, just as the call for a Feminism which is feminism(s) invites the re-figuration of feminist literary criticism.

Because of its intricate convolutions, Marguerite Duras's novel *The Lover* (published in France in 1984 as *L'Amant* and winner of the prestigious Prix Goncourt) is the site of very unsettling experiences, *liter*-ally and figuratively, as it explodes the simple representation of otherness (even the project of representation itself) in which a writing and a reading respect the hierarchical relation of (op)positions where male/female, white skin/dark skin, rich/poor—and by analogy, theorist/feminist—stay on their (as)signed sides of the bar of dominance and submission, the One and the Other. Duras, her work admired by Lacan, enacts through her characters a much-neglected corollary elaboration which Lacan sets forth in "Guiding Remarks for a Congress on Feminine Sexuality" (omitted from the English selections in *Ecrits*). Here he recalls "a basic principle": the accession to language, assuming one's subject position, occurs through "the subjectivity of the Other as the place of its law. The otherness of sex is denatured by this alienation. Man here acts as the relay whereby the woman becomes this Other for herself as she is this Other for him. . . . Perhaps all that this conceptualization [which Lacan characterizes as "monstrous"] shows is how everything gets ascribed to the woman in so far as she represents, in the phallocentric dialectic, the absolute Other" (*FS* 93–94). We can read the limits of the Lacanian paradigm, as perhaps Lacan himself did, for sexual (non)relations—"the woman becomes this Other for herself"—as Duras sets in motion the elaborate system of relay switches which are supposed to regulate the dialectics, not only of phallocentrism but of racism (particularly in colonialism) and classism. Through the simultaneous play of multiple subject positions and infinite reduplication, signification takes (its) place and is disturbed, thwarted, as the Law which powers the system is both demonstrated and violated. Its "limits" exposed, the regulative capacities or technologies of the signifying chain are exceeded, and recalling Gordimer's epigraph in *Burger's Daughter*, something takes (its) place.

The Lover works with several settings—French Indochina (now Vietnam) during the 1930s; the frame (Duras's signature, a brief meditation on the "otherness" of her "ravaged" face, the recurring figure of the older woman) that locates writing in the scene of memory; the site of the "knot," of desire and the Other, or of the unconscious, through which, in the interest of (exploding) fictitious constructions of identity, like mine for Feminism, the Other speaks. Sharon Willis speculates provocatively on how "A text that begins with the face of its author, although it contains no images, and that elaborates a prolonged description of the author as a subtext to the love story, is, in a sense, a book about shaping a figure. This disfiguration of the face (figura) may be its real subject" (5). Perhaps the "subject" here is writing, how the face, a simulacrum of Identity, is written and read, a process in which, as the narrator tells us, she takes "the same sort of interest I might have taken in the reading of a book" (4).

The narrative slips and slides, with infrequent demarcating signs, between and among these scenes, across their boundaries and back. The narrator (re)crosses the Mekong River into a time when she is fifteen-and-a-half, living in Saigon and attending a French high school. Her father dead, her mother and the children are poor but white: "We were white children, we were ashamed, we sold our furniture, but we weren't hungry, we had a houseboy and we ate. Sometimes, admittedly, we ate garbage—storks, baby crocodiles—but the garbage was cooked and served by a houseboy, and sometimes we refused it, too, we indulged in the luxury of declining to eat" (6–7). These events which Duras also chronicled earlier in the more conventional narrative entitled *The Sea Wall* (1950) are "both different and the same" in this new text, which cannot resist its intertextual relations to Duras's earlier works (her face is "ravaged," recalling the woman in *The Ravishing of Lol Stein;* the mysterious beggar woman and Anne-Marie Stretter of *The Vice-Consul* and other works, reappear), a process Carol Murphy describes as one "wherein a text 'remembers' other texts in the same corpus" (67): "Text remembers or reads texts and boundaries between works disappear" (72). The difference between *The Sea Wall* and *The Lover* resides in Duras's effort in the latter to move across the river of consciousness, to "the hidden stretches of that same youth, of certain facts, feelings, events that I buried" (8) and into a textuality which escapes the reticence imposed by conventions of family morality and the letter: "Sometimes I realize that if writing isn't, all things, all contraries confounded, a quest for vanity and void, it's nothing. That if it's not, each time, all things confounded into one through some inexpressible essence, then writing is nothing but advertisement. But usually I have no opinion, I can see that all options are open now, that there seem to be no more barriers, that writing seems at a loss for somewhere to hide, to be written, to be read" (8). *The Lover* explores the space beyond the barrier, the space beyond consciousness, through a (re)reading of the family drama and through a writing of desire that acknowledges the inadequacy of the bar separating signifier and signified, as it ostensibly conjoins them, of the father's "no" which separates child-subject from her (m)other, and of the barrier, like the wall the girl's mother constructs to separate the family from the devastating tidal floods, that barrier to the Pacific of the earlier title—the French title of *The Sea Wall* is *Un barrage contre le Pacifique.* As such, these texts, each one or taken together, may be read as lessons concerning the limits of identity politics and a monolithic Feminism. The meditation resembles Silko's consideration of the "half-breed" and Gordimer's reflection on pleasure and politics vis à vis the color bar. Instead of respecting the structures which make signification possible and defending territorial boundaries (enforced separations), the Durasian text pursues the course of desire, as though it wants nothing and everything, the going (everywhere and nowhere) of desire as it ebbs and flows like the tidal floods, creating as it circulates in/as the only imperfectly channeled pathways of language. No respecter of (textual) identity, desire moves in, on and beyond the substitution of signifiers that occasions narrativity, showing itself as both a textual and a thematic concern (Murphy 86).

Duras signals the Other's function early in the novel in the moment of crossing the river. Like the unconscious that erects the figure of the Other at/as the installation of subjectivity and the accession to language, the significance of this crossing over or splitting of the subject is only represented (takes representatives) retrospectively: "The photograph could only have been taken if someone could have known in advance how important it was to be in my life, that event, that crossing of the river. But while it was happening, no one even knew of its existence. Except God. And that's why—it couldn't have been otherwise—the image doesn't exist. It was omitted. Forgotten. It never was detached or removed from all the rest. And it's to this, this failure to have been created, that the image owes its virtue: the virtue of representing, of being the creator of, an absolute" (10). Thus, the Law speaks itself: the subject has been installed in language, and its (con)fusing representational capacities come into play. The passage recalls Lacan's sidestepping in "The Signification of the Phallus" as he describes the process of subject constitution: "*It* speaks in the Other, I say, designating by the Other the very locus evoked by the recourse to speech in any relation in which the Other intervenes. If *it* speaks in the Other, whether or not the subject hears it with his ear, it is because it is there that the subject, by means of a logic anterior to any awakening of the signified, finds its signifying place. The discovery of what it articulates in that place, that is to say, in the unconscious, enables us to grasp at the price of what splitting (*Spaltung*) it has thus been constituted" (*Ecrits* 285). As we shall see in the next chapter on Rigoberta Menchu's struggle to enact a revolutionary politics based on the "pure" Indian, the Other is always already there in the speaking subject, in both terms— "speaking," as a language activity made possible through the Other to whom it is addressed, and "subject" (position), as a place in language and an identity construct projected from the field of the Other. In this sense, the Other is (in) me, representing my difference from myself—and it speaks, whether I listen or not.

Duras's text plays through the register of subject positions with little regard for fixity or stability of position in the signifying chain. Duras's character speaks in the first person, "I," is spoken of in the third person, "she," or as "the girl," "the child," an effect of what Trista Selous observes as the text's lack of a controlling point of view (145). The first-person speaker addresses us from the narrative present of the older woman looking back, and then later as the girl. With respect to this feature, Sharon Willis observes that in the "text's strategy of veiling and unveiling, where 'I' veils herself as 'she,' but where 'she' just as frequently masquerades as 'I,' we cannot maintain a rigid and secure separation of same and other, interior and exterior" (6). This is a well-practiced strategy for Duras as she exposes the sexual (non)relations in/of the subject. In an astute observation, Marcelle Marini says of *Hiroshima Mon Amour*, for example, "A woman with fixed eyes looks at a man with closed eyes and sees a young woman with closed eyes in front of a young man with fixed eyes. Something always escapes the gaze or the subject always escapes the inscription of the scene" (*Territoires* 19).[1] Stability of image and locutionary place are elusive, placed and displaced repeatedly, as "woman," the Other, object of man's desire, circulates: "Suddenly I see myself as another, as another would be seen, outside myself, available to all, available to all eyes, in circulation for cities, journeys, desire" (13). Like Rosa Burger standing before the prison gate, Duras's character is available for viewing, awaiting the gaze that creates her as "woman," as the Other that constitutes her as subject. She readies herself. Speaking of the masculine subject whose "Other" is "woman," Lacan explains in *Four Fundamental Concepts of Psycho-Analysis*: "it is in the space of the Other that he sees himself and the point from which he looks at himself is also in that space. Now, this is also the point from which he speaks, since in so far as he speaks, it is in the locus of the Other that he begins to constitute that truthful lie by which is initiated that which participates in desire at the level of the unconscious" (144). Duras, however, also enacts a writing of desire through the substitutability of the shifting, signifying place of the female subject—where "I" is taken up variously by one and then another. Contrary to law, her female speakers meditate on one another as her text performs a choreography of substitutable positionality and object choice. In a radicalizing gesture, it is "she," the narrator that the girl (who wants to be a writer, to be "Duras") has become, who structures this circulation of female image, body, and language, this study of/in a "photograph . . . never taken" (13). Hers is the body writing, re:writing.

Inevitably, writing disguises, reduces, and covers up as it produces, expresses, and creates (see Kauffman 112). This is the treachery at the heart of any discursive representation of feminist literary criticism. Desire is the hallucinogenic effect (affect) of the Other in the writing/speaking/reading subject. It is the displaced and displacing affect moving from one site to the next from its irreducibly obscure and inaccessible origin. This circuitry leads Barthes to observe that "there are no first figures, no last figures" (*Lover's* 8). The girl/woman's place in the family drama, the feminist critic's place in the critical/ theoretical field, is never "figured out." The characters continue to live out their roles "in that common family history of ruin and death which was ours whatever happened, in love or in hate, and which I still can't understand however hard I try, which is still beyond my reach, hidden in the very depths of my flesh, blind as a newborn child. It's the area on whose brink silence begins" (25). The place before the door, before the law that installs the subject in language, serves as a barrier to the enigmatic silence of the *before*, motivating one story after another in search of whatever "it" is that lies buried deep in the flesh.

In the interest of this question, Duras situates her reader in a psychic topography. The rivers are flat, large, almost fixed, but rush, like the rivers of desire, "into the caves of ocean," and the narrator constructs her text, like a seawall, on that temporary shore, but in memory of her mother's failed enterprise, "always afraid . . . [that] we might be swept out to sea. In the terrible current I watch my last moments. The current is so strong it could carry everything away— rocks, a cathedral, a city. There's a storm blowing inside the water. A wind raging" (11). She too is swept along in the current, part of the flotsam and jetsam, the detritus of everyday life, on the surface of water, moved along by the force of desire, that inner current of the unconscious at work; accordingly, the desiring text composes and extends the signifying network just as its effort to make meaning, to signify some thing, is con-founded (founded against "itself"). Thus, even as I write, in pursuit of feminist literary criticism's meaning, I write against myself, against it.

Crossing the river, Duras's character experiences the Other's gaze: the man, who is not white, looks at her—not because she is beautiful, though she can be that if he (or she) wants, but for something else he looks. She can be constructed to please the Other, "can become anything anyone wants me to be" (18). In this scene, on the border between bodies (of land, of subject positions) we read the difference between desiring and desired, where desire, as Marini points out, "carries in its shadow jouissance and the impossibility of jouissance" (*Territoires* 21). Textuality (the text of desire) is the space between, the crossing. But in a strike against the woman as lack, Duras also gives the girl the power of the gaze, as the older narrator's voice comments: "I can see it in the eyes, all there already in the eyes" (21). From their first meeting in the apartment, the girl takes control of the scene (seen): "Suddenly, all at once, she knows, knows that he doesn't understand her, that he never will. . . . It's up to her to know. And she does" (37). The narrator, in retrospect, says that the girl understands that "it's already desire" (36). She sees "it," reading what she interprets as desire in the other's eyes. Knowing, seeing, reading are never enough: she asks for "it": "She says, I'd rather you didn't love me. But if you do, I'd like you to do as you usually do with women. He looks at her in horror, asks, Is that what you want? She says it is" (37).

The peculiar, inhuman world of colonial French Indochina separates races and classes as it does sexes, complicating the reading of desire. The girl sits by the driver in a part of the "native bus" reserved for white people (9). The man in the black limousine is "not white" (17). The Chinese man, no monodimensional masculine subject as he exists in the text of colonialism, approaches the white girl with fear: "His hand is trembling. There's the difference of race, he's not white, he has to get the better of it, that's why he's trembling. She says she doesn't smoke, no thanks. She doesn't say anything else, doesn't say, Leave me alone. So he's less afraid" (32). She knows in advance her part in the play of desire, the power she can wield: "From the first moment she knows more or less, knows he's at her mercy. And therefore that others besides him may be at her mercy too if the occasion arises" (35). Her mother embarrasses them in the poverty of her dress and appearance, "like a Chinese woman's" (23). Racism dictates her family's response to the Chinese man, "the man from Cholon," his color a mark which money can't bring them to overlook. While gorging on sumptuous meals at his expense, they refuse to look at or to speak to him even though they need him and this particular relationship of the One and the Other in order to construct their supremacy narrative.

For the family, he wears the invisibility of the racially different; for the one who reads and writes, he (re)presents the unrepresentable other of desire. He is insubstantial, and the love between him and the girl is perceived as a matter of economic exchange: "This because he's a Chinese, because he's not a white man. The way my elder brother treats my lover, not speaking to him, ignoring him, stems from such absolute conviction it acts as a model. We all treat my lover as he does. I myself never speak to him in their presence" (51). Through her character, Duras displays the effect of woman standing before the Law. The girl also participates in this betrayal of the Other. He becomes an empty shell, the husk of a sign: "My desire obeys my elder brother, rejects my lover. . . . In my brother's presence he becomes an unmentionable outrage, a cause of shame who ought to be kept out of sight" (52). But this is more than a narrative of phallocentrism and racism, of the Other (the Chinese man) as simply a member of another race, or the girl (the "woman" as the Other who permits man to found "himself"). In the powerful circuit of economic exchange, controlled by the Chinese man's wealthy father, the girl is "the little white whore from Sadec" (35), another kind of spectacle in her man's hat, makeup, and gold lamé shoes—not a fit marriage partner for his (pure-breed) son. The son is too weak to oppose his father, an/other representative of the Law (49). As desire writes itself, each becomes an other as "the lover," the poor white girl and the rich Chinese man, and the text transform, for a time, another figured as "the Other."

Displaying the complex operation of "the Law," Duras's text recalls Kafka's parable, "Before the Law," on which Derrida comments in his essay "Women in the Beehive": "[Kafka] describes a powerful structure, and then he deconstructs all the systems of the Law and shows you how impossible it is to see the Law, to enter the Law, to transgress the limit past the door. But what he is doing, in the meantime, is writing a text which in turn becomes the Law itself. 'Before the Law' *is* the Law. We are in front of it as in front of the Law. He reproduces the situation, and the Franz Kafka signature, or the signature of the text, makes the Law" (197). This too is the gesture of my text as I write my narrative against feminist critical narratives. A law is (re)produced. Thus, Duras's narrator reflects on what she has written in her life, and summarizes: "I've never written, though I thought I wrote, never loved, though I thought I loved, never done anything but wait outside the closed door" (25). Just as the man from the country waits outside the door, stands before the law, the speaker waits (a situation which, if we return to Kafka, will not change whether one is male or female, black or white, rich or poor, feminist or theorist, or, indeed, whether the door is open or closed). Furthermore, it is only in retrospect that we can read (as on Freud's mystic writing pad) the significance of our experience since it is always part of what is being performed, "(incorporated in an act, a doing) and to that extent precisely it is not transparent to itself" (Felman, *Jacques Lacan* 15). To this degree, I do not know what I want, what my writing means. In this way, too, I am (like) an American Feminist Literary Critic.

The figurative quality of Duras's text is underscored by similar structural exchanges in position. In the absence of the father, his part as her mother's lover is assumed by the elder brother, "the child-killer of the night" (6), the tyrannical, death-dealing lawgiver and war-maker from whom the girl wishes to save her vulnerable younger brother, her "child," "from that black veil over the light, from the law which was decreed and represented by the elder brother" (7). He represents the paradigm for how the family relates to the Chinese man. Like the Chinese lover before the white girl, the narrator remembers her fear of the older brother's law. Fear and rage—"I wanted to kill him, to get the better of him for once, just once, and see him die" (7). She reads this story of "an animal law" in retrospect, trying now to speak of the gaps, the silence, the dark moments of family life. This is the Law as something that we can never elude, caught up in that multilocal, omnipresent and multidirectional forcefield of power which Foucault depicts so captivatingly (see, for example, *The History of Sexuality*). We are "in" it, writing "out" of it.

This effect becomes clearer when, in Duras's text, we consider who the nameless "lover" is, this "other" who refuses to speak, yet is spoken. We encounter an array of possibilities—Tournier says this is a masquerade for incest, the lover as father (67). But then perhaps Solomon is correct in saying that the lover of the nubile fifteen-year-old girl is the younger brother (the Chinese man and the brother both fear the elder brother [52]; the girl can only oppose the elder brother, not to protect her lover but her younger brother [53] from the Law of the elder brother [7]), or perhaps in this story the lover is the mad, elusive mother ("The beast, my mother, my love" [22]) whom all three of her children love "beyond love" (55). Or is the object of desire rather all of these and none, no *one* at all, and everyone, the substitutable "other" according to which the girl com-poses herself, as she narrates her narrative and the writing writes her? The figures fuse and displace one another in the chain of desire/signification:

> The shadow of another man must have passed through the room, the shadow of a young murderer [the elder brother (6–7)]. . . . The shadow of a young hunter must have passed through the room too, but that one, yes, I knew about, sometimes he was present in the pleasure and I'd tell the lover from Cholon, talk to him of the other's body and member, of his indescribable sweetness, of his courage in the forest and on the rivers whose estuaries hold the black panthers [the younger brother (26)]. Everything chimed with his desire and made him possess me. I had become his child [as the narrator's son takes the place of the girl in the

photo never taken (13)]. It was with his own child he made love every evening. (100)

These circulating representatives of desire, which Lacan calls "the *non-representative representative*" (*Four* 218), swirl ambiguously, overlapping, repeating, and returning, demanding that I intervene in the interest of explanation, but making my explanatory intervention just another production in the interest of my obscure desire.

Even after the girl's departure for France, desire continues to materialize its desiderata. On the ship she believes she sees her younger brother, the one she loves, as she almost did the Chinese man from Cholon, her love for them approaching a pain like death when a brilliant and inexplicable melody, like this controlled (going off in paths) but explosive (exceeding its structure) text itself, bursts across the night sky (113–14). The other as absence, as lack in the "self," is driven by desire, the animating force in/of language. The result: more text. She imagines the Chinese lover, able only after a long time to consummate his marriage to a sixteen-year-old Chinese girl from Fushun: "For a long time she [the girl] must have remained the queen of his desire, his personal link with emotion, with the immensity of tenderness, the dark and terrible depths of the flesh. Then the day must have come when it was possible. The day when the desire for the little white girl was so strong, so unbearable that he could find her whole image again as in a great and raging fever, and penetrate the other woman with his desire for her, the white child" (115–16). The vertiginous convergence of the nearly homonymic— brother, father, mother—in the lover/other overwhelms as it tips us off. The self split in two—me and the other; four—my other, my (m)other, an/other me, the Chinese girl/the Chinese man; six, eight. . . .

In *The Ravishing of Lol Stein*, when Jacques Hold asks Lol V. Stein "What is it you want?" (Freud/Lacan's question: "What does woman want?" and the Chinese lover's question, "Is that what you want?"),[2] she answers, "I want" (102). Her (non)answer, Martha Noel Evans explains, "is more truthful than any object she might name. Desire has no direct object, not because there is nothing in that place but because everything is in that place. The direct object of desire is an infinite chain of interchangeable nouns and names" (144). These writers encourage us to ask as well, "What do you/I want for feminism? What is it?" The direct object of desire, while perhaps not everything, is anything that can hold, even for a moment, the object position in the sentence "I want 'X.' " As such then it is always *something* and never some *thing*. And the "X" is never "it"; rather "X" creates the gap where demand fills in for the unspeakable need, resulting in more desire, or desiring more. The logic of the propositional or declarative sentence is ill suited to desire, which refuses to be so confined, con-forming as it speaks (seeks) an/other grammar. At the opening of *The Lover*, Duras writes that she is telling a story which is the same and different: "The story of my life doesn't exist. Does not exist. There's never any center to it. No path, no line. There are great spaces where you pretend there used to be someone, but it's not true, there was no one" (8). While there is in this story of a life a desire for someone, no one is ever there. The speaker alone with the figure of a life, *figura*, a face which can be ravaged or beautiful, murderous or sexual, loyal or treacherous. In *The Lover*, Duras offers as a figure for narrative the story of the face—the obscurely precomprehended life there to be read in the visage: "Now I see that when I was very young, eighteen, fifteen, I already had a face that foretold the one I acquired through drink in middle age. . . . I acquired that drinker's face before I drank. Drink only confirmed it. The space for it existed in me. . . . Just as the space existed in me for desire. At the age of fifteen I had the face of pleasure, and yet I had no knowledge of pleasure" (8). How then can one read and write the story (of) writing a woman's face?

Through a discursive practice which admits the course of desire, Duras offers a lesson for Feminist Literary Criticism by complicating our understanding of "the other" and "identity." She writes and rewrites the place of woman in the Lacanian system: "Set up as the guarantee of the system she comes to represent two things—what the man is not, this is [sexual] difference, and what he has to give up [renounce], that is, excess [jouissance/pleasure]" (Jacqueline Rose 219). She stands for the *pas tout*, the "not all" of the system of representation (see Jacqueline Rose 188). She is the mark re-marked, gone over again, that cancels as it underscores. She rewrites the family history (25), the story of her encounter with the lover (27), the "place of woman" with respect to desire. She criticizes the white colonial women who wait, who "save themselves up" and betray themselves as they repress desire. Through her re-marks on women, Duras stages a version of what Derrida calls double inscription which offers a strategy for negotiating the boundaries of this double bind, for moving in the between of the simultaneity of the One and the Other to help us conceive of the other-as/in-us as we theorize identity in language: "whenever any writing both marks and goes back over its mark with an undecidable stroke . . . [this] double mark escapes the pertinence or authority of truth: it does not overturn it but rather inscribes it within its play as one of its functions or parts. This displacement does not take place, has not taken place once as an *event*. It does not occupy a simple place. It does not take place *in* writing. This dis-location (is what) writes/is written" (*Dissemination* 193). The narrator's imagination defies the one-directional as(sign)ment of woman as the object of man's desire and identity. She plays her part, or writes it, through the Chinese lover but she imagines an/other experience, one of ultimate pleasure for woman mediated through the pleasure of another woman, her schoolmate Hélène Lagonelle: "I want to take Hélène Lagonelle with me to where every evening, my eyes shut, I have imparted to me the pleasure that makes you cry out. I'd like to give Hélène Lagonelle to the man who does that to me, so he may do it in turn to her. I want it to happen in my presence, I want her to do it as I wish, I want her to give herself where I give myself. It's via Hélène Lagonelle's body, through it, that the ultimate pleasure would pass from him to me" (74). Duras signals a partial disruption in the subject/object relation as she usurps "man's" role in the system of exchange. She will change places with Hélène. Hélène will change places with the man from Cholon. Although the narrator refuses an/other move—the unthinkable lesbian writing where she and Hélène comprise the lovers' pair, it is nonetheless through Hélène's body that she imagines "A pleasure unto death" (74).

Like many of Duras's novels, *The Lover* speaks the haunting language of the Other, of desire, of the unconscious. As the subterranean current swirls and eddies while it propels the narrative surface, and the subject negotiates its place on the other side, things are no longer what they seem in the rational place of consciousness. Nothing stays in place; the categories give way. In fact, the "present," the real, is always already re-constituted (re:written, trans/lated), as is its unconscious Other text (see Derrida, *Writing* 211–12). The other/lover shows itself as a site of difference, of loss, of desire that too frequently escapes us in a monodimensional (monolingual, monotextual) discourse of power, which includes the discourse of Feminism, that produces the simple, stereotypical representations of man, woman, poverty, or race—the (confounding) assumptions that Feminist Literary Criticism frequently uses to "found" or to elaborate its meaning.

For Duras, the condition of being an other, of being an "outsider," is, in Dina Sherzer's view, "a breakthrough, not a breakdown" (144). Actually, it serves a dual function, breaking open the closed system of representation and breaking down the illusion of the controlling logos.[3] The bar—barrier or seawall—stands on one side and the other, in the space between which are both places and no (one) place. To acknowledge the "other" in the "self" is to stage a break with the fundamental philosophical principle of contradiction at work in the law of identity: a thing cannot be A and not A at the same time, or, in concrete terms, one cannot be a feminist and not a feminist at the same time. But Duras's texts write (to) the limit of its obverse: one is simultaneously A and not A, the one and not-the-one, the Other from which the notion of the One can neither be distinctly derived nor absolutely separated. The narrative of desire is a narrative of the death of representation—what is repeated replaces/displaces/dis-figures previous repetitions—just as it is death in representation, an absence re-marked. There is, then, always an/other body. Always an/other writing, other feminisms.

Writing the "Other" is, for Duras, a way of theorizing both the "Other" and (in) the "self." Her texts make a question of Baudrillard's claim: what is the "radicality of desire which, in its non-meaning, cuts through all finality"? (*Mirror* 155). In response her texts perform desire's unsettling and productive work, the perpetual un-ease of (ex)tension and change in the "subject." The writing of desire is a writing of expenditure, not one that waits or saves itself up but "spends": "He calls me a whore, a slut, he says I'm his only love and that's what he ought to say, and what you do say when you just let things say themselves, when you let the body alone, to seek and find and take just what it likes, and then everything is right, and nothing's wasted, the waste is covered over and all is swept away in the torrent, in the force of desire" (42–43). The girl is one who, after she has experienced it, will, as the Chinese lover says, "love love" (42). She asks for it over and over, she spends herself until she is exhausted, he says he will love her "unto death." There is a bitter pleasure in this unending repetition, in the search for the right word in the face of desire's radical (non)meaning.

Discussing Lacan's elucidation of this point through his reading of repetition, Felman writes, "For Lacan, what is repeated in the text is not the content of a fantasy but the symbolic displacement of a signifier through the insistence of a signifying chain; repetition is not of *sameness* but of *difference,* not of independent terms or of analogous themes but of a structure of differential interrelationships, in which what *returns* is always *other*" (*Jacques Lacan* 43). It is always another case of the "purloined letter."[4] The lover to whom the language, the letter of love, is addressed never materializes. The love letter is a fugitive letter (in) the (pre)text of desire. It shares the properties of other "purloined letters" like those Derrida describes in "The parole soufflée," "The *letter*, inscribed or propounded speech, is always stolen. Always stolen because it is always *open*. It never belongs to its author or to its addressee, and by nature, it never follows the trajectory that leads from subject to subject" (*Writing* 178). The fugitive letter speaks from the unconscious which is always beyond mastery or control. And when it speaks, it requires of the listener, the Other, the kind of attention Duras seems to expect of her readers and that she accords to the languorous Hélène Lagonelle: "She has the matchless attentiveness of those who don't understand what is said to them" (102). They hang on one's every word, follow without following.

The Durasian text, as an alternative performance of the letter's trajectory, offers a method from which feminist literary criticism stands to benefit greatly. Here the text insists on a writing which is always a re:writing (a text which recalls and reconsiders past texts), a re-vision of the idea of closure where the text's discursive field can never be counted on to be the end (since character and story may appear in an/other text yet to be written and read). Shoshana Felman explains the value of leaving open the fundamental feminist problematic: "The allegorical question 'She? Who?' will thus remain unanswered. The text, nonetheless, will play out the question to its logical end, so as to show in what way it *precludes* any answer, in what way the question is set as a trap. The very *lack of the answer* will then write itself as a *different* question, through which the original question will find itself dislocated, radically shifted and transformed" ("Women" 7). So chapter after chapter I ask and answer what might be taken as the "same" question. Duras gives us, in effect, a demonstration of Peggy Kamuf's notion that what feminist literary criticism can do is to write itself so that it makes way for the replacement of a given discourse by another "yet-to-be-determined level of feminist critical practice" (45). These texts of expenditure re:write themselves endlessly— as the discourses of the madwoman, the beggar woman who laughs (84–89), "the little slut," and the woman who in other texts is Anne-Marie Stretter: "they are alike in themselves. Both isolated. Alone, queenlike. Their disgrace is a matter of course. Both are doomed to discredit because of the kind of body they have, caressed by lovers, kissed by their lips, consigned to the infamy of a pleasure unto death, as they both call it, unto the mysterious death of lovers without love" (90). The only real sentence for/of desire is the death sentence. Period. This accounts for the lover's last words, the text's last words—no "last" words at all, as there are no first and last figures, as there is always an/other writing: "Then he didn't know what to say. And then he told her. Told her that it was as before, that he still loved her, he could never stop loving her, that he'd love her until death" (117). The endless play, the circulation of texts, of repetition, memory, and rewriting that make "more/text" as they destabilize not only this text but the text of Feminism, presents for us the very writing practice that we might describe as re-figuring feminist literary criticism. Not once, here in this text for either the first or even the last time, but in each text we receive from before or later. Feminist criticism, re-figuring itself, performs "itself," but in a manner that re-cognizes the radical potential of the psychoanalytic discovery: "the unconscious is no longer the difference between consciousness and the unconscious, but rather the inherent, irreducible difference between consciousness and itself" (Felman, *Jacques Lacan* 57).

Duras reminds us that it is in the (in)essential nature of desire for the Other not to be caught or expressed in/by "nature." Writing writes and re:writes desire, never capturing it and always supplementing it as it goes. Always writing, passionately (desiringly), even obsessively. She reminds us that another, like the other in us, offers no consolation, no remedy for lack: the Chinese crowd goes "along together without any sign of impatience, in the way they are alone in a crowd, without happiness, it seems, without sadness, without curiosity, going along without seeming to, without meaning to, just going this way rather than that, alone and in the crowd, never alone even by themselves, always alone in the crowd" (47). It is a going on, like the girl's mother— "through to the bitter end without ever dreaming she might give up, abandon—the cousins, the effort, the burden. . . . It's in this valor, human, absurd," Duras says, "that I see true grace" (96). Language performs its desire in the letter. Her text enacts the dissemination of desire in the Derridean sense where "dissemination affirms the always already divided generation of meaning" (*Dissemination* 268). The "Other" is always a party to, a part of, this great expenditure. The letter (writing) of desire produces desire. More desiring. The desire of/for desire. Duras's *The Lover* suggests a way of rethinking feminist literary criticism's dedication to the figuration of woman, of the Other and "the One," to our desire to capture that elusive Other, (re)presented here as black, there as lesbian or Indian, and always as "our selves," just as we figure the feminist criticism that we want, often not knowing as we enact it what "it" is, and the feminist critics we might want to be(come). Duras's nautiluslike text of imploded but erupting desire suggests that perhaps the only "dark continent" is the domain of discourse from within which the radically other, captured and colonized, is perpetually escaping. The other shows herself. What we are called to do, as Marini says so well, is "neither to write like . . ., nor to write on . . ., but perhaps to write oneself with ["(s') écrire avec"]" (73). In this way, feminist literary criticism is always beginning again, (re)writing what it thinks it wants to be.

(Dis)Locations: Reading the Theory of a Third-World Woman in *I . . . Rigoberta Menchu*

The enemy says that the guerillas are in the mountains, so they are
with us because we are the mountains.

> —Elderly Indian man, *Guatemala in Rebellion*

Desaparecer, formally an intransitive or reflexive verb, has another
meaning in Guatemala: *lo desaparecieron* means "they disappeared him."
To kill someone is *darle pasaporte*, literally to "give someone a
passport." The terms *volar al pájaro*, "to make the bird fly away," *darle
agua*, literally to "give someone water," *mandarle para el otro lado*,
literally, "to send someone to the other side," *irse con Pancho*, literally,
"to go with Pancho," and *mandarle a uno a vers las margaritas desde abajo*,
literally, "send someone off to look at the daisies from below," all
mean "to kill."

> —Jean-Marie Simon, *Guatemala: Eternal Spring, Eternal Tyranny*

My role is to be alive.

> —Luisa Valenzuela, *Other Weapons*

Adrienne Rich concludes her essay "Notes toward a Politics of Location" with a critical summary of white North America's (by which
she must mean primarily the United States' and perhaps Canada's)
construction of the "Third-World Woman" as one who "doesn't think
and reflect on her life," whose ideas are "not real ideas like those of
Karl Marx and Simone de Beauvoir," and whose spiritual philosophy,
ethical talents, legal skills, and political decisions are "merely instinc-
tual or conditioned reactions." From this white, middle-class, U.S.
feminist position, Rich observes that one might conclude: "That only
certain kinds of people can make theory; that the white-educated mind
is capable of formulating everything; that white middle-class feminism
can know for 'all women'; that only when a white mind formulates is

97

the formulation to be taken seriously" (*Blood* 230). While I have already argued that feminist theory cannot, indeed should not, attempt to formulate everything or to "know for 'all women' " (the gesture of colonial imperialism), neither can Feminism (the proper name) speak without such an interest in inclusion, speak as though what it knows exists for all women. Feminism's double bind is that it cannot speak "for" other women, nor can it speak "without" or "apart from" other women.

Rather, it must create a space where women who are not these white, middle-class Anglo-American or European feminists can speak or write. Only then can negotiation occur and the larger, necessary alliances present themselves in full, orchestral proportion. The positions of the third-world woman (that is, the monolithic "Third-World Woman" of that other monolith, Feminism) and woman of color cannot be generalized with any more success than can Feminism. Nonetheless, the need to elaborate similarities and differences in the world community of women represents feminism's most compelling human and theoretical project; it is the project required to open Feminism toward the possibility (which can only ever be a possibility) of global feminisms. Here I want to reiterate Gayatri Spivak's comment in "French Feminism in an International Frame" with respect to the " 'colonized woman' as 'subject' ": "However unfeasible and inefficient it may sound, I see no way to avoid insisting that there has to be a simultaneous other focus: not merely who am I? but who is the other woman? How am I naming her? How does she name me? Is this part of the problematic I discuss?" (150). In the double step—who am I? who is she?—Spivak's questions point us in the direction of negotiating mutual respect across boundaries. Furthermore, it would seem that Marguerite Duras's French text, "French" in its affinities with high theory and an/other kind of feminism, has little to offer us when we approach the more representational discourses of revolutionary identity politics from speakers in other traditions; still, it is in the con/text of Rigoberta Menchu's contrary testimony that I wish to apply the lesson derived from Duras as a way of writing myself with the other woman, naming myself as she tells me her name.

In this chapter I propose to explore a space between the written (the texts of Feminism and the theory of the "Third-World Woman") and the unwritten (the theory and practice of a nonhegemonic, negotiating feminism and the autobiographical chronicle, *I . . . Rigoberta Menchu*) in the interest of calling this space, a place of exile, a Guatemalan Quiché Indian woman's theory of her position as an Indian and as a woman—that which I want to call her theory of feminism. My exploration centers on (re)presentations of identity—of feminism as a space within which woman, who cannot be spoken, speaks; of the Quiché Indian whose concept of identity depends upon the conviction that identity must be kept secret from the other, the non-Quiché; and of both the speech and the silence that the personal and collective identities of political revolutionaries require for their very survival. These three interlocking identities show themselves as they hide and are hidden from themselves and others. Despite Doris Sommer's assertion—"Testimonials never put the referentiality of language into question" (119)—I know that there is always "more," some otherness that exceeds the simple projection of identity, no matter how carefully controlled. There are gaps and slippages between the way in which the symbolic order does (not) (re)present woman, and the effort of woman to bring herself into representation, to show herself. Further, the unresolved and evident contradictions within permit the construction of these categories (feminism, Quiché Indian woman, revolutionary collective) and the categories respond to them. The geopolitical repositionings this inquiry requires for the feminist, the Indian woman,[1] and the political revolutionary challenge the fundamental oppositions upon which we shape both thought and action, theory and praxis, masculinity and femininity.

I will begin with what appear to be the simplest questions which are at the same time the hardest ones to answer. Who are these Quiché people, and what is the position they inhabit? First, a demographic response. The Mayan Indians, Guatemala's indigenous peoples, are the majority of the country's inhabitants. In Guatemala, life expectancy is fifty-nine for urban residents, forty-nine for rural peoples; 40 to 60 percent of the children die before the age of five. Guatemala has 79 infant deaths per 1000 live births (Simon 42), second only to Haiti in the western hemisphere. In 1978, the wealthiest 5 percent of the population received 59 percent of the country's total earnings, while the poorest 50 percent of the population received 7 percent of the total earnings. In Guatemala, 52 percent of the population does not have the estimated 68 cents per day required for food to sustain life, even though the country is the wealthiest nation in Central America (supporting "over 300 firms with U.S. interests" [Simon 19]). In 1980, only 37 percent of the population over fifteen years of age could read and write. While the official language is Spanish, it is the second language for the twenty-two Indian groups (55 percent of the total population) that comprise the country's majority (WIRE 35). In these details of an overwhelming oppression and an almost incomprehensible difficulty to survive, I read a demand for solidary identity and a rationale for revolution.

How can I understand such a different circumstance? The editors of *Guatemala in Rebellion* (re)pose the question as though it were inevitable. They offer me a way to situate the resistance Rigoberta Menchu chronicles in her testimony:

> To comprehend a popular movement for radical change, such as the one contending for power with the military and the oligarchy in present-day Guatemala, at least two kinds of intellectual effort are necessary. First, a level of misery and oppression such as few readers of this book will have personally experienced must be imagined: malnutrition so severe it approaches mass starvation; inadequate sanitary water supplies so that diarrhea is a main cause of death; violence so extreme that thirty to forty mutilated bodies turn up daily; a government so devoid of legitimacy that, aside from invocation of anticommunist faith, it hardly has any other justification of its rule, and so must practice and condone terror to retain the existing distribution of power. . . . The second important concept necessary to comprehend contemporary Guatemala, one that follows almost logically from the perception of the grim reality of that country, is that these conditions generate an opposition. (153)

I understand the production of opposition, the constitution of identity by negation or reversal, but I know that there is always more, some otherness that exceeds the simple projection of opposites.

The undeniable complicity of the United States government in Guatemala's ongoing regime of political murder and oppression cannot be separated from my position as writer and my production of the Quiché Indian as both the tragic victim and the courageous opponent of my country. But when the U.S. feminist tries to examine and revise the imperialist position Rich describes, she risks an/other limitation which Chandra Mohanty and Biddy Martin describe very well:

> what is increasingly identified as "white" or "Western" feminism unwittingly leave[s] the terms of West/East, white/nonwhite polarities intact; they do so, paradoxically, by starting from the premise that Western feminist discourse is inadequate or irrelevant to women of color or Third World women. The implicit assumption here, which we wish to challenge, is that the terms of a totalizing feminist discourse *are adequate* to the task of articulating the situation of white women in the West. We would contest that assumption and argue that the reproduction of such polarities only serves to concede "feminism" to the "West" all over again. The potential consequence is the repeated failure to contest the feigned homogeneity of the West and what seems to be a discursive and political stability of the hierarchical West/East divide. (193)

If, as I hope to have demonstrated in earlier chapters, I cannot identify myself, declare my own desires, and expose my interests, with any reliability or certainty, how can I then presume to differentiate from or relate my "self" to an/other? Even more problematically, doesn't this difference/(non)difference between me and the other that is created in/through language and thought, their oppositions, their subject/object relations, end up producing both the discourse of "Western feminism" and the (its) Other as the "Third-World Woman"? Further, how does the speaking of an/other woman escape this difficulty? Through these questions which motivate my discussion here, I hope to recuperate the experience of the feminist project's desire for writing the other woman—in this case, another version of the relation of the personal to the political.

Perhaps as important as the grim catalogue of facts for understanding the Indian's position in Guatemala is the way in which traditional culture serves a complex authorizing function for (an)other discourse and (an)other action. Rigoberta Menchu's role in theorizing and enacting revolution exceeds the simplistic conceptualization that reduces it either to victimization or to opposition with respect to the colonial ethos. Although she learns the colonizers' language, Spanish, in order to tell this particular story, she constructs her resistance according to her (mis)reading and (re)writing of the values and behaviors prescribed by Quiché tradition as well as of the common opposition of theory and practice represented in Western philosophy. The initial difficulty I have in reading Rigoberta Menchu's theory is that I must read it through the frame, structure, and selection of her Latin American amanuensis, Elisabeth Burgos-Debray, and I cannot determine how "slavishly," how faithful a job of copying, this "(slave) at hand(writing)," herself from another culture ("knowing nothing about Rigoberta's culture" [xix]), gives us: "I allowed her to speak and then became her instrument, her double by allowing her to make the transition from the spoken to the written word" (xx). Translations never offer us the perfect, "slavish" copy of an/other text (this persistent problem of non/identification inhabits texts as well as their speakers and writers). How close has she come to occupying Rigoberta Menchu's position? Is this even possible? She acknowledges her complicity: "We Latin Americans are only too ready to denounce the unequal relations that exist between ourselves and North America, but we tend to forget that we too are oppressors and . . . *colonial*. Without any fear of exaggeration, it could be said that, especially in countries with a large Indian population, there is an internal colonialism which works to the detriment of the indigenous population" (xii). Burgos-Debray, when contemplating her project, realizes that its quality will depend largely on the relationship she is able to establish with the "other woman." At the same time, however, Burgos-Debray and Rigoberta Menchu replicate the age-old colonial (non)relationship. The former describes the Indian woman in terms reserved for the dominated: she has a "childlike smile" and a "guileless" expression (xiv); Rigoberta plays the domestic, a role she also performed in Guatemala, as she prepares their food while the "other" watches:

> A woman friend had brought me some maize flour and black beans back from Venezuela. . . . I cannot describe how happy that made Rigoberta. It made me happy too, as the smell of *tortillas* and refried beans brought back my childhood in Venezuela, where the women [some unnamed women, not "my mother," not "I"] get up early to cook *arepas* for breakfast. . . . The first thing Rigoberta did when she got up in the morning was make dough and cook *tortillas* for breakfast; it was a reflex that was thousands of years old. She did the same at noon and in the evening. It was a pleasure to watch her. (xv-xvi)

Burgos-Debray wants to believe that a trusting relationship can be based upon sharing food, but she refuses to question that other age-old relationship enacted in her Paris kitchen: some people cook and others watch. She also wants to believe that for the week of interviewing, she "lived in Rigoberta's world" (xv), but it is a place "cut . . . off from the outside world" (xv), a place in Paris, that only the "theorist" would call "Rigoberta's world" even as she advances the Eurocentric claim, one Rigoberta Menchu never suggests, that "Paris is their sound box. Whatever happens in Paris has repercussions through the world, even in Latin America" (xvii). Fundamental differences inhabit these positions, Paris and Guatemala, the one who cooks and the other who watches, the Latin American and the Quiché Indian woman. The "theorist" mis(re)presents the differences; the "activist" appropriates them.

Rigoberta Menchu has a "mission"; a purpose (a form of theorizing?) under/ or over/writes her actions. She comes to Paris as a representative of the Popular Front to speak to solidarity groups.[2] Unlike the anthropologist/interviewer/"theorist" Burgos-Debray who speaks her own language, Menchu conducts this speaking in Spanish, the language of the servant's colonial master, of her exile in Mexico, and not her "own." She speaks in "other words," from "inside" the discourse of the colonizer. She takes on this language in order to speak from their position, an/other subject position, but to occupy it as an Indian, in the interests of her people. The interviewer explains:

"Rigoberta learned the language of her oppressors in order to use it against them. For her, appropriating the Spanish language is an act which can change the course of history because it is the result of a decision: Spanish was a language which was forced upon her, but it has become a weapon in her struggle. She decided to speak in order to tell of the oppression her people have been suffering for almost five hundred years, so that the sacrifices made by her community and her family will not have been made in vain" (xii). So, this text that is Spanish, created by Rigoberta Menchu and Elisabeth Burgos-Debray, the language of which is not entirely "natural" (spoken by an Indian and written by a Latin American anthropologist), has been translated (though not entirely) into English by Ann Wright, who describes it as follows: "Rigoberta's narration reflects the different influences on her life. It is a mixture of Spanish learned from nuns and full of biblical associations; of Spanish learned in the political struggle replete with revolutionary terms; and, most of all, Spanish which is heavily coloured by the linguistic constructions of her native Quiché and full of the imagery of nature and community traditions" (viii). Many texts from other cultures come to us in this way—in another language, translated in two or three (re)moves from the "original" language, and presented through the optics of alien discourses, languages against which the speaker speaks. These are only a few of the reading problems the text presents, but not uncommon ones because they simulate woman's position in general, always speaking in an/other language, in an/other relationship to the language of power (the "original," author-ized speaking), and they ask us to confront the troublesome status of texts in general, those "mixed bloods," the origin and meaning of which remain unsettled and open to discussion.

Not unrelated to this is Rigoberta Menchu's discussion of the theory/practice opposition, part of a longer conversation between "theorists" (feminist intellectuals of the elite class) and "political activists" (poor and working-class women engaged in fundamental struggles). If Doris Sommer is correct in her assertion, "To be an intellectual is precisely not to come from the people or . . . not to return to them" (113), the tidy opposition of the first chapters which permits Feminist discourse to represent some feminist nontheorists as "pure" or "proper" feminists, is further con/founded. Because this division (one of many) between intellectual (elite) and working-class women in Latin America characterizes relationships between them, Menchu can be expected to declare herself as one-without-theory—aligning herself with the peasant class. "Theory" is that which is spoken or written from the position of the colonizers—a view which holds for many U.S.

feminists as well. The Indian elders relate a history which differs from that presented in books and schools: "When our children reach ten years old . . . they remind them that our ancestors were dishonoured by the White Man, by colonization. But they don't tell them the way that it's written down in books . . . No, they learn it through oral recommendations, the way it has been handed down through the generations" (13). The institutions of culture are controlled by the colonizer, in the interest of (re)producing a particular relationship between the colonizer and the colonized which represents for the Indian a "false education." Rigoberta Menchu's father views education as a "ladinizing" process in which the "mixed-breed" replaces the "pure Indian."

Colette Guillaumin forcefully exposes the theory/practice dilemma—reflective of the position of the Indian as well as the feminist—in terms of a domination/oppression opposition:

> Is theory a fortress? Or is it a private preserve? Or, rather, what is theory? In any society minorities—and here I mean not those who are perforce the least numerous but rather those who have the *least power*, whether economic, legal, or political—are in a peculiar position as regards products of the intellect. Most often they hate theory, recognizing it for what it is: the sacred verbiage of those who dominate them; that which emerges from the head and mouth of those who dispose of power (tools, weapons, the police, the army) and nourishment (wages, lands, goods, etc.). Since in the majority/minority relationship, the power, goods, and individual freedom which flow from this relationship are the distinctive features of the dominators, the institutionalized expression of *their* consciousness and *their* view of the situation is the only one to be transmitted, diffused, and expounded. This then is what is called theory. (23)

Like "Theory," and existing in a specific relationship to it, books, schools, ideas are suspect because they are controlled by the agents of oppression. But it is a mistake to accept this self-characterization as the singular "truth" of Rigoberta Menchu's discourse. A line from the *Popul Vuh*, the anonymous written sacred Mayan text, directs the reader's attention in another way: "There is the original book and ancient writing, but he who reads and ponders it hides his face" (33). Here the readers are the writers who hide their identities; there are similarities in this positioning, in relation to texts, that Rigoberta and I share. A more complex relationship is being suggested: if theorists pose this theory/practice (not theory) opposition (as we often do), she will choose the side of "practice" for reasons suggested above. She inherits this need to make a choice, not from her cultural text but ours (or that of her Spanish colonizers), and the mandate to choose sides within the terms the opposition offers, as well as the choice which the revolutionary Indian woman can make.

Rigoberta Menchu offers her own people, and through them feminists in other places, an opportunity to reconsider the theory/practice opposition, to participate in the theoretical revolution with respect to social relationships. In Guillaumin's description of sexual relationships, this theoretical revolution has two primary characteristics:

> The first . . . it is the *direct expression* of the group concerned (without mediation by anyone else). It is women, individuals belonging to the group of women (and not an individual from another group setting himself up as the mediator and interpreter of a group to which he himself does not belong), who have produced this reversal and are continuing to develop its consequences. The second characteristic is that it is not the work of one particular person. Rather than being *the* unique and signed work of an individual, which is the way theory is ordinarily produced, it is the work of a vast ensemble of individuals doing a variety of political jobs, ranging from direct action to writing tracts, from writing articles to legal projects, from consciousness-raising to writing books—in fact, *truly collective* work. The fact that this is taking place within and against a relationship of domination results in the process being sorely shaken by divisions and contradictions and scarcely having the look of a linear—or harmonious—development. (37)

Rigoberta Menchu's theorizing goes beyond the unrecognized or unacknowledged limits of Guillaumin's observation, in that the latter's Feminism leads her to overlook the sexual opposition ("he" who is the enemy, "we" women who form solidarity) essential to the differentiation she makes, betrayed by the pronouns she chooses.

Menchu's engagement with the theory/practice opposition involves a more elaborate struggle with other oppositions, finding parallels in the dualities of gender—feminism/*machismo*, race—Indian/*ladino*, and class—the poor *ladino* and the rich *ladino*. She demonstrates precisely the view Chandra Mohanty advances concerning the need to disrupt the monolithic construction of the "Third-World Woman" produced by "Western feminist discourse":

> An analysis of "sexual difference" in the form of a cross-culturally singular, monolithic notion of partriarchy or male dominance leads to the construction of a similarly reductive and homoge-

neous notion of what I call the "Third World Difference"—that stable, ahistorical something that apparently oppresses most if not all of the women in these countries. And it is in the production of this "Third World Difference" that Western feminisms appropriate and "colonize" the fundamental complexities and conflicts which characterize the lives of women of different classes, religions, cultures, races and castes in these countries. (335)

Rigoberta Menchu's explanation (defense) of machismo provides a useful point of departure:

> When a male child is born, there are special celebrations, not because he's male but because of all the hard work and responsibility he'll have as a man. It's not that *machismo* doesn't exist among our people, but it doesn't present a problem for the community because it's so much part of our way of life. . . . This doesn't mean girls aren't valued. . . . The girl and the boy are both integrated into the community in equally important ways, the two are interrelated and compatible. Nevertheless, the community is always happier when a male child is born and the men feel much prouder. (14)

Perhaps we can say that what is most important in Menchu's context is the preservation of her "Indianness," that her Indian Otherness occasions her oppression more than her sexual difference. So that the fact of observing the "customary" is more important than the desire to abandon it in the interest of some more limited "liberation."

If "the usual custom is to celebrate a male child by killing a sheep or some chickens," it is less important that the birth of a male child is cause for a greater observance than that of a female, and more significant that another Indian is born and the celebration conducted in the customary way, (re)marking one's traditional life on the earth. Rigoberta (re)defines the traditional or (re)interprets it so that from the start the preservation of life begins with or includes the Indian. These interpretations signal her difference from the intellectual Feminists, every one of whom would be regarded as a theorist, whose self-definition requires in the "first place" a critique of *machismo*. Rigoberta Menchu does not lack an analysis of *machismo* and the relationship between multiple layers of oppression, however. Evaluating the strategy of forming women's groups to focus on sexual oppression, she observes:

> For the time being, though, we think that it would be feeding *machismo* to set up an organisation for women only, since it would mean separating women's work from men's work. Also we've

106

found that when we discuss women's problems, we need the men to be present, so that they can contribute by giving their opinions of what to do about the problem. And so that they can learn as well. If they don't learn, they don't progress. Our struggle has shown us that many *compañeros* have clear ideas, but if they don't follow in the footsteps of their woman, they'll never have the clarity that she has, and they'll be left behind. (222)

For Rigoberta Menchu, to have "clarity," the "clear" idea, is what it means to theorize-as-an-Indian. If the culture is to theorize its sexual politics in the interest of change, both men and women, in solidarity, must have clear, consonant ideas concerning sex role expectations.

Rigoberta Menchu describes both her father and mother as having "clarity" but not "theory." Her father teaches her his theory, which is "not theory." She explains: "His views were as clear as any theoretician, as if he'd studied and all that. All his concepts were clear" (183). Similarly, her mother conveyed clear ideas, without "theory": "Women must join the struggle in their own way. My mother's words told them that any evolution, any change, in which women had not participated, would not be a change, and there would be no victory. She was as clear about this as if she were a woman with all sorts of theories and a lot of practice" (196). In a sense, Rigoberta Menchu's theory of *machismo* is like her mother's—(re)presented as "non-theory": "There was something my mother used to say concerning *machismo*. You have to remember that my mother couldn't read or write and didn't know any theories either. What she said was that men weren't to blame for *machismo*, and women weren't to blame for *machismo*, but that it was part of the whole society. To fight *machismo*, you shouldn't attack men and you shouldn't attack women, because that is either the man being *machista*, or it's the woman" (216). There are ways to know from practice rather than from theories; this is her mother's way: "My mother, of course, didn't know all these ideas, all these theories about the position of women. But she knew all these things in practice" (221). The relationships between men and women that surface in the discussion of *machismo*, as it occurs in theory versus how it occurs in practice, show the complex interlocked nexus of multiple oppression. Knowing that these contests between identities and oppressions are dangerous to engage, I also see how Rigoberta Menchu's actions, despite her words, enact what I call *feminism* through independence, courage, and self-display. But when pressed to take sides, to make what appears to her to be a choice between her people, men and women, and the Other (me and my feminism or the feminism of Latin American women), Rigoberta Menchu chooses against the feminism of the Other, just as she chooses (her) practice against (my) theory. At the same time, however, her defense appears to mask an important contradiction. She hides her face.

Recalling the multiple gestures that negotiation requires, the Bolivian woman Domitila Barrios de Chungara presents, more explicitly, her sense of the differences that inhabit the women's community. At the International Women's Year Tribunal in Mexico, the president of the Mexican delegation enjoined her to focus on similarities between women rather than on cooperation with *compañeros* and class analysis. Domitila responded:

> All right, let's talk about the two of us. . . . Every morning you show up in a different outfit and on the other hand I don't. Every day you show up all made up and combed like someone who has time to spend in an elegant beauty parlor and who can spend money on that, and yet I don't. I see that each afternoon you have a chauffeur in a car waiting at the door of this place to take you home, and yet I don't. . . . Now, señora, tell me: is your situation at all similar to mine? Is my situation at all similar to yours? So what equality are we going to speak of between the two of us? If you and I aren't alike, if you and I are so different? We can't, at this moment, be equal, even as women, don't you think? (202–3)

The effect of such a difficult speaking (out) of difference is that, upon reflection, or upon "theorizing," Domitila sees a painful similarity between imperialism and this monolithic, exclusive Feminism which seeks, perhaps unwittingly, to separate and divide. She comments in an interview: "But I think at this moment it's much more important to fight for the liberation of our people alongside the men. It's not that I accept *machismo*, no. But I think that *machismo* is a weapon of imperialism just like feminism is" (234). When pressed to take sides, to make what appears to her to be a choice between her people, men and women, and the Other, including women historically complicit with class oppression, Domitila, like Rigoberta, chooses against this Feminism of the other woman.

The situation is problematic from a feminist/theoretical position when the traditional culture appears, through the defense of *machismo*, to replicate the structure of inequality which can be read in the history of its past class, race, and gender oppression. But in this scene, the arbitrariness of theory-caught-in-opposition—"pure" Feminism—demands that women like Rigoberta Menchu and Domitila Barrios de Chungara oppose *machismo* through a critique of gender by showing the limitations of their *compañeros*, in reaction to whose "shortcomings" the imperialist system has ostensibly justified itself and its domination for centuries. The graphically depicted scenes of torture to which Rigoberta Menchu's mother and brother are subjected illustrate Theory's nearsightedness. Let us read how *machismo* is written in the following parallel passages; first, the torture of her brother: "They tied him up, they tied his testicles, my brother's sexual organs, they tied them behind with string and forced him to run. . . . They cut off his fingernails, they cut off his fingers, they cut off his skin, they burned parts of his skin. . . . They shaved his head, left just the skin, and also they cut the skin off his head and pulled it down on either side and cut off the fleshy part of his face" (174). They are careful not to kill him there; instead he and other prisoners are doused with gasoline and burned in front of their families and friends. And then the story of her mother: "My mother . . . was raped by the officers commanding the troops . . . they cut off her ears. They cut her whole body bit by bit. . . . my mother began to lose consciousness and was in her death throes. Then the officer in charge sent for the medical team . . . to bring her back to life again. . . . They gave her food. Then they started raping her again" (198–99). The brother's Indian skin is cut from his face, his testicles mutilated, and the mother is raped—annihilation of the site (sight) of otherness, in the place where difference (re)produces itself. Rigoberta conflates these incidents as part of the collective agony of the Indian people. She unites the experiences, part of the "same" story, of her mother with the earlier one of her brother: "It was her turn to suffer the terrible pain her son had suffered too" (198). While we know that no two stories are the same story, the similarities are as instructive as the differences. Certainly the repeated rape of the mother underscores her multiple victimization, her oppression as a woman. But in the face of such extreme hatred, of genocidal extermination, her rape, though a gendered violation, is simply one more form of racial persecution she shares with her son. The complexities of positioning, where the Indian woman as compared with the non-Indian feminist stands and how a different location engenders a different view, are themselves obstacles to "seeing," to theorizing. The lesson of Rigoberta Menchu's life stories, then, is that the Quiché man falls unmistakably on the side of Sameness—he is her brother—an ally in suffering and in struggle, rather than an opponent, the *cause* of suffering or struggle.

The text presents a familiar lesson for feminists in multiracial and multiethnic societies like the United States. We have encountered it in the texts of black women and *latinas*. One might even think that the lesson, because familiar, is not too difficult to read. However, writing is not always written in a familiar language, so that it can be read, and reading does not appear to be the same as theorizing; perhaps this underscores another difference between Theory, which wants to generalize, to "fix," and practice, which wants to express itself in specific local instances. It may be one of the limits of theory that it privileges the book, the written word, which offers only an illusion of stability, over speech, the only partially fluid, changing utterances of daily life. Rigoberta Menchu's story begins with her declaration: "My name is Rigoberta Menchu. I am twenty three years old. This is my testimony. I didn't learn it from a book and I didn't learn it alone" (1). Theory, read in solitude from a book, suggests that there is one way to answer, once and for all, the question of who this other woman is, that the woman sitting alone can speak for someone else, but praxis (the theory in action of politics) seems to refuse such a generalizing capacity, and instead determines only the question—who is this other woman?—never its answer, demanding that I ask it again and again.

My asking grows more obsessive in this case because of the traditional Quiché culture's restrictions on answering. How can I know or what am I allowed to know of Rigoberta Menchu when I who am asking am a non-Indian from a country complicit with Guatemala's genocidal terrorism, and the identity of the Quiché Indian is based on the conviction that it must be kept secret from the non-Indian? In this instance I must read a text about which I cannot even make the provisional assumption that it wants to say what it "knows," or that it "knows" what it says (even though I also understand that neither the text nor I can establish this or our "identities" with any reliability). As Homi Bhabha correctly points out, "Colonial power produces the colonised as a fixed reality which is at once an 'other' and yet entirely knowable and visible. It resembles a form of narrative in which the productivity and circulation of subjects and signs are bound in a reformed and recognizable totality" (199). Obviously, I can only "know" (and only partially) what Rigoberta Menchu chooses to tell me—never all of her story, never, from my position as reader (itself obscure), how to read this (other) discourse perfectly or even well. She resists complicity in the production of a positive sign of Indian visibility as a knowable presence that can be read by the other. I will always perform inadequately; I will only ever be able to tell the story of my own interrogation—a doubling in which I ask questions of the text (of) "Rigoberta Menchu" and of the text of who "I" am as producer of this interrogation. But I can also assume of this and other texts that it tells both more and less than its author might presume, more and less than its reader can read (or admit).

At the end of her long narrative, Rigoberta Menchu describes the stories she has and has not told us: "Of course, I'd need a lot of time to tell you all about my people, because it's not easy to understand just like that. And I think I've given some idea of that in my account. Nevertheless, I'm still keeping my Indian identity a secret. I'm still keeping secret what I think no-one should know. Not even anthropologists or intellectuals, no matter how many books they have, can find out all our secrets" (247). Especially not by intellectuals, and particularly not in the written record of their many books, can the identity of the Indian woman be read. Here is the unreadable, unspoken theory of the Indian woman (and I suspect of every other woman), though, like Duras's character, I desire it nonetheless. These secrets have been with us from the beginning (9). Rigoberta Menchu's disclaimer presents the ultimate contradiction with respect to her Indian identity: the compulsion to speak herself (the anthropologist notes Rigoberta's "desire to talk") and her insistence on secrecy, on hiding herself: "But we have hidden our identity because we needed to resist, we wanted to protect what governments have wanted to take away from us. They have tried to take our things away and impose others on us, be it through religion, through dividing up the land, through schools, through books, through radio, through all things modern. . . . they are weapons they use to take away what is ours" (170–71). In this apparent contradiction of speaking and not speaking, Rigoberta Menchu offers a strategy of theorizing (speaking *of*) and of praxis (taking her opponents by surprise). She presents an example of discourse as sociopolitical practice, an/other kind of book, an instance of *exteriorismo* where the boundaries separating the public and private, political and artistic, self and collectivity are doubly (con)founded.

In a world populated with powerful oppressors, secrets conceal, protect, and preserve the "Other," which in any case conceals as it reveals. Secrets of identity are consciously kept not from the similar, but rather from the dissimilar. Rigoberta Menchu explains, "We Indians have always hidden our identity and kept our secrets to ourselves. This is why we are discriminated against. We often find it hard to talk about ourselves because we know we must hide so much in order to preserve our Indian culture and prevent it being taken away from us" (20) Secrets are, at once, the means of survival, self-preservation, and the cause of persecution and discrimination. Related to the system of passing on ancestral wisdom, both secrets and speaking preserve Quiché culture. The dying and the guerilla leaving for the mountains pass on their secrets (203)—they speak; the living speak and keep silent. Rigoberta Menchu explains this in a lesson from her father: "My father used to say: 'There are many secrets we must not tell. We

111

must keep our secrets.' He said that no rich man, no landowner, no priest, or nun, must ever know our secrets. If we don't protect our ancestors' secrets, we'll be responsible for killing them" (188). The secrets, necessarily spoken of and to members of the community, are withheld from those outside, remaining veiled in a gesture which both exercises and protects their power. As Juana, another Guatemalan Indian woman, comments, "When more than four hundred fifty years ago the Spaniards came to conquer and invade Guatemala, they wanted to destroy our customs, our entire culture, but this was not possible because it is something within our very hearts, it is very deeply rooted within us that they go wherever we go. And now we are struggling for this entire culture" (286). Identity is discussed as though it were stable and fixed, as though it could be specified either fully (like theory) or selectively, again with complete control, revealed, and concealed, but the talk about cultural values (the foundation for Indian identity) shows the ways in which it is fluid and changing (like praxis). In fact, we can see that mutability, its deviation from traditional values, accounts for the very continuity of the culture and for its capacity to adopt new, life-preserving forms. Through change, by being for itself but not "itself," Indian identity retains its ability to mark (as it masks) its difference from the oppressor.

In an important gesture of self-definition, Rigoberta Menchu defines herself "as a woman, as a Christian, and as an Indian" (168), identities the convergence and divergence of which are evident in the following explanation of the marriage ceremony: "Our vows aren't made before God, though, but before our elders. The girl says: 'I will be a mother, I will suffer, my children will suffer, many of my children will die young because of the circumstances created for us by white men. It will be hard for me to accept my children's death but I will bear it because our ancestors bore it without giving up. We will not give up either" (70). It is as a woman and an Indian that these mothers suffer their children's deaths at the hands of *ladino* and white men. They are her opponents, her adversaries in the context of the wedding ceremony where an Indian man and woman are joined for the purposes of procreation and racial survival, in opposition to and as an antidote to the genocidal politics of the non-Indian. The Indian man and woman state their shared purpose: "We will try to leave two or three seeds to reproduce the lineage of our ancestors. Although some of our children will die young, others will live on. From now on we will be mother and father" (70). Even in this ceremony, the individual is subsumed in the interests of the collective, the preservation of a race threatened with extinction. As such, then, marriage and procreation, as the enactment of ancestral law, are the Indians' ultimate responsibility.

Rigoberta Menchu's decision not to marry and have children, not to fulfill this ultimate responsibility, illustrates how she crosses over, contra/dicts the oppositions. By crossing over the oppositions, contradicting the contradictions, she both manifests solidarity with her people and acts out a difference (within) which revolution requires. Despite her repeated references to her forefathers' teachings as a source of authority for Indian life, Menchu, as a woman engaged in a specific historical struggle against oppression, finds herself in conflict with these teachings and violates their prescriptions. But she takes care to represent this violation in a particular form: as though the Law itself provides for the violation-of-the-Law. A childhood recollection establishes the parameters:

> because I was a girl, my parents told me: "You're a young woman and a woman has to be a mother." They said I was beginning my life as a woman and I would want many things that I couldn't have. They tried to tell me that, whatever my ambitions, I'd no way of achieving them. That's how life is. . . . and then they said I shouldn't wait too long before getting married. I had to think for myself, learn to be independent, not rely on my parents. . . . They gave me the freedom to do what I wanted with my life as long as, first and foremost, I obeyed the laws of our ancestors. (59)

What is certain here is that Rigoberta Menchu wants to show respect for ancestral law and to represent her parents as fulfilling their traditional responsibilities: they convey the ancestral wisdom to their children. The mandates do not, in themselves, appear to be contradictory: get married soon, think for yourself, be independent, obey the ancestral laws.

A similar experience occurs at the final meeting as the family is dispersing, when, unlike the traditionalists in Silko's *Ceremony*, Menchu's father, who is leaving the community perhaps never to return, pronounces his farewell and once again offers advice to his daughters: "Then my father told us girls who weren't married that we had absolute freedom to do as we wished, that we should be independent, and give everything we could to the struggle without anyone behind us ordering us about or forcing us to do anything. He said he gave us total freedom, but that he would like us to use that freedom for the good of the people, to teach the people what he had taught us" (155). Here her father, in the context of impending familial and political crisis, uses his authority to relinquish authority by dispersing and disseminating it. He sets his daughters free, but qualifies and circumscribes that freedom: it must be used in the service of the people. It is like feminism(s) which permit transgressions and nonconformity, but somehow remain loyal to their own interests. Freedom (the opportunity to act *against* the Law) is exercised curiously, in other words, in the same interest *as* the Law, even though it takes an/other form. There are other limits to this "freedom"—it is not the daughters' "right" to take it; rather, it is the father's right to grant it. And he gives it only to those daughters who are not married (those still subject to *his* Law and not to the Law as manifest in or through some other man).

Ancestral law, as received from her father, contains the possibility for its own undoing in the interest of preserving both the Quiché people and its own authority. While it is tempting to consider the Law as an inflexible and abstract codification of behavior, Rigoberta Menchu represents it as rooted in the exemplary, the lived experience, which, though not written in books, when told or demonstrated is "like an education for us" (189). Parents instruct the children as they grow up: "They talk to their children explaining what they have to do and what our ancestors used to do. They don't impose it as a law, but just give the example of what our ancestors have always done" (16). Her father, as a leader of the people in the community, as a father to everyone, "must lead an exemplary life" (17). As Certeau notes, in most Indian societies,

> The law functions . . . as the *tacit coordination of traditional practices.* The law is the very functioning of the group—an authority that is embedded in practical norms, not set above them. Since the alliance with the land minimizes the role a system of representations can play, and is expressed through gestural relations between the body and the mother earth, the totality of social practices and functions constitutes an order that no singular figure can detach from the group, or make visible to it in such a way as to impose obligations of obedience or offer all of its members supervisory or oversight possibilities. (230)

The Law has an adaptive plasticity that protects it from attacks from without as well as from within. She acknowledges and eludes her "place," thus becoming an effective revolutionary agent and spokeswoman for her people. To the extent that she is able, Rigoberta Menchu at once reveals and conceals her identity, and similarly, is (and must be) the "ideal Quiché woman"—the one who unquestioningly abides by the rule of the Fathers—and its contradiction—the woman who thinks for herself and decides her own life, breaking or exceeding the Father's law in the process (244). In this sense, we can also read her as offering a prototype for the feminist woman.

Such strategic self-positioning can be illustrated by returning once again to the circumstance of the marriage law: "you're a young woman and a woman has to be a mother" (59). Rigoberta Menchu's position in revolutionary struggle conflicts with the traditional position of "the Indian woman": "Well, in my case, I analysed my ideas about not getting married with some of my *compañeros*. I realized that what I said wasn't crazy, that it wasn't some personal mad idea, but that our whole situation makes women think very hard before getting married, because who will look after the children, who will feed them? . . . But knowing that I had to multiply the seed of our ancestors and, at the same time, rejecting marriage . . . that was a crazy idea" (223–24). This conflict is not resolved easily—the logic of revolution at odds with the tribal custom and the harsh circumstances of raising children to adulthood: "It is terrible to know that such a hard life awaits you, with so much responsibility to make sure your children live" (224). Rigoberta Menchu makes what she carefully marks as a provisional decision to remain single when her parents die (the literal death of the representative of law and custom within her own family): "That's when I decided [not to marry or have children], although I can't say that it's a final decision because I am open to life" (224). Following this, she comments: "I am human and I am a woman so I can't say that I reject marriage altogether, but I think my primary duty is to my people and then to my personal happiness" (225). Still, reiterating the earlier refrain, she refuses to foreclose her future: "But, as I said, I'm open to life. It doesn't mean that I reject everything because I know that things come in their time" (225). She works her way through the contradiction by siding with an as-yet-to-be-determined future of her people and by choosing "against" her personal happiness as specified by her forefathers and "against" her personal experience of love. In other words, she validates the Law of marriage, and instead of refuting it, chooses "against herself" in favor of the collective well-being which ostensibly authorized the law. Echoing the opening statement, "I'd like to stress that it's not only *my* life, it's also the testimony of my people" (1), she wants to exchange her individual identity for a collective one: "at the moment I wouldn't feel happy having a *compañero* and giving myself to him while so many of our people are not thinking of their own personal happiness" (224)—and as such, the position from which she speaks may at this point encompass men, *ladino* women, all poor Guatemalans: "My personal experience is the reality of a whole people" (1). (This suggests as well the irony implicit in the

115

choice of the English, ego-centered title, *I . . . Rigoberta Menchu* as compared with the Spanish, *Me llamo Rigoberta Menchú y así me nació la conciencia* [My Name Is Rigoberta Menchu and This Is How My Consciousness Was Born/Raised].)

Perhaps even greater than the struggle over marriage is Rigoberta Menchu's effort to come to terms with the *ladino*, whose structural position resembles the feminist theorist, and whom, as part Indian and often marginalized, she inherits when she claims identity and solidarity with the poor. It would be easy to offer the argument that, since she is first and foremost an Indian, the *ladino* is necessarily the enemy. Her people have been objects of genocide, exploitation, and torture in which this enemy has been complicit. Further, the Indian people's sense of a "pure" identity provides racial, cultural, and political cohesiveness, the collective identity one needs in order to survive and to struggle. This places Menchu in opposition to the *ladinos*, whom the interviewer defines as "any Guatemalan—whatever his economic position—who rejects, either individually or through his cultural heritage, Indian values of Mayan origin. It also implies mixed blood" (249). In a sense the opposition between the terms *ladino* and *compañero* founds Rigoberta Menchu's struggle. The *ladino* or *caxlan* represents a personal threat in the form of the "ladinized Indians" who speak Spanish and identify with the powerful—what Rigoberta Menchu refuses to become. She presents her grandfather's (189), her father's, and her own view of these go-betweens: "Many of them are *ladinos* from Oriente. But there are also many of our people from the *Altiplano* among them. My father used to call them 'ladinized Indians.' When we say 'ladinized' we mean they act like *ladinos*, bad *ladinos*, because afterwards we realized that not all *ladinos* are bad. A bad *ladino* is one who knows how to talk and steal from the people. He is a small-scale picture of the landowner" (24). Rigoberta Menchu's struggles to liberate the racial or ethnic term from economic and moral connotations of the opposition are instructive to feminist criticism as it negotiates other (con)founding oppositions such as masculine/feminine, theorist/feminist, political/personal. Her contribution to the discussion of *ladinos* is the retrospective awareness ("afterwards we realized") that *ladinos* can be human (like Indians), good and bad depending on how they behave rather than on any essential (blood) nature. This is a profoundly un/settling awareness for the revolutionary who needs to be clear about who the enemy is (119).

As the translator, Ann Wright notes the subtleties of shifting nominalization with respect to the *ladino/compañero* opposition. Again the definitions of the oppositional terms refuse to stay put, to stay on their respective sides of the divide. Wright remarks: "Although ladino ostensibly means a person of mixed race or a Spanish-speaking Indian, in this context it also implies someone who represents a system which oppresses the Indian—first under Spanish rule and then under the succession of brutal governments of the landed oligarchy. So a word like 'half-caste' would be inadequate. Hence Rigoberta's father's invention 'ladinizar' (to ladinize, or become like a ladino) which is a mixture of ladino and latinizar (to latinize), and has both racial and religious connotations" (viii). Rigoberta Menchu does not easily abandon her ancestors' view of ladinos. She meets groups of Achi and Mam Indians who try to disabuse her of the conventional wisdom: "They all told me: 'The rich are bad. But not all ladinos are bad.' And I started wondering: 'Could it be that not all ladinos are bad?' I used to think they were all bad. But they said that they lived with poor ladinos. There were poor ladinos as well as rich ladinos, and they were exploited as well. That's when I began recognizing exploitation" (119). The transgression of carefully and strategically erected boundaries is difficult since her initial experiences (an important proving ground) with ladinos who are glad they are not Indians and look down on them differ from the experiences of the Indians she meets later, who challenge her long-held views. She summarizes her initial position as follows: "being ladino is something important in itself: it's *not* being an Indian" (167).

To arrive at an understanding of the poor ladino as an ally in the political struggle confounds the difference that in part structures Rigoberta Menchu's identity and gives purpose to her revolutionary politics. She explains, "*Ladinos* are *mestizos*, the children of Spaniards and Indians who speak Spanish. But they are in the minority. There is a larger percentage of Indians. Some say it is 60 per cent, others that it's 80 per cent. We don't know the exact number for a very good reason—there are Indians who don't wear Indian clothes and have forgotten their languages, so they are not considered Indians. And there are middle-class Indians who have abandoned their traditions. They aren't considered Indians either" (167). The recurring elaboration of identities—who is an Indian and who is a ladino—renders problematic some aspects of Rigoberta Menchu's own relationship to her language and traditions. And here she engages the personally vexing threat of the ladino.

In addition to the discussions of marriage, the story we are given contains many other instances in which the narrator discloses her' departures from traditional culture. In a brief discussion of prostitution, she states, "This is something which doesn't exist among Indians, because of our culture and the traditions we preserve and respect. In the eyes of our community, the fact that anyone should even change the way they dress shows a lack of dignity. Anyone who doesn't dress as our grandfathers, our ancestors, dressed, is on the road to ruin" (37). Here, the Indians who don't wear proper clothes are conjoined with those who have forgotten their language. Dress is an external marker of one's identity and standing (respect) within the community. Yet in an interview with Jim Stephens she comments, "The most difficult thing for me was when my parents had to let me join the struggle, when I was older. At the beginning it was very difficult for my father to understand—he had a lot of attitudes concerning how we dressed, how we wore our hair, and I had to ignore a lot of them. But once he understood, he didn't give me any more trouble" (Menchu and Stephens 51). She uses herself as a somewhat transparent example of the individual who exceeds the boundaries of community control, whose past activities are unknown and therefore threatening to group identity: "The community is very suspicious of a woman like me who is twenty-three but they don't know where I've been or where I've lived. She loses the confidence of the community and contact with her neighbours, who are supposed to be looking after her all the time" (61). Those with clear, pure ideas are the Indians who have never left the village; they are neither con/fused nor con/founded. Her father, however, freed her from this expectation: "I was free in those days. My father told me: 'You are independent, you must do what you want to, as long as you do it for our people.' That was my father's idea. I was absolutely free to decide, to leave for another village" (141). Neither Rigoberta Menchu nor her father are "conventional" people ("pure" followers of the Law). He too acknowledges her difference as well as both his complicity and approval when at a meeting in El Quiché of the Committee leaders, he tells the *compañeros,* "This badly brought up daughter has always been a good daughter" (183). She does not conform to convention, he failed his responsibility as a "proper" father (she is "badly brought up"), but he is pleased with her (she is a "good daughter") nonetheless.

The most marked incursion into the space of the *ladino* occurs when Menchu tells this story of her (non)identity in Spanish, becomes a "Spanish-speaking Indian," stepping dangerously near that category she resists. She signals her accommodation of the *ladino* through the shift in the positive designation *compañero.* Wright comments as follows on the transformation of the word, literally meaning "companion," in the course of the narrative: "Rigoberta initially uses it for her friends, and her neighbours in the community. But as the political commitment of both Rigoberta and her village grows, it becomes 'comrade', a fellow fighter in the struggle. She uses it for the militants in the trade unions, the CUC [Comité Unidad Campesina or Peasant Unity Committee], and the political organisations. The *compañeros de la montana* are the guerillas. From these two words comes the rather unwieldy *compañero ladino*" (viii-ix). The *ladinos* can never become Indians (as "pure bloods"), even when loosely defined, but they can become "like Indians," companions in struggle. In secret meetings, she discovers this from her *ladino* Spanish teacher, who worked with the CUC. From his actions, not his ideas, she learns "to love *ladinos* a lot" (165). So, as one who desires to represent "the poor"—"my story is the story of all poor Guatemalans" (1), Rigoberta Menchu necessarily engages the contradiction of the poor *ladino*, the "unwieldy," confounded category of the *compañero ladino* (160), neither strictly one nor the other, terms and identities which refuse to stay put in the very space of her own speaking—the telling of her Indian/*compañera* story in non-Indian or *ladina*/Spanish. She learns this through the greater lesson of union rather than division: "the example of my *compañero ladino* made me really understand the barrier which has been put up between the Indian and the *ladino*, and that because of this same system which tries to divide us, we haven't understood that *ladinos* also live in terrible conditions, the same as we do" (165). So the terms *compañero*, reserved initially for the designation of Indian compatriots, and *ladino*, used exclusively at first for evil oppressors, are conjoined to form the unlikely, the "unwieldy" identity of a "half-breed," the *compañero ladino*, and the possibilities for negotiating broader networks of engagement is established.

Before returning in a more general way to the question of reading (or how I have produced) a "theory" of Rigoberta Menchu (and how, at least implicitly, it seems that she has theorized me), I want to trace the more treacherous, but I hope instructive, path of her relationship to her mother, as compared with her father/companion, and what the identity of the mother/woman represents in traditional Quiché culture. Rigoberta Menchu describes her parents' role in the community early in the narrative: "In our community there is an elected representative, someone who is highly respected. He's not a king but someone whom the community looks up to like a father. In our village, my father and mother were the representatives. Well, then the whole community becomes the children of the woman who's elected" (7). The Quiché woman, even when she is not an elected representative, has special (different) roles and responsibilities. Her identity is understood in a particular way that links her to the earth as well as to the perpetuation of the race through procreation, functions which should not be separated in a discussion of traditional Quiché culture. Thus, Rigoberta explains: "Indians think it is dreadful to sit on chairs, women especially, because the woman is the mother of the home and the earth is the mother of the whole world—the mother of all our indigenous people. The importance of the mother is related to the importance of the earth" (73). Woman is part of the earth, the renewing and guarding spirit of the people. Menchu elaborates on this point slightly when she discusses the subject of women in Guatemala, and particularly the Indian woman:

> There is something important about women in Guatemala, especially Indian women, and that something is her relationship with the earth—between the earth and the mother. The earth gives food and the woman gives life. Because of this closeness the woman must keep this respect for the earth as a secret of her own. The relationship between the mother and the earth is like the relationship between husband and wife. There is a constant dialogue between the earth and the woman. This feeling is born in women because of the responsibilities they have, which men do not have. (220)

But neither does Rigoberta Menchu have this special responsibility born into her, since she follows her father's side rather than her mother's. This subject, perhaps like much of what her mother did, is veiled, almost exclusively the site of sacred and secret rituals, and as such delimits the feminist critic's ability to come to terms with the other woman.

Her mother possessed special powers, illustrated in the unelaborated reference to her mother's choice when she was young to be a *chiman*. Rigoberta Menchu explains: "she said she was going to learn from a *chiman*. That's what we call a man who tells the Indians' fortunes. He's like a doctor for the Indians, or like a priest. My mother said: 'I'm going to be a *chiman* and I'll learn with one of these men.' And she went to the *chiman* and he taught her many things out of his imagination connected with animals, with plants, with water, with the sun. My mamá learned a great deal, but who knows, perhaps that wasn't to be her role in life. Nevertheless, it helped her a lot to learn and dedicate herself to other things" (213). We cannot discern what relationship her mother had as an adult to such secret wisdom. Her daughter's comment leads us to believe that she carried away some details about plants and weather, leaving the more substantial aspects of the diviner/priest/doctor's role behind her; "As I said, my mother was brave but, nonetheless, I learned more from my father. I regret this very much now because my mother knew many things that I

120

don't know, things like medicines and what she knew about nature. I know this as well, of course, but only on a general level, not at all profoundly" (219). Her mother followed the strict traditional way, which made her courageous. Perhaps her adherence to conventional mores created a distance between them, or perhaps Rigoberta Menchu was in this instance too, free to choose: "There were many estimable things in my father; many things which he could face but also many things he couldn't face. And my mother too. She could face many things, but there were other things she couldn't do. So I love them both the same. I love them both but I have to say that I grew up more at my father's side. My mother taught many people many things, but I didn't learn as much from her as I should have learned" (219). What Rigoberta Menchu failed to learn from her mother we do not know; we are only told those things she did learn and chooses to reveal.

I believe, however, that there is more to this story. Dennis Tedlock, in his notes to the sacred Mayan text, the *Popol Vuh*, provides some information that is useful in considering the community status of Rigoberta Menchu's parents. Tedlock explains that the men who are heads of patrilineages, then and now, are called " 'mother-fathers,' since in ritual matters they serve as symbolic androgynous parents to everyone in their respective lineages" (47). Tedlock elaborates on this term later, noting that it is

> pronounced as a single word. In this context, "mother" and "father" are complementary metonyms that together produce the sense of "parent," but without any final reduction of the difference between motherhood and fatherhood. In the *P.V.*, the composite term thus produced is used as a metaphor for the gods called Maker and Modeler and less figuratively for the first four human males, three of whom became founders of patrilineages. In several present-day Quiché towns the heads of patrilineages, who are daykeepers and are also responsible for lineage shrines, are called mother-fathers even though they are all males. (350)

Tedlock provides one more note pertinent to the matter: "contemporary daykeepers (of either sex) are symbolically androgynous, female on the left side of the body and male on the right. . . . To this day, a daykeeper ideally has a spouse who is also a daykeeper, and the divinations with the clearest outcomes are the ones they do together" (370). The female daykeeper is also, like Rigoberta Menchu's mother, frequently a midwife (8, 215) and a woman who possesses powers of divination and responsibility for the care of the earth and its inhabitants. This strange, once again unwieldy and con/founded notion of the "mother-father" reminds me of other odd hybrids, the *ladino com-*

pañero, the feminist man, the (com)passionate U.S. feminist theorist—
each an instance of being neither one thing nor the other, somehow
both in an uncanny identity of man and woman, enemy and friend.

In "The Politics of Silence: The Long March of the Indians," Michel
de Certeau conflates the Latin American Indian's "*tortured* body" and
"the *altered earth*" in the figure of the page upon which the histories
of oppression and resistance are written (*Heterologies* 227). He attributes the Indian's political power to the specifics of the geo-*graphical*,
their geocultural positioning:

> their communities continued to return periodically to the home
> village, to claim their rights to the land and to maintain, through
> this collective alliance on a common *soil*, an anchorage in the
> *particularity* of a place. The land, serving as a reference point, in
> addition to preserving local representations and beliefs (often
> fragmented and hidden beneath the occupiers' system), is also a
> ballast and defense for the "own" [*le propre*] against any superim-
> position. It was, and is, a kind of palimpsest: the gringos' writing
> does not erase the primary text, which remains traced there—
> illegible to the passersby who have manipulated the areas for
> four centuries—as a silent sacrament of "maternal forces," the
> forefathers' tomb, the indelible seal joining the members of the
> community together in contractual agreement. (229)

Such is the nature of secrecy, the guarded silences of speakers like
Rigoberta Menchu. Their secrets are connected to the earth, the place
of the Law of the Forefathers, a land inscribed with historically rooted
and materially significant (signifying) graphics. The Indian's "secrecy"
issues from the ethos of silence, the unspoken recognition of the
Eternal. Certeau continues:

> It enables the resistance to avoid being disseminated in the occupi-
> ers' power grid, to avoid being captured by the dominating, inter-
> pretive systems of discourse (or by the simple inversion of those
> discourses, a tactic which remains prisoner to their logic). It "main-
> tains" a difference rooted in an affiliation that is opaque and
> inaccessible to both violent appropriation and learned co-optation.
> It is the unspoken foundation of affirmations that have *political*
> meaning to the extent that they are based on a *realization of coming
> from a "different" place* (different, not opposite) on the part of those
> whom the omnipresent conquerors dominate. (229)

In this resides the error of carving new marks, routes of escape,
tunnels and ditches, on the earth's body.

The secrecy, or "discretion," of native peoples finds reinforcement in oral tradition. Within this context, one listens to the earth and the animals who speak like teachers or father-mothers. Speaking is not so much a right as it is a presumption of sorts. Rigoberta Menchu recounts the following episode: "my father told us all about the marvellous things there were in our land (and thinking of our ancestors of course), and the closeness of the peasant to nature. We kept quiet and listened to the silence of the mountains. It's a pleasant silence. And in that silence, birds and animals were singing" (191). Through the silence one attends to many voices.

But what happens when the silence is broken, when a "third-world woman" speaks? What kind of theory or practice is spoken? Rigoberta Menchu, having taken over the toolbox (the Spanish language), seizes the power to speak—a property previously reserved for the intellectual, the capitalist, the colonizer. At the same time, when the oppressed begin to speak, they speak their own theory of oppression, of economy and land rights, of cultural dignity—or, as Foucault terms it, a *theory of* rather than a *theory about* (Foucault and Deleuze 209). What, then, is this *theory of* a Quiché woman?

What if we turn again to the objection, presented by the Feminists, that Rigoberta Menchu's theory, if it survives the onslaught of wealthy landowners' power, will ultimately leave intact the culture's traditional *machismo*. I hope that by now this position is more difficult to insist upon. It is plausible that the Quiché man and woman, and Quiché tradition, will return from struggle changed, that this current phase of life may represent the equivalent of the Derridean reversal, while the ultimate, or next, (displaced) position of women remains, like life for Rigoberta, "open." The Indian culture in which woman will be (re)placed is not itself remaining static. The community's response to the army's attempt to force them off the land further illustrates the adaptability of Law and culture with respect to tradition. The community digs ditches and escape routes into the mountains to avoid being slaughtered: "We broke with many of our cultural procedures by doing this but we knew it was the way to save ourselves. . . . The community elects its leader but everything he does has to be approved by the others. What the community does not approve cannot be carried through. Everyone plays an equal part: men, women, and the children as well" (128). The comment demonstrates how the collective responds to the political necessities of life in Guatemala today. The women are not "women," the children not "children." Instead, women and children literally "act like men"; "men" act like "women" and "children": their roles in the revolution are indistinguishable, as is the sociocultural value attributed to them. Their work is survival.

Menchu elaborates: "Children had to behave like grown-ups. We women had to play our part as women in the community, together with our parents, our brothers, our neighbours. We all had to unite, all of us together" (120). In an interview with Jim Stephens, Rigoberta Menchu explains what is at stake: "There are things you have to do in the struggle and there's no way around that. That's why we emphasize that our culture is being endangered, because we're losing a number of things. But that's a risk we have to run if we're going to defend it; there's no other way" (51).

This situation is not unique to the Quiché culture. In *Risking a Somersault in the Air*, the Nicaraguan poet Giaconda Belli describes the difficulties of changing gender relationships even in the context of revolution: "sometimes I think it's easier to face an enemy army in combat than to confront the inheritance of concepts and prejudices we carry inside ourselves and transform it. . . . It produces enormous contradictions, and we don't have any models at hand because it's something new that has to be created" (150). A characteristic of traditional cultures under/writes these new responsibilities accorded women, men, and children. As the soldiers are hunting people in their homes, the people change their rules, the grounding principles of their collective "identity": "now we have good cause to find new methods. That's how the community itself looks for ways of improving certain things that weren't any good. We did everything together because there were no longer specific tasks for men and others for women" (129). Historical contingencies require that the Law change the Law, and it is a process of collective decision-making in which women and children (often widows and orphans) participate along with the surviving forefathers. In this sense, then, women are not merely subject to the Law, they, to a degree, are the Law. As Commander Maria Tellez comments in Randall's *Sandino's Daughters*, "How could values *not* change in families where loved ones were lost? What can't change? Anything, even the role of women—so deeply rooted—can change" (197).

Rigoberta Menchu's mode of theorizing is not particularly occulted. In some respects, her way is rather like mine. With her friends and *compañeros* she thinks about the experience of her people (116), poses questions (117), speaks with others (119, 162), identifies the enemy (122), generalizes her experience—"I just tried to turn my own experience into something which was common to a whole people" (118). The process is a familiar one: "when we're all together, amongst ourselves, we discuss, we think, we give our views" (170). But there are profound differences, how she is not like me and never will be.

She believes most fundamentally in the validity of her lived experience: "We know this is true because we live it every day, not because someone else tells us" (121). She has and demands another kind of credentials: "you can only have a real consciousness if you've really lived this life" (223)—a requirement that I permit her only provisionally but that I am afraid to allow Feminism because I think I understand what Feminism means and wants, the kind of tensions which inhabit it, when it (im)poses the criterion of knowledge through experience, as though one could be kept separate from the other. In addition, her transmutation of the *ladino* into the *ladino compañero* makes me suspect her ability to hold firmly to other oppositions like feminist-(theorist)/ Indian. Rigoberta Menchu's authorizing text is the life of her people, and her aim is to create "a real change inside people": "That is my cause. As I've already said, it wasn't born out of something good, it was born out of wretchedness and bitterness. It has been radicalized by the poverty in which my people live. It has been radicalized by malnutrition which I, as an Indian, have seen and experienced. And by the exploitation and discrimination which I've felt in the flesh" (246). I want to believe her when she claims to be able to speak for all of her people, and, even, finally, the "good *ladino*." We occupy vastly different relationships to the oppositions I have been discussing. For her, the stakes are immeasurably high: theorizing practice and practicing theory are a life or death affair. She can say, "I am convinced that the people, the masses, are the only ones capable of transforming society. It's not just another theory" (246). When I talk about theory, it feels and sounds like it *is* "just another theory." When she talks about practice, it sounds like revolutionary theory, a revolution in theory. Guillaumin explains this as a process of breaking away from the always already given,

> the belief that if things are thus, they are naturally thus and fated to remain so; therefore there is nothing particularly unusual about it, it cannot be analyzed, and there is nothing there to be discovered or understood, since the only reason for analyzing something is to change it, to interfere with it. (Thinking already means changing. *Thinking about a fact already means changing that fact.*) It is obvious that the long-standing blindness of theory, whether psychological or sociological theory, simply resulted in attesting to belief in the natural ineluctability of these relationships. (38)

I want to read Rigoberta Menchu's text as enacting a theory which cannot be circumscribed, accommodated, and recolonized because it remains a radical, unspecifiable projection into the future, a future which is understood differently from my linear differentiation of the space that follows past and present. In *I . . . Rigoberta Menchu* feminist critics can read the story of a theory/practice relationship which escapes the entrapping opposition of the metalogic, one in which the exigencies of daily life (practice) require a rewriting of Law (theory), and the authorizing function of Law redefines or corrects the already constituted actors, their relationships, and their arena.

Rigoberta Menchu "shows" herself and her mother to be women speaking without Theory, concealing in that gesture the way in which this practice is a moving theory, a theory in action. In doing so, she con/founds the very idea of theory's difference from practice. For example, her mother tells her,

> "My child, we must organise. It's not something I demand of you because I'm your mother. It's your duty to put into practice what you know. The days of paternalism, of saying 'poor girl, she doesn't know anything,' are over." My mother made no distinction between the men's struggle and the women's struggle. She said: "I don't want to make you stop feeling a woman, but your participation in the struggle must be equal to that of your brothers. But you mustn't join as just another number, you must carry out important tasks, analyse your position as a woman and demand a share. A child is only given food when he demands it. A child who makes no noise, gets nothing to eat." (219)

Both Rigoberta and her mother pretend to speak only the language of experience, of practice and representation. It is in their interests to conceal any authorizing capacity other than their traditional culture (already wearing a disguise) which is, after all, their rallying place— what they hold out for us to see as clearly as they wish us to see it. But representation, whether of "idea" or "experience," as commonly and erroneously separated, is always representation of an idea, the already there in the speaking about (from) experience. This is the excess, the "something else" in these stories and the stories within the stories: the something else that their language of practice speaks of relentlessly, pointing to itself, as it conceals, among other equally important things, its theoretical excess, its identity as theory.

So what then is this *theory of* a third-world woman? Domitila Barrios de Chungara, commenting to her amanuensis, on her own narrative as presented in *Let Me Speak!*, sees her text's function and value as that of returning material to the people. "I think it's correct that you've understood and not changed what I wanted to say and interpret. I hope that in Bolivia and in other countries the people's experiences are gathered up not only to elaborate theories on an intellectual level, alien theories, but to be used, as the title you gave this book says, so that the people can be allowed to speak" (235). If we attend to the logic of the ancient Mayan books, the parent father-mothers, as well as that of the *ladino compañeros*, and the theory in action model of practice, we might see how the absoluteness of opposi-tions, as we understand them in Western philosophy and as Rigoberta Menchu sees them in political practice, requires revision.

Rigoberta Menchu's text, through its example, offers feminist literary critics other more general but important lessons. As radicals gain power through discourse (in this case, a "place" for feminist criticism within the academy), we grow unwilling to give up the discourse that made us powerful; we base our permanence, our "place" at the "center," "with the permanence of the discourse that founded [us]" (Radhakrishnan, "Post-Modern" 55). In our own way, we become "*ladinized*," a term which in itself suggests no more, but no less, than the precariousness of our function in revolutionary strug-gle. To enact the "contra/dictoriness" of its discourse, feminism must struggle to remain a radical practice. That is to say: feminist criticism cannot set itself up as "Theory" or "Non-Theory"; nor can it manifest itself in some way other than as an eruption in a local instance. This is the paradox of radicality: that it cannot assent to assent. As Deleuze maintains, "A theory is exactly like a box of tools. . . . A theory does not totalize; it is an instrument for multiplication and it also multiplies itself. It is in the nature of power to totalize and . . . theory is by nature opposed to power. As soon as a theory is enmeshed in a particular point, we realize that it will never possess the slightest practical importance unless it can erupt in a totally different area" (Foucault and Deleuze 208). Feminist literary criticism's power de-pends upon its ability to remain dis-located, without a home in cul-ture's institutions. The location or "place" of feminist criticism, then, is the "some place" of guerilla fighters, like the *compañeros de la montana* who steal, hide, attack, and set up camp somewhere else, awaiting the unpredictable moment when they will strike again.

The future of feminist critical theory depends upon its negotiating capacity—how we are to engage the struggle of competing denomina-tions—Rigoberta's rejection of the words "feminism" and "theory," and my desire, admittedly violent and imperialistic, but also admiring and loving, to attach those names to her. This raises the question of respect, addressed so powerfully by Bernice Johnson Reagon in "Coalition Politics: Turning the Century": "Respect means . . . allow-ing people to name themselves. And dealing with them from that perspective" (366–67). To deal with a person in their name is not, however, to forget the name I have for them. It is, instead, to speak in the gap. When I call her a "feminist" and a "theorist," I (only) call her that in a gesture of representation which, nonetheless, I know to be both formation and deformation, but through which no essential identity is articulated. All I can recount at this moment is the rationale for and the relationship between our names, and my own desire for feminism and (with) a Quiché Indian woman. Perhaps all I can do is "write myself with her" (Marini, *Territoires* 73) as a way of negotiating and weaving the differences and similarities into a complex discursive fabric where we both realize that neither speaks what she does without the other. And I wonder, if she can grow to love the *ladino compañero*, might she someday learn to love the feminist theorist?

In *I . . . Rigoberta Menchu* feminist critics can read the story of a theory/practice relationship in which the exigencies of daily life (practice) require a rewriting of Law (theory), and the authorizing function of Law redefines or corrects the already-constituted actors and their relationships. The effectiveness of feminist literary criticism rests in contra/diction, its ability to remain incomplete, to be a moving energy of practice, the enactment of tactics not intended to survive their occasion (Radhakrishnan, "Post-Modern" 57), struggling against the singular identity of Feminism that makes nominal representation possible, that permits me to think even for a moment that the Quiché Indian woman, despite what she might choose to tell me, has no theory, and that makes it impossible for me to say what the "place" of feminist criticism is or might be. Likewise, according to this (il)logic, it impossible for me to formulate, to fix as literary history, or to predict the implication of a feminist critique that erupts, attacks, disappears— appears, now here, now here again, occurring and recurring ir/regularly, unpredictably, and contra/dictorily.

CHAPTER SIX

(Trans)Forming the Grammar of Racism in Sherley Anne Williams's *Dessa Rose*

beyond sisterhood is still racism
—Audre Lorde, *Sister Outsider*

In the same way that the ideology of Apartheid is only an aberration—
a stillness—of what is potentially present in all of mankind, the
butchers and the interrogators are not monsters but people like you
and me. That is what makes them so horrible and so pitiful. And that
is exactly why we must continue condemning and combating their
acts. I believe that the torturer is as depraved by his acts as the one
who is tortured. We will be fools and mere objects of history if we go
looking for the causes of depravity in "human nature" only. We make
society and society makes us, all of us. But there are certain fabrics
once torn that cannot be mended again; certain transgressions that can
never be condoned.

—Breyten Breytenbach, *The True
Confessions of an Albino Terrorist*

I learned very early that in the realm of the imagination all people and
their ambitions and interest could meet.
—Ralph Ellison, *Shadow and Act*

White feminists have been urged for over a decade to examine and to
come to terms with our racism which presents itself as an exclusion
in the spaces we call "Woman" and "Feminism." The grammar of race
is, in this country and many others, a grammar of racism. Hatred,
fear, and ignorance under/write an elaborate discursive (syntactical
and lexical) complexity that produces the text of racism out of race, in
a way analogous to the text of sexism incessantly produced by sex. In
this light, Hortense Spillers warns, "We might concede, at the very
least, that sticks and bricks *might* break our bones, but words will most
certainly *kill* us" ("Mama's" 68). Physical features "figured out" as
racial difference are (re)presented in such a way that they assume

129

intellectual, moral, and even metaphysical difference in a treacherous economy of the Same where value is invested on the side of the powerful, those presumed to be racially "unmarked." The matter of race is never simply that; it is always "more." Henry Louis Gates, Jr., argues that race is "a dangerous trope" rather than "an objective term of classification": "Race has become a trope of ultimate, irreducible difference between cultures, linguistic groups, or adherents of specific belief systems which—more often than not—also have fundamentally opposed economic interests" ("Writing" 5). It is easy to agree on this point, but I find myself wanting to stop before his next sentence: "Race is the ultimate trope of difference because it is so very arbitrary in its application" (5). Recalling the arguments advanced in my discussion of *Burger's Daughter,* where Gordimer enacts a similar move, I want to reserve judgment concerning the primacy of race, its supreme arbitrariness over other differences, specifically, the irreducible capriciousness of sex.

While the black writing of race has not eliminated racism (see Gates, "Writing" 12), women's writing of sex has not eliminated sexism, and too often one writing practice perpetuates the problems against which the other writes. To this we can add as well, taking account of Susan Willis's fine work, the relation of class to race and sex. Gates's assertion throws us back into the dilemma of the hierarchy of oppression where one is asked to designate the primacy of racism over sexism (or class or sexual choice) as arenas of struggle. This is not a choice that I have constructed, and is therefore a choice that I refuse to make. Rather, I am personally sympathetic with Barbara Smith's trenchant observation, materialized in her example of forced sterilization, that "Black and other Third World women's relationships to the systems of oppression in this society are, by definition, different from those of other oppressed groups who do not experience both racial and sexual oppression at the same time. The effect of this double, actually triple oppression because of class [she later adds sexual choice as well], is not merely arithmetic—one plus one plus one—but geometric. There is such a thing as racial-sexual oppression which is neither solely racial nor solely sexual" ("Notes" 123). I choose to focus on this difference, the excess in choosing the two, racial-sexual, plus the third, class, as inseparable rhetorical properties in what Spillers calls "an 'American grammar' " ("Mama's" 68), and that Sherley Anne Williams presents as a lesson for reading in her novel *Dessa Rose.*

Race as a trope is written in/by language which is a space co-(in)habited by the one and the other(s). Speakers designate me as they wish, to suit their intentions and interests. Unless I speak myself, language will not serve me, and only then does it throw me and the other(s) into a negotiating relationship so that we can bargain with each other and with language over our shared property, our respective investments in signification. This idea of negotiating figuration, the (re)presentation of the self, identity, and community, characterizes the work of black men and white and black women writers. In fact, it provides the scene of struggle for writers historically excluded from representation.

While it is easy to see these writing projects as simple additions, the representation of the un(der)represented, a matter explored in some length in Chapter 2, more is at stake than this additive economic metaphor suggests (the ruse of critical pluralism and the "melting pot"). What I am talking about is the addition that makes (a) difference in its resistance to the recovery of the same in a dialectical sublation of difference. The aim is the (trans)formation of this hierarchically oppositional grammar into an intense, sometimes conflictual, sometimes pleasurable and pleasureful commingling of opposites (Duras's project) in a "free" zone or "borderland," where anxieties about identities (which we have when we must maintain difference or sameness) and the noncoincidence of self and other (including the other that is the "self") are affirmed for the purpose of negotiation. This activity involves, in the instance of race, for example, the (un)writing of historic (re)presentations of race as racism, to work an/other (trans)formation, not back to the impossible ground of some neutral, objective origin—the "real" of "race"—but a (re)valuation, an undoing of the rhetoric (structure) of racism that wants to stand for/as race in imperialist ideology. My particular concern in this chapter is how black and white women can negotiate the thicket of conflicting and contending pressures of race, class, and sex (and if my example were different, sexual choice) in the interest of striking a relationship between "black feminism"/"black" women's studies and "white feminism"/ "white" women's studies in such a way that they do not stand in fixed opposition to one another.[1] Through a reading of Sherley Anne Williams's *Dessa Rose*, I want to suggest some ways in which the historic tensions characterizing our (non)relationship might be (re)written so that we can be open to one another through ex/posure, ex/change, and ex/position.

The (re)figuration of the received figure of the black woman has been the project of black women from the time they could speak and write. Sojourner Truth's powerful unanswered query—"and ain't I a woman?"—resonates across the decades. Michele Wallace ironically summarizes the rhetorical field into which the black woman has been

inserted: *"Sapphire. Mammy. Tragic mulatto wench. Workhorse, can swing
an axe, lift a load, pick cotton with any man. A wonderful housekeeper.
Excellent with children. Very clean. Very religious. A terrific mother. A great
little singer and dancer and a devoted teacher and social worker. She's always
had more opportunities than the black man because she was no threat to
the white man so he made it easy for her"* (*Black* 153). Emphasizing the
"overdetermined nominative properties" of the "names" for black
women, Hortense Spillers opens her brilliant analysis of the African-
American woman, "Mama's Baby, Papa's Maybe: An American Grammar Book," with the following ex/posure of received identities: "Let's
face it. I am a marked woman, but not everybody knows my name.
'Peaches' and 'Brown Sugar,' 'Sapphire' and 'Earth Mother,' 'Aunty,'
'Granny,' God's 'Holy Fool,' a 'Miss Ebony First,' or 'Black Woman at
the Podium': I describe a locus of confounded identities, a meeting
ground of investments and privations in the national treasury of rhetorical wealth. My country needs me, and if I were not here, I would
have to be invented" (65). As we find in the case of other Identities such
as "feminist" or "lesbian," these as/signed names are so overloaded, so
excessive, they must be under/mined and stripped away (at) before an/
other, a "self"-invention, a "self" to be invented, can be discursively
(re)figured, even though our "new" names will always bear the traces
of other names and times, and of the naming practices that produce
them. A rhetorical violence stands in for centuries of literally and
figuratively murderous violence against African-Americans. There is
not simply one name for the black woman but a proliferation of them.
A violence on and against the body, on the figure of/for the body
and, Spillers reminds us, of the flesh, "that zero degree of social
conceptualization" ("Mama's" 67), is (re)formed by a "dehumanized
naming" (69) that authorizes physical as well as psychological mutila-
tion. What will it take in the discourse of literary criticism alone in the
United States to (un)write the grammar of such willful and calculated
protocols for subjugation and genocide? This is a question which, for
many reasons, I wish to keep open rather than to close through posing
an answer. I want to re-pose it when I read Silko, Gordimer, and
Menchu, to leave it open in front of me to protect myself from myself.

In my desire for a (pro-spective) dialogue and dialectical relationship, I want to turn the tables on white feminist critics, on Gordimer,
Duras, Rich, and myself, to examine how the black woman figures
the white woman. Gloria Wade-Gayles writes: "White women are
fragrant, dainty, and feminine ladies whom white America has placed
on a pedestal" (10). She moves from monolith (citing the same inven-
tory from Wallace) to monolith, in her effort to (un)write the (re)pre-

sentation of black women. The difficulty here is that the figuration of the dainty, fragrant, venerated white woman is no more adequate as a representation of white women—the women, for example, of *Burger's Daughter*, *The Lover*, and Rich's poetry—than the images of the black mammy and field hand are for black women. The figure (works because it) denies ethnicity (the Swedish- and German-American farm women), religion (the Jewish immigrant women from Eastern Europe), class (the Southern white women mill workers), and sexual choice (many white lesbians in America). So, we might ask again, aren't there white women without the pedestal who existed or can exist in some other relationship to African-American women? Aren't there also white women that Amerikan Kultur would like to keep invisible?

Doris Davenport, writing in a sense of outrage that devastatingly reverses the terms of discourse, redirects the pain that runs through the figures the white world has constructed for black women. She writes that black women find white women aesthetically "repulsive," culturally "limited and bigoted," socially "juvenile and tasteless," and politically (especially feminists) "naive and myopic." These aversions are the result of black women having seen "through the 'myth' of the white womon. The myth was that white wimmin were the most envied, most desired (and beautiful), most powerful (controlling white boys) wimmin in existence. The truth is that black people saw white wimmin as some of the least enviable, ugliest, most despised and least respected people, period. From our 'close encounters' (i.e., slavery, 'domestic' workers, etc.) with them, white people increasingly did seem like beasts or subnormal people" (87). The (re)presentation of others as subhuman and bestial characterizes the racist rhetoric (under)writing the enslavement of African-Americans as well as the hostility directed toward "other" women. But why am I saying this? I am not interested in guilt, "sin," or increased animosity. I cite these texts to make trouble in the logic of identity, to say I *am* this (a white woman), to say that I do not want to be *this* white woman (racist betrayer). I say: I am (not) this. I want to study how these words inscribe both possibility and impossibility, relationship and identity.

There is an issue here worth pursuing, and it is a matter crucial to Williams's text and our collective future: the question of respect. Toni Morrison, in an essay from 1971, spells out precisely the historic animosity between black and white women: "[Black women] look at white women and see them as the enemy—for they know that racism is not confined to white men, and that there are more white women than men in this country, and that 53 percent of the population

133

sustained an eloquent silence during times of greatest stress" ("What the Black Woman Thinks" 15). The history of the betrayal of black women by white women has been elaborated in its painful specifics (see, for example, Spillers, Hooks, Wade-Gayles, Giddings, Carby, Davenport), contrary to the claims of disloyalty to racist ideology often advanced by white feminists. The "intimacy" of our (non)relationship has been one that breeds distrust and contempt. Morrison continues, "black women have always considered themselves superior to white women. . . . Black women have been able to envy white women . . . they could fear them . . . and even love them (as mammies and domestic workers can); but black women have found it impossible to respect white women. I mean they never had what black men have had for white men—a feeling of awe at their accomplishments" (63). The contempt that characterizes this relationship, that stands as an obstacle to alliance in the name of feminism or racial dialogue, is itself inseparable from sexism which dictates that women, black and white, are (the) ones without respect. What, we need to ask, has the white woman accomplished, earned, built, run, organized? Sexism and racism are inextricable. But we continue to struggle with one another in the interest of constructing mutual interest or, as the Reverend Jesse Jackson states it, "common ground." I can't help reading this struggle over relationship in terms of another, contradictory comment Morrison makes here: "you don't fight what you don't respect" (63). Black and white women would not produce this explosive discourse, so much talk, so many years of it, if there weren't something in it, if we didn't want something from/in one another.

Gates's observation concerning the dangers inhabiting the trope of race applies as well to the names that black women give white women. I do not propose to deny the economic reality that black women, as a group, are at the bottom of the ladder in the United States, or the genocide and race warfare of "Apartheid U.S.A." in ethnic neighborhoods and schoolyards of Boston and Hampton Beach, the MOVE house in Philadelphia, the U.S. invasion of Grenada, or the obscene cover-ups related to the Atlanta child murders and the Guyana tragedy.[2] Nor can we, after Spillers's powerful explication, diminish the rupture, the shock waves of which are still felt, occasioned by the loss of maternity and paternity rights/rites of the African-American parent and child in bondage. Rather, we might consider, following her lead, the ways in which the "African-American women's community and Anglo-American women's community, under certain shared cultural conditions, were the twin actants on a common psychic landscape, were subject to the same fabric of dread and humiliation.

Neither could claim her body and its various productions—for quite different reasons. . . . In fact, from one point of view, we cannot unravel one female's narrative from the other's, cannot decipher one without tripping over the other" ("Mama's" 77).

In *Dessa Rose* Sherley Anne Williams creates a break in the grammar of racism. The intercalation of the discourses of slavery makes the textual work of *Dessa Rose* where the author opens a space, creates a day in the calendar of discursive history, for the African-American woman's text. Williams (un)writes the plantation novel, separating the white woman from white racism (the socioeconomics of the planter class) and the white academic and literary discourses of slavery; she (dis)places white stories of black men's and women's lives (the "authoritative" written texts by which African-American experiences have been "known"), and, in a project sharing certain features with Silko's in *Ceremony*, (re)writes the slave narrative, freeing the black woman so that she can figure her story. She converts the monolithic character of group and generic identity (black woman/white woman)—moves instructive to me as I try to unsettle the oppositional terms feminist and theorist—to individual identities (Dessa/Ruth) in order to destroy the mechanics of stereotypes, the very machinery by means of which they work. Through structural intervention, Williams creates a break, a potential for relationship beyond the historical monolithic (white) master/(black) slave dialectic of oppression. She writes (in) the gap: a romance of race, a u-topic fiction of hope and a "happy ending."

In an author's note, the novel's pre-text, Williams situates her narrative in intertextual relation to other narratives—two stories, one of an African-American woman and the other of a white woman (a track that led Williams from Angela Davis's landmark essay on black women in the slave community to Herbert Aptheker's *American Negro Slave Revolts*). Her text creates the occasion upon which these two narratives come together as difference within a text: the women "meet" (5). Another revisionist energy infuses *Dessa Rose*: Williams's outrage at William Styron's *The Confessions of Nat Turner* "that travestied the as-told-to memoir of slave revolt leader Nat Turner," a work symptomatic of how "Afro-Americans, having survived by word of mouth—and made of that process a high art—remain at the mercy of literature and writing; often, these have betrayed us" (5). More betrayals. An un(re)marked betrayal of another sort might also be considered. In *William Styron's Nat Turner: Ten Black Writers Respond* (1968), black writers published their reactions to Styron's novel. Curiously, every one of the ten writers is male, as though the term "black writer" encoded the masculine gender. We can read Williams's "Meditations on History" and *Dessa Rose* as the eleventh voice,[3] her texts as an/other response. Williams gives us a fiction which blends two "real life" stories as a new writing of race in the story of the African-American woman rather than the "travestied" story, a ridiculing, grotesque imitation of the story.

Williams also offers an/other writing of her own writing; she has been preoccupied with her character for many years, as early as Odessa in "I Sing This Song for Our Mothers" from *The Peacock Poems* (1975), who appears with the novel's cast, Nathan, Cully, Harker, Jemina, and the rudiments of her part in the story, the chain gang and the pregnant woman's escape. Williams contemplates the place of the African-American (in) history, how it writes them and is there to be written by them: "History is them; it is also theirs to make" (34). Already considering the power of naming and the life of language, she remarks in "I see my life . . ." on the need to keep the name(s) one gives one's self secret, another version of the life-preserving capacity of secrets in Quiché culture. The poem's speaker says that even if she could say the name her son gives himself in secret, she wouldn't (87).

More directly related to the novel is Williams's story, "Meditations on History," published in 1980 in *Midnight Birds,* edited by Mary Helen Washington. She dedicates the story to Angela Davis, the source of the first fiction and subject of the story, Odessa; it is Davis who first suggests that the slave woman has a story to tell. "Meditations on History," which is later rewritten in the novel as the "Prologue" and "The Darky," takes the form of a journal kept by a white male historian, reminiscent of Styron's Thomas Gray. Williams begins the exploration of nomination: the white man designates Odessa as the negress, the wench, the virago, the she-devil, the darky, the "raging nigger bitch" (211). The story also continues Williams's long meditation on the inscription of African-Americans in the work of white (male) writers. She takes her title, "Meditations on History," from the author's note with which Styron begins his novel: "Perhaps the reader will wish to draw a moral from this narrative, but it has been my own intention to try to re-create a man and his era, and to produce a work that is less an 'historical novel' in conventional terms than a meditation on history" (ix). Surely the moral Williams cares to draw differs from the one Styron, or many of her (white) feminist readers for that matter, must have envisioned, just as her "meditations on history"—spoken (of) in the plural and from an/other perspective—take a radically different form and meaning from his. Her reflection brings to mind the epigraph from Merleau-Ponty chosen by Lerone Bennett, Jr., the first black writer in the collection of responses to Styron's *Confessions:*

"History takes still more from those who have lost everything, and gives yet more to those who have taken everything. For its sweeping judgments acquit the unjust and dismiss the pleas of their victims. History never *confesses*" (3). Putting feminist literary historians on notice, Williams (re)writes this (white) discursive "give and take" economy (where some give and others take and take again) in her effort to (trans)form the grammar of racism, as a way of wresting a "confession" out of history.

In addition to the author's note, another feature marks this novel (both devices are used by Styron). It begins with a table of contents, a "telling" outline that suggests the novel's perspectival shifts and progressions: "Prologue," "The Darky," "The Wench," "The Negress," "Epilogue." Between the "Prologue" (a second pro-logue if we count the note, or a third if we begin from "Meditations") and the "Epilogue," we read more names for the "Afro-American" woman, the name Williams, as author of the note, chooses for herself. These names record a history and a present of perspectival difference called the "African-American woman," reminding us of the many names (as)signed, not chosen, providing both a thematic and a structural focus for the novel and a complex field within which feminist literary critics can observe Williams's strategic engagements.

The text's "Prologue" and "Epilogue" constitute a narrative frame, the envelope of pleasure and autonomy, the love between Kaine and Dessa, and the future in freedom of Dessa and her offspring. The opening situates us in the tradition of the romance revised in the tradition of the blues, Dessa and Kaine, her lover, a blues man and the father of the child Dessa is carrying. Dessa is neither bred nor raped by design of the white master, but the frame of personal pleasure and control is nonetheless framed once again by slavery. These characters desire to stay in the pleasure of the intimate moment—"*To be always in this moment, her body pressed to his, his warm in the bend of her arm*" (13). The need to find "*the right word*" to engage and sustain this passion between the black man and black woman, contained behind the rickety door of the slave shack, shut away in a tenuously private place from the master and slave boss, but in a domestic space only fragilely demarcated and not their own. Lucille Clifton's *Generations* recalls the powerful tension between human love and the machinery of slavery: " 'Oh slavery, slavery,' my Daddy would say. 'It ain't something in a book, Lue. Even the good parts was awful' " (22). The love story's ironic figure for the tenderness of Kaine's lips, "*firm and velvety as the tip of a cat-tail willow*" (14), (trans)forms or (re)forms itself into the slave story's cat-o-nine-tails, the whip that the slave boss uses "to note you" (37). The personal narrative of the black man and the black woman is dispersed, fractured by the socioeconomic organization of slavery and the (white) narrative of its recapitulation. A love message, but "Chilly Winds took it, / Blowed it everywhere" (14). The epilogue is the limit text, the love story that this will not be, italicized as an originary memory trace that endures for a future that wasn't, in contrast to the narrative present of loss and pain, or reflection beyond racism. As Mary Helen Washington asserts in her note to "Meditations on History," this (re)writing of the African-American/white (non)relationship is one white men still want to suppress: "I think it is significant that a number of white male editors took personal exception to Sherley Anne Williams' story 'Meditations on History,' most probably because of the unflattering portrait of white males in that story. Much of the story's meaning is conveyed—unwittingly—through the writer-interviewer, a white male historian—ultimately betrayed by his own presumptions of superiority to the slave woman" (198–99). This is only one more reminder of how certain perspectives will not be tolerated, despite what we believe we hold as our cultural ethos—the same ethos that author-izes Feminist Literary Criticism to repress or dismiss feminist post-structuralist theory, or to relegate black and lesbian writing to a barely mentioned, nondifferentiated subset.

In the trajectory of the text, Williams performs a number of functional (trans)formations with/in the structure of racism. She moves from inside the slave house to inside Dessa's house, from the plantation house to the plantation house (trans)formed, to the liberated Dessa's house. Through a strategy that blends a certain simultaneity and coextensivity, bearing certain resemblances to the one Silko employs with respect to oral and written literatures, several narratives are juxtaposed: the text (trans)forms someone else's textuality to the (re)presented orality of the slave narrative, to the text of a white woman, to an/other discursive practice through the telling and recording of Dessa's story. The African-American woman's identity changes from the undifferentiated collective or group identity in the grammar of racism, what Memmi calls "the mark of the plural" (85), to individuated identity which can (re)dedicate itself to collective well-being. The social relations change from self-interest to collective well-being, protection, and preservation, in the name of a future where the positioning which situates the slave man's remark—"*I don't want to love . . . where I can't live*" (33)—no longer holds.

"The Darky," set in Marengo County, Alabama, in 1847, begins with a brief excerpt in which Dessa, an African-American woman, suggests the tragic context of the drama about to unfold. The text contrasts Dessa's reaction to the news of her lover's death to that of the hysterical fainting spell of the mistress. She marvels "how one lil sickly white woman turn a House that big upside down" (17). The quotation begins with an ellipsis, a story in midstream, that (re)marks its marked difference immediately: ". . .Was I white' " (17). And the quotation is set apart from the heading, which designates time and place, and is abandoned shortly, as if placed there for the purpose of explication, as if there were a sense in which this inexplicable story could be explicated. Then the section commences: "The darky had sat on the floor of the root cellar, barely visible in its shadow" (17).

It is particularly shocking to encounter a white character like Adam Nehemiah speaking in the fiction of an African-American woman writer. Immediately one wonders, as earlier with Rigoberta Menchu's Spanish testimony, why Williams would want to write "from inside" a character like that, to give him part of her text. What is on her mind? We discover in his voice the provenance of the chapter's title, "The Darky." Dessa's narrative is intercalated with a third-person limited narration told from Nehemiah's perspective, and passages of his writing: "He hadn't caught every word; often he had puzzled overlong at some unfamiliar idiom or phrase, now and then losing the tale in the welter of names the darky called. Or he had sat, fascinated, forgetting to write. Yet the scene was vivid in his mind as he deciphered the darky's account from his hastily scratched notes and he reconstructed it in his journal as though he remembered it word for word" (18). He cannot comprehend the significance of black utterance—humming, moaning, Dessa's "absurd monotonous little tune in a minor key" (35), the ritualistic, historicizing grammar of the blues (Williams/Tate 208), or the politicizing codes of the spiritual he (mis)takes for "a quaint piece of doggerel" (52).

These limitations do not interfere with, indeed may even contribute to, his success among the white readers of his first book, *The Masters' Complete Guide to Dealing with Slaves and Other Dependents.* Nehemiah is at work on the next, *The Roots of Rebellion in the Slave Population and Some Means of Eradicating Them.* Williams (con)structs her response to Styron and others engaged in a white and to a degree male writing of black (women's) history, the differences within the story of history, through the juxtaposition of Dessa's and Ruth's comments and Adam Nehemiah's journal entries. She performs a fictional polyvocality that offers both identity-as-representation and the potential for negotiating relationships. Similarly, the performance of the clever Jemina, when asked to disclose the details of Dessa's escape, masks the truth by parodying the "Aunt Jemima" figure her white audience needs (and reinvents) to satisfy their expectations: "we finally pieced together, between the darky's throwing her apron over her head and howling, 'Oh, Masa, it terrible; they was terrible fierce' " (70). This mimicry, however, conceals a revolution in the letter: "Jemima" is really Jemina. In a sense, all revolutions in the letter take place in and against some "other" discourse.

Dessa Rose concerns itself with an/other writing—the story of the cleverly concealed scars on Dessa's body, marks of a deeply intimate subjugation kept hidden from the white woman, perhaps as the sign of a vulnerability and pain one only discloses, and even then at great cost, to those most respected. The white writing of slavery on the black flesh—"the horror that scarred her inner thighs, snaking around her lower abdomen and hips in ropy keloids that gleamed with patent-leather smoothness" (58)—inscribes the story Williams wishes at once to reveal, to bring out into the open for reading, and then to (dis)place by means of her character's story and her own function as storyteller. Through her narrative strategy, Williams exposes an/other story of the economics of slavery and of revolution in the community of slaves, and as such she provides a critique of exclusionary and separatist principles that is useful to feminist criticism. The fundamental principle of slavery— "buy cheap and sell dear" (27)—is synonymous with surplus value in a commodity capitalism where the commodity is chattel or "animate property": "They were bred for market, like the cows mammy milked, the chickens that she fed" (58). Human "value" is measured in dollars. Nehemiah, for example, figures insurrection in terms of economic loss: "Four free negroes and nine of the slaves—over ten thousand dollars in property!—had been hanged" (27). While a Creole man is depicted as "increasing his capital" through intercourse with slave women, the slaves use the contraceptive root to abort the products and proliferation of capital: "baby murder" (46), as the astonished Nehemiah puts it. Revolutionary acts begin with the body, the slaves' control over the (re)production of slavery through their control over reproduction itself, or a woman's decision to think through her body as well as her mind. The economy of slavery also produces a certain textual economy where the slave's body actually occasions textuality, making the white writing of history black in its hieroglyphic scars or providing a productive site of exploitation (a writing without respect), reflected in Nehemiah's exclamation, "Pray God this darky don't die before I get my book!" (32).

Through this and other means, Dessa discovers the nature of agency, how "white folks didn't need a why; they was" (56). To do and to be are synonymous, and multiply so (as) "to speak." Her revolutionary activity begins in the economy of the Same, with the interruption in the logic of slavery: "White Man Can . . . Nigga Can't" (50). When asked what the death of Kaine has to do with the slave uprising, Dessa says, "I kill white mens cause the same reason Masa kill Kaine. Cause I can" (20). Her action demonstrates the reversal she learns from Kaine's song. After he says, "Nigga can't do shit. Masa can step on a nigga hand, nigga heart, nigga life, and what can a nigga do? Nigga can't do shit" (38), he shows through an ironic application what he can do: make a song in which the inaction attributed to and forced upon the African-American applies equally well when the master's house catches on fire. Williams's interests echo mine in the first chapter but from a different perspective. By (re)fashioning meaning through art, by taking the white man at his word and acting accordingly, the system can be (trans)formed. Through the diverse and contrasting activities of her creative characters, Williams suggests what the telling of her story demands; she gives us a reading/writing lesson. Nehemiah writes an outline of "the facts of the darky's history" and hesitates: "the 'facts' sounded like some kind of fantastical fiction. Had he but the pen of a novelist—And were darkies the subject of romance, he thought sardonically, smiling at his own whimsy" (39). Williams in the name of Dessa takes over the activity her white character mockingly rejects as he positions himself between the blank (whiteness of the) page "and the darkness of her [Dessa's] face" (44). Nehemiah fails as an interpreter of African-American discourse because he refuses to learn the language of other speakers or more fundamentally even to regard them as speakers. When Dessa asks him why he writes, he says, "I write what I do in the hope of helping others to be happy in the life that has been sent them to live" (45), and she takes him literally, that is, at his word, asking if he thinks her story will make people happy, and if so, she wonders, "why I not be happy when I live it?" (50).

Dessa Rose chronicles the deconstruction of the white man's text of black womanhood and slavery. In this writing "against the grain" (22) of American literature and history, there are two scenes in which the narrating capacity of white men is devastated. They suggest ways in which one (person's) Identity or place in a structure of relationships is contingent upon another's remaining in "place." The first involves Wilson, the slave dealer against whom Dessa revolts, who is left maimed, deranged, raving, and delusional (22) by the insurrection, a pre-view of the historian's fate at the end of the novel. In the second instance, Nehemiah's position also changes suddenly and begins to break up when Dessa escapes, thereby removing herself as his object and unsettling his place as subject. Kimberly Benston comments on a similar effect, " 'Nigger,' as the white name for the blackness of blackness, is a name for difference which serves the ideological function of imbuing 'whiteness' with a 'sense' it primordially lacks" (157). When the black slave as prop to the master's identity (as white and master) refuses her or his place in this relationship, the significance of whiteness and mastery (including its contingent linguistic competence) is threatened. Similarly, when a feminist theorist insists on being both a feminist and a theorist, or a white woman insists on hearing the black woman speak to her in her own words, the possibility for structural disruption is produced in the tensions.

The African-American is the marked subject that permits the unmarked's existence; Dessa generalizes about Harker's relationship with Ruth, "All he did was make them look whiter. He wasn't nothing but a mark on them. That's what we was in white folks' eyes, nothing but marks to be used, wiped out" (171). When Hughes abandons the search for Dessa, Nehemiah records, "Hughes, in giving up the hunt, charged that I acted like one possessed. I know this was merely his excuse for failing in his own lawful duty. But the slut will not escape me. Sly bitch, smile at me, pretend—. She won't escape me" (71). True, he has been deceived, the victim of her ruse, but more effectively, her escape (re)presents the disappearance of the other that the signifying system of enslavement requires to do its work. Nehemiah is "possessed" by what he has lost control over, the other of whom he has been (dis)possessed and whose function as other he requires for the constitution of his own identity as a "masterful" speaking subject.

In "The Wench," where Dessa finds herself in a white woman's bed, having escaped Hughes and Nehemiah, Williams reverses the spatial (and racial) positioning; now Dessa rests in the light and the white woman, Ruth, regards her "from the shadows of some room" (82). Unlike Nehemiah, Ruth is not "fearful of being drawn into the shadows" (30). Dessa contemplates this dreamlike vision: "A white woman—Is that your enemies? . . . could be . . . *could be*" (83). This time the African-American regards the white person not in the bestial terms Nehemiah used to describe Dessa; rather, Dessa sees Ruth's face as a peculiar whiteness, an absence of color, "a milky glow" with a "bloody gash across it" (86)—a nothing waiting to be something. She discovers that Ruth may be crazy but is "not a killer. No, not a killer" (115). Harboring a distinct distrust of the African-American women surrounding her, and prey to the stereotypical views of the black woman, Ruth rejects Ada's story of the lecherous and abusive slave masters. In anger, she reverts to Nehemiah's words, calling

Dessa a "wench" and an "Uppity, insolent slut!" (121). But what is it that saves Ruth from recapitulating the grammar of racism as betrayal? Instead of rejecting other people's stories, Ruth establishes her difference by engaging in dialogue with critical attention and personal reflection, encouraging others to tell their stories whether she believes them or not. Somehow she is able to see one individual in an/other, to discover "Mammy" in Dessa, rather than seeing "Mammy" as the individual(ized) exception to the generalized, plural identity of the "bestial darky."

Williams creates a white woman who, despite her many limitations, (re)signs her position as mistress. She does a "crazy" thing, bringing a runaway slave and her baby into her house, and harboring other slaves, according to an obscure reasoning rather like Dessa's "cause I can." Making herself an agent (with the responsibilities that entails), she responds on a level "beyond" racism but in (re)cognition of race: "But she could do something about this, about the baby who continued to cry while she waited in the dim area back of the stairs for the darkies to bring the girl in. Something about the girl, her face— And: She—Rufel—could do something. That was as close as she came to explaining anything to herself. The baby was hungry and she fed him" (95). This radical shift, where the white woman plays nursemaid for the African-American woman and wet nurse to her infant, is more than a reversal since the former plays her part because she can, because she *chooses* to act, to interpret, and to respond to the black baby's call: "it had seemed to her as natural as tuneless crooning or baby talk" (101). Spillers's reading of relationships between characters in James Baldwin's work can be profitably considered here. Spillers discusses the more subtle opposition and oppression between black men and women, an opposition which, because it occurs on the "same" side of the racial divide, one might presume to reflect a shared belief in unity against the white oppressor:

> Outside fiction, the question is: What are the terms of relationship to be worked out between partners when the social and moral condition, given a change of slope in the landscape, conforms to other than traditional life patterns? . . . These changes [of women's status in relation to black men, or, I want to add, of black women in relation to white women] in the propositions of relationship, the soil from which they spring, lead us to perceive the "politics of intimacy" as a dialectical encounter rather than an antagonism of opposites—in other words, the situation requires *conversation*, the act of living among others, in all the dignity and concentration that the term implies. It is this tension in our

dynamic experience which shocks mythic expectations. ("Politics" 103–4)

The intimacy of nursing and sharing a bed, of (com)posing a common story, presents the site for a dialogue as (con)figuration across difference that results in a narrative of respect; although it is perhaps only a fiction, particularly the romance that can write such a "happy ending," if for no other reason than because it *can* produce it—through its occasion, the "right" words, the coherence and pleasure of an affirmative resolution.

Both Ruth and Dessa are characters with a difference. In fact, so are a number of the others—Nathan, Dorcas (Ruth's "Mammy"), and Rose (Dessa's Mammy). They are individualized, made distinctive, that is, human, by the fact of narration. Each one who is given a story is removed from the economy of the Same, distinguished and thereby differentiated. They are arguments for the value of the very (f)acts of narrating and listening (reading or "writing with"). Their stories constitute their difference and constitute them as different. The small, particular details permit readers and characters to figure (out) "common ground," the similarities in their socioeconomic and personal positioning that override the larger, cruder divisions along racial (or sexual) lines. Ruth's husband, for example, is a "scoundrel, wastrel, gambler" (109) who has deserted her and their two children, and caused Ruth's estrangement from her family. Like Dessa, Ruth has become a woman alone with a baby to nurse and no resources except her skin color and two rooms of a house. The "slaves" at the Sutton place are not slaves in the usual sense of the word. As runaways they have a different relationship to Ruth: "Neither Ada nor her daughter belonged to the white woman; none of them did" (115). These white people are so poor they don't own slaves, and Ruth shares the proceeds from the crops with the men and women who plant and harvest them. These ambiguities blurring the categories of race and economy also carry over into their social relationships: "She had never met darkies who seemed so unversed in what was due her place as these" (132). The fact is that Ruth has no "place" since she has neither the power of capital nor of sexual standing to compel obedience or "respect" or "place." Like Rigoberta Menchu in her decision to choose against herself (her traditional role and its rewards) in the interest of revolution and the preservation of "identity," Ruth has skin privilege, which, if she chooses not to exercise it, has only the "value" others assign to it. Through dialogue and (self)reflection, she begins to realize that her husband's return would mean the reinstitution of human subjugation, and despite her desire to interrupt the classical grammar of slavery, "She would have no more rights than they when Bertie came back" (150), thereby in her awareness aligning racism and sexism, or their economies. In contrast, Nehemiah forestalls change by refusing to personalize the names of the African-Americans populating Dessa's story; they are a distraction and a nuisance. Dessa tells him, "niggas just only belongs to white folks and that be's all. They don't be belonging to they mammas and daddies; not they sister, not they brother" (37).[4] The destruction of the slave family facilitates the appropriation of slaves as property and the usurpation of the African-American's name, giving rise to what Benston calls the practice of "an act of radical unnaming" for the purpose of deconstructing the "enslaving fictions" which hold blacks in bondage (151); this unnaming or (un)writing can be read back through "the semantic lineage stretching from 'nigger' to 'Colored' to 'Negro' to 'black'/'Afro-American' " (152). Working through this lineage, Williams in *Dessa Rose* transforms property into personality (Spillers, "Mama's" 78) and, as such, requires that whites divest themselves as "property owners," and that new names suggestive of (self)-possession be written.

Through her u-topic ("no place") fiction, Williams presents a paradigm for the ideal, dialogic access to knowledge of the racial other. Shoshana Felman's description of the unsettling process of teaching and learning offers a keen insight into the dynamics of alterity in relationship and suggests indirectly what is at stake for feminism and feminist literary criticism: "knowledge is what is already there, but always in the Other. Knowledge, in other words, is not a substance but a structural dynamic; it is not contained by any individual but comes about out of the mutual apprenticeship between two partially unconscious speeches that both say more than they know. Dialogue is thus the radical condition . . . through which ignorance becomes structurally informative; knowledge is essentially, irreducibly dialogic" (*Jacques Lacan* 83). In this respect, both Dessa and Ruth learn the other and herself from the other as an object of (self)reflection. The process is a difficult one that demands the letting-go of "pure identity" and objectivity by (re)signing "place," and, with it, distrust and misprision. Each teaches the other what she does not know she knows about herself and the other woman.

This critical aspect of Williams's work occurs through the (trans)-formation of how notation and nomination are produced with respect to African-American women, and to a lesser, though no less important, degree, to white women. Dessa's Mammy provides the following comment on the black woman's position in the discourse of slavery: *"Another one want to be noted, huh? Note ain't never got a nigga nothing*

145

but trouble" (78). Williams intends to undo the trouble that noting and naming have created for African-American women as objects in an institution (slavery and authorship) controlled by whites. Three of the central characters (in different ways I also count Mammy Rose, "Mammy" Dorcas, and Kaine as "central" to the narrative) have problems with their names. When Ruth calls Annabelle, a "servant" girl, "nigger," the girl retorts with the pet names "Mammy" had given Ruth, "Mistress 'Fel? Miz *Rufel?"*(99), which aggravates the older woman: " 'Miz Rufel' was a slave-given name, discarded by white people when they reached adulthood. Annabelle had put Rufel almost on the same level as herself by its use now, making Rufel appear a child, Young Missy in tantrum, rather than Mistress of the House. Shaking, Rufel screamed, 'My name is "Mistress" to you!' and fled before the silent laughter in the girl's eyes" (99–100). This scene where Ruth is "called out of her name" begins a series of nominative struggles with issues of domination and control, the means by which Ruth loses her name/Identity as Mistress (her ability to compel work, "respect," and "love") and gains her name as a respected friend—precisely the (trans)formation of the structural relation between black and white women feminism(s) desires. Dessa's and Ruth's discussion of "Mammy," as mother (biological and familial) and mother-figure (surrogate/function), provides one of the text's pivotal struggles with discourse's contra/dictory signifying capacity.

The contest (and contestation) of signification assumes particular currency since a cliché of white feminist discourse has been the description of their intimate relationships with blacks as predicated on their affection as children for the African-American women who were their family servants (an/other writing of economic bondage). In her review of *Dessa Rose,* Michele Wallace discusses the conflation of significance attached to the (no)name "Mammy," at once a slave name for mother and a slaveholder's name for "either a servant or a slave with a huge domestic responsibility": "At the center of the interaction between the white Rufel and the black Dessa lies the myth versus the reality of 'Mammy.' . . . In *Dessa Rose,* both aspects of Mammy are explored as both Rufel and Dessa make proprietary claims on her" ("Slaves" 4). Ruth's altercation with Dessa over "Mammy's" identity produces a shift in signification, leading the white woman to recall "Mammy's" real name, Dorcas, and to discover some of the dimensions of Dorcas's life outside the white family. Dessa's challenge sets off a chain of liberating questions: "Had Mammy minded when the family no longer called her name? Was that why she changed mine? . . . Was what she had always thought loving and cute only revenge, a small reprisal for all they'd taken from her? How old *had* Mammy been? Why had they gone to France? Rufel had never asked. Had she any children?" (129). Finally, Ruth has to call "Mammy" by her real name, her "tongue stumbling over the familiar name" (125), introducing a stutter in the economic and linguistic machinery. For the familiar, comforting, and comfortable "Mammy," "her treasured 'weddin gif' " (108), Dessa substitutes a stranger without a name—" 'Mammy' ain't nobody name, not they real name" (119), forcing Ruth to (re)figure the woman through her name as that once-familiar figure "subtly altered so the face seemed that of a stranger" (125). Ruth's greatest desire, a symptom we might call the "White Woman's Desire," is to believe that "Mammy had loved her not only fully, but freely as well" (138), that the unfree slave freely loves the one who demands and (mis)directs her love. In the process of figuring (out) the stories of Dorcas and Dessa, and how those stories are bound up with her own, Ruth discovers her complicity and asks the fundamentally unsettling question: "How could you love someone who used you so?" (143).

Dessa, likewise, struggles to revise her idea of the white woman who has been a necessary opposition in the founding of her own black identity. She reflects, "the white woman nursed her baby; she had seen her do it. It went against everything she had been taught to think about white women but to inspect that fact too closely was almost to deny her own existence. That the white woman had let them stay— Even that was almost too big to think about. . . . Why had they all run here? Because she let them stay. Why had she let them stay?" (117). But when Dessa discovers Ruth having intercourse with Nathan, she joins Ada and Annabelle by calling her "Miz Ruint" in spite. Ruth has come to signify the ruined white woman/Identity, not in the simple sense that Dessa means, that she makes love with a black man who by all rights should belong to a black woman, or that she is financially ruined, but in the suggestion as well (one that Dessa will later come to recognize) that she has ruined Southern White Womanhood as a force underwriting the grammar of slavery and racism. Dessa recognizes how the name fits: "Way she was living up there in them two rooms like they was a mansion, making out like we was all her slaves. For all the world like we didn't know *who* we was or how *poor* she was. . . . We all knew *some*thing wasn't right up there" (164). The "not right" like the "no place" tolls the ruination of the structured master/slave relationship. Gates comments on this logic of black discourse in Frederick Douglass's use of irony in his autobiographies, the only position, he maintains, that is available to the African-American speaker: "The relation of the speaking black subject to the self figured in these languages must by definition be an ironical relation, since that self exists only in the 'non-place of language,' and since these languages encoded figuratively the idea that blackness itself is a negative essence, an absence" (*Figures* 117). Dessa enacts her first move in the (trans)formation of language as a "non-place" to language in which she holds a place through her recognition that she can assign or refuse others their names; assigned meaning can be at least partially (re)signed or evacuated. In this preliminary gesture, she allows Ruth her uncontested feeling that, while she wasn't actually "Mammy's" child, the servant loved her as though she were a "friend." Both women learn to engage the other by speaking in a way that changes subject/object relations and (re)defines structural terms that keep the other in the position of an other, a "not me." The changes in Ruth's name signal a significatory shift from the ruined "mistress" to the white woman without the pedestal, a friend in/beyond slavery.

Appropriately, "The Negress" opens with Dessa speaking in the first person: "I never *seed* such a thing!" (163), her exclamation at the shock of discovering Nathan and Ruth in bed together, a parallel to seeing Ruth nursing her black baby. Because her story articulates the terms of the entangled relationship between them, Dessa is forced to acknowledge her debt to Ruth even though she "didn't know nothing about no good white folks" (165). Ruth's difference "is exactly that she *could* betray them, or at least make them all leave" because "she was white and it was her place" (165). Analyzing the text of her past experience, Dessa aligns all goodness with blacks and all evil with whites, lines of demarcation that she needs to keep clear from motives analogous to Menchu's desire to separate the Indian and the *ladino*. Ruth's difference, her ability to (trans)form the grammar of racism into a grammar of race, is an effect of her ability to see color as difference (without hierarchical opposition): "She did know the difference between black and white; I give her that. She wasn't that foolish. But where white peoples look at black and see something ugly, something hateful, she saw color. I knowed this, but I couldn't understand it and it scared me" (170). Nathan, who has the capacity and insists on his right to love both women, helps Dessa differentiate Ruth from the generalized white oppressor: "You know, Dess, Ruth ain't the one sold you; her husband ain't killed Kaine—" (173). Nonetheless, Dessa resists admitting Ruth to the company of those who "risked something" for her, part of the "knot" of blood kin (174–75)—a position Ruth must earn by action rather than attribution (race/class privilege). Dessa counters Harker's description of mutual trust between Ruth and the blacks with the astute assessment that Ruth trusts "in her whiteness and not our blackness" (189).

Williams's (trans)formational text works on many fronts at once. Through the mediation of French, her characters (re)figure the politics of race, the difference color makes, just as I am urging feminist literary criticism, through the intervention of the "French" Duras and post-structuralist theorists, to rewrite our founding oppositions. Harker explains that in this other tongue, " 'Negro' meant black man; 'negress' was black woman; 'blank' was white" (185), a conversion of the blank invisibility of blackness to the blank whiteness of Ruth's skin and of Nehemiah's eyes. Similarly, the blacks manipulate the economic ruses of slavery to finance their own escape, selling themselves back into slavery as a scam. The white writing, the history of slavery etched on the black body, a hidden impairment of "value" in the slave economy, is recalculated through the romance where the African-American man and woman can live a new economy of value. When Harker kisses the "R" branded on Dessa's thigh, his lips are "like fire on fire," and he says, "It ain't impaired you none at all. . . . It only increase your value" (191). Together they claim the right to a future in which the "R" (Romance? Racism?) is rewritten, "made beautiful with his lips" (223). Such structural/semantic twists and ruptures (trans)form the grammar of slavery as a discursive historic event. Recalling Gordimer's tricky hermeneutics of apartheid's "between the lines," the African-American project, according to Spillers, might be interpreted "in light of the *intervening, intruding* tale, or the tale . . . 'between the lines,' which are already inscribed, as a *metaphor* of social and cultural management" ("Mama's" 79). In this sense, Williams, through the intercalation of Dessa's and Ruth's stories, constructs an interruption, or intervention, in (as) the African-American woman's discourse about white women.

Williams's novel offers instruction in intragroup and intergroup coalition politics. She extends a tendency in black women's writing that Susan Willis has identified as the capacity to imagine "the future in the present. It sees the future born out of the context of oppression. It produces utopia out of the transformation of the most basic features of daily life, everything we tend to take for granted" (159). Working along (or between) these lines, Williams's u-topic romance (trans)-forms the domestic place and the workplace. The "common ground" is the commonplace—sex, work, domestic space—a shared bed, a collaborative plan of escape, a mutually contingent future, trust overcoming at least for a moment our fears of betrayal. (Williams sidesteps the issue of black and white women fighting for the same man by having Dessa profess her love for Harker.) Ruth's decision to act "against the grain," (in)formed by her perception of Dessa's courageous decision to escape the coffle, frees both of them from repeating the narrative of historic dependence Morrison describes: "The one great disservice black women are guilty of (albeit not by choice) is that they are the means by which white women can escape the responsibilities of womanhood and remain children all the way to the grave" (63). How precisely Sherley Anne Williams works this out is one of the significant lessons of *Dessa Rose.*

Several events in the third section signal turning points in Dessa's view of Ruth, and, as such, are instructive as feminists consider their identities and those of other women. First, Dessa realizes that she and Ruth, as women, share the same position in the sexual opposition. When the drunk Mr. Oscar tries to rape Ruth, Dessa sees that, like the black woman, the "white woman was subject to the same ravishment" (201), and the only protection each had was "ourselfs and each others" (202). Their relationship, however, is held back by Ruth's inadequate analysis of how most whites treat blacks. Ruth wants to believe that only lower-class whites are cruelly oppressive, yet Dessa knows that poor whites (Ruth, for example) don't even own slaves. Dessa situates the grammar of slavery within the nexus of power and capital, remarking that (rather like the Germans who claim ignorance and innocence of concentration camps in their backyards) "As far as white folks not knowing how bad slavery was—they was the ones made it, was the ones kept it. Master could've freed me anytime and I wouldn't've never said him nay" (212). Elizabeth Schultz summarizes her exploration of relationships between black and white women in American fiction with a description of *Tar Baby* and *Meridian* that applies equally well to Williams's process in *Dessa Rose:* "when the effects of racism and sexism can be identified and acknowledged, then forgiveness is possible, then hope is possible, for then change is possible" (82).

The multiple meanings of "place" act as switch points in the grammar of racism. As a dream that powers their activity, the fugitives invest "West" with the idea of freedom. They know little about this u-topic no-place except that it is marked off by "the river where slavery couldn't cross over cause everybody on that side was free" (171). "West" is a place in the imagination, across the bar, beyond the split (in the) subject. Ruth's decision to leave the South, as the "place" of slavery, and to join the blacks in their journey west enrages Dessa. Her distrust and resentment surface again when Ruth asks for her opinion of the idea. Dessa covers her tracks by saying that, while it was a ridiculous notion, it wasn't her "place to speak." Ruth counters with " 'Place,' she say, 'place'. . .'That's how they answer every-thing.' she say, 'Ain't my place, Missy,' mocking us, you know, 'Morning, Mammy'; 'Ain't my place.' 'Afternoon, Dessa'; 'Ain't my place.' 'Well, I ain't talking no "place," ' she was yelling now, 'no "mistress." . . . I'm talking friends' " (218). In a double gesture, Ruth abandons her place in the mistress/slave dialectic and wants to take the place of friend to Dessa as she wants Dessa to abandon her place in the discourse of slavery and to take (her) place freely beside Ruth, together beyond slavery.

In the final pages of the third section, the nominative struggle reaches its climax. Just as the fugitives prepare to leave for the West, Nehemiah succeeds in his obsessive-compulsive search to find Dessa. His deranged mental state manifests itself in his language and behav-ior, his disheveled clothing, and his unwashed, unshaven body, as he attempts to realize his vendetta to enforce slavery and prohibit Dessa's freedom. Dessa is saved by Ruth and Aunt Chole, a black woman brought in to inspect her for identifying scars, who through her in/sight, and perhaps blindness, refuses to read the black signs produced by the (white) writing on Dessa's body.

Dessa calls Nehemiah out of his name, designating him Nemi, her nemesis. Nehemiah's reading from his slavery book, which only spells out one "place" for Dessa, makes her even more afraid of him and his story. But the (un)writing of his text occurs as the unbound pages are scattered on the floor, and the sheriff concludes, "ain't nothing but some scribbling on here. . . . Can't no one read this" (232). Nehemiah's text is further erased when Ruth claims that the pages she holds are blank. The nemesis text of Dessa's "confession" by the Styron-like author is ex/posed as a work of non-sense rather than sense. Nemi without Dessa, without the other, cannot function as a speaking subject; he has no language without her to under/write his symbolization. Nehemiah's text is, therefore, illegible, unreadable at the end—because of his obsession but also because the object, Dessa, has moved to the subject position, escaping her place(ment) as object of his "Science. Research. The mind of the darky" (232). He is destroyed not so much by what he made of her but by what she makes of herself in a conspiracy of blacks and women, and by what she makes of him as she speaks as a subject of/in her own sentence/ text. The grammar of slavery breaks down.

In this moment of triumph, the women each insist on their "real" names—"My name Ruth. Ruth. I ain't your mistress," and "My name Dessa, Dessa Rose. Ain't no O to it" (232).[5] In "Hidden Name and

Complex Fate," Ralph Ellison reminds us of the importance of names and naming in African-American culture and thus the significance of this exchange: "We must learn to wear our names within all the noise and confusion of the environment in which we find ourselves; make them the center of all of our associations with the world, with man and with nature. We must charge them with all our emotions, our hopes, hates, loves, aspirations. They must become our masks and our shields and the containers of all those values and traditions which we learn and/or imagine as being the meaning of our familial past" (151). Both "slaves" and "mistress" abandon their places in the place of slavery. In another finessing move (the prerogative of romance?), Williams has Ruth go east and the others west. Dessa explains in the "Epilogue," "she went on to . . . Philly-me-York—some city didn't allow no slaves" (236). Dessa speaks her real "confession" that she misses Ruth and dignifies the white woman's choice with her respect and friendship: "Negro can't live in peace under protection of law, got to have some white person to stand protection for us. And who can you friend with, love with like that? . . . but none the equal of Ruth" (236). This is the "happy ending" of the romance of interracial relations between the African-American and the white woman, although it is not, we can be sure, the ending of the grammar of racism in the United States or within feminism or feminist literary criticism.

Clearly, Williams's novel brings the races together in a radically different way from Styron's southern white (male) repetition-compulsion tale, a white man's fantasy of a pseudo-black man's fantasy of intercourse with a white girl. It is worth asking if Bennett's observation about Styron can be applied equally well to Williams: "Styron tells us he is meditating on history. But we are not fooled. We know that he is really trying to escape history. We know—he confesses it—that he is trying to escape the judgment of history embodied in Nat Turner and his spiritual sons of the twentieth century" (4). In a sense, Williams too, with her "happy ending," presents a distortion of history (all that writing ever is or can be, or that history as text also is), but unlike Styron's text, Williams's (re)figures the lessons of the slave narratives, as the black story of history which the white story has un/written and denied in the process of writing itself. The issue, as Bennett goes on to explain, is again one of respect, or its obverse—the willful blindness this (white) writing cultivates in order to produce its insights—since Styron, who reviewed Aptheker's book on slave revolts, should know better than to represent compulsively and unquestioningly the southern white male story of slavery. He chooses to recast Turner's confession, already mediated by a white man, in order to present a (white) fiction in support of which, according to Bennett, "not one shred of evidence [exists] to indicate that Nat Turner was obsessed by the traditional obsession of the white male, [and] we can only wonder why William Styron dreams of black revolutionaries dreaming of white thighs" (12). In this sense, the outrage of enslavement is recuperated and perpetuated in *The Confessions of Nat Turner* through a writing of racism in the "place" of race: the African-American is once again, in a discursive repetition-compulsion, (re)presented as the victim of representation. Nat Turner's story is held captive by Styron's, and the revolution against both the oppressor and his discourse are (un)written.[6]

Spillers's description of the unending status of slavery suggests that the grammar of racism is inescapable. The enslaved body's possible reinscriptions are collected in the body: "The captive body, then, brings into focus a gathering of social realities as well as a metaphor for *value* so thoroughly interwoven in their literal and figurative emphases that distinctions between them are virtually useless" ("Mama's" 68). Williams's choice of the "romance" permits a very slight separation from the almost-deterministic position Spillers articulates with respect to the representation of enslaved African-Americans. We are always victimized by/in representation, even though or because it is the only way we have of speaking identity. In her discussion with Claudia Tate, Williams comments on the strategic function of writing as "a process of ordering the world. . . . a process of bringing insight, playing around with possibilities, solutions, in a way I could never play around with actual life" (Williams/Tate 211). Through the play of signification, the u-topic possibilities, the imagination of life beyond life, can be (em)bodied.

It is, therefore, of some consequence that the one thing Dessa won't forgive slavery is "the ignorance they kept us in" (208). This ignorance, primarily in/of the letter, how the letter is concealed and withheld, guarantees the repression of African-American discourse, which we could call a discourse of (an/other) race produced by a grammar where both blacks and whites hold positions of subjects (speaking) and objects (spoken of). Guarding against the tenuous position she occupies, even in the West where blacks still require white intermediaries, Dessa has her story recorded by her black grandchild, the new scribe who is required to say it back. She concludes her narration, "*I will never forget Nemi trying to read me, knowing I had put myself in his hands. Well, this the childrens have heard from our own lips. I hope they never have to pay what it cost us to own ourselfs. Mother, brother, sister, husband, friends . . . my own girlhood all I ever had was the membrance of a daddy's smile. Oh, we have paid for our children's place in the world*

153

again, and again . . ." (236). This new place for generations of African-Americans has cost dearly. In the suggestion that the price of freedom is (to be) levied and paid again and again, Williams seems to abandon her romance, in favor of a narrative suggestive of our enduring failure to write an American grammar (inclusive) of race, and, I would add, other differences. It is *Dessa Rose* as an "out of place" romance that comforts us, black and white women alike—the black woman because she reads a story of her people's bondage rewritten by a woman of courage, promoting her dream of a liberation (without quotation marks), the white woman because she can read a text in which women of strength and perseverance (re)figure opposition and alienation in the form of mutual respect and acceptance, reinforcing the dream that, even though one goes "West" and the other "North," an/other kind of coalitional feminism is possible, and reminding us that feminism would not mean much without the simultaneously encouraging and challenging voices of Barbara Smith, Simone de Beauvoir, Adrienne Rich, Audre Lorde, Alice Walker, Tillie Olsen, Sojourner Truth, Lillian Robinson, Leslie Silko, and Gloria Anzaldua. Placing the discourses of the woman and the other woman side by side gives us an (inter)textual proving ground where we can (re)formulate identities and enact relational strategies of respect and responsiveness that re(in)cite once more the play of (de)constructing identities and relationships.

CHAPTER SEVEN

Negotiating the Metalogic: (Re)Figuring Feminism in the Works of Adrienne Rich

Revolutionary demands and literary demands are one and the same.
> —Marguerite Duras, "Interview with Germaine Bree"

To write *I am a woman* is full of consequences.
> —Nicole Brossard, *L'Amèr*

But poems are like dreams: in them you put what you don't know you know.
> —Adrienne Rich, "When We Dead Awaken"

Adrienne Rich, the philosopher-poet, is one of the foremost feminist theorists of our time. Her work, spanning a period of more than thirty years, serves as both a touchstone against which we test ideas and feelings today and a beacon that casts its light into the uncertainty of tomorrow. Whether she contributes most significantly as a poet, a critic, a friend, or a citizen is not of concern here, and reflects the problem of generic conventions which entrap as much as they enable. To speak of the poet Adrienne Rich as a feminist critical theorist requires certain differentiating moves, on her part as poet and ours as readers. We could consider here only her prose works—her three books and numerous other essays—allowing us the comforting illusion of separating the critical theorist from the poet. But Rich assists us by resisting the stasis and security of such delimiting categorical boundaries. The value of her writing, in any form, is that it represents a thoughtful response to these decades of momentous change for women (especially for feminists and lesbians), American intellectuals, and literary critics. In particular, Rich's works to date explore the figuration of woman along a continuum of familiar identity positions

155

that represent horizons of future possibilities: heterosexual lover, wife, mother, daughter, daughter-in-law, lesbian lover, artist, intellectual, social activist. The splendor of her writing is the result of a kaleido-scopic positioning and repositioning as thinking, feeling, and writing subject, uncovering the breaks in the stitching, the flaws and the cracks in the apparently smooth surface of our literary and sociopolitical text. The trajectory of Rich's theorizing deserves exploration as a useful record of the development of feminist critical theory in our time—the paths we have and have not taken, how we stand, and where positions are assumed, resisted, or abandoned.

In this chapter, I want to explore an idea about Rich's movement from an uncritical heterosexuality to a lesbian feminism with a global commitment. My remarks can be taken as a demonstration of Walter Benjamin's view in "The Author as Producer" that the literary or aesthetic tendency of a work is inseparable from its political tendency, which means that the revolutionary artist presents us with both an "improved" politics and an "improved" apparatus (a "better" writing practice); and that the revolutionary dimension in art and politics— what constitutes "improvement"—involves the articulation of one's position in relation to the mode of production. We can see this conver-gence in Rich's writings through her simultaneous critique of language (the writer's means of production and point of relation to the mode of production) as both *form* (demanding a certain kind of verbal structure) and *sociopolitical ethos* (demanding a certain kind of relation between the woman writer and the world). Furthermore, her expression of this critique takes the form of a radical repositioning of the subject in relation to her audience as well as to the demands of the artist in society—a positioning which we might call a certain kind of "lesbian feminist method."

The early stages of this narrative are familiar to Rich's readers and critics. Her first book of poetry, *A Change of World* (1951), published the year she graduated from Radcliffe, marks a point of departure for her lifelong artistic and analytic quest. Despite its title, very little of the concern for social transformation which characterizes her later work is apparent in this volume of youthful, highly formalistic "school poetry." Rich, the good student and dutiful daughter, positions herself carefully in the place of the writer in a literary tradition that constructs the poet as a masculine speaker. She earns the Yale Younger Poets Prize and Auden's praise for her mastery of form and voice, for a notable "self"-restraint that obscures "Rich-as-woman" so successfully that she can present herself as the "poet" in (harmony with) tradition. Citing Yeats and Frost as progenitors, Auden places her in that tradition: "In a young poet, as T. S. Eliot has observed, the most promising sign is craftsmanship for it is evidence of a capacity for detachment from the self and its emotions without which no art is possible" (Rich/ Gelpi 126). The poet does what is needed. As Deborah Pope observes, "Making oneself small, passive, and sheltered was a way to handle the weather abroad and in the heart, but it was also the way to pass successfully as a feminine woman in Rich's time" (123). Through craft and self-positioning, the fashioning of an apparently objective, detached, and gender-neutral voice which speaks to the "fathers" (a figure for the powerful arbiters of tradition), these early poems win their place.

The story we tell of a literary career or an author's canon requires the same narrative strategies as those involved in relating a literary history. We choose to produce its continuity or discontinuity as reflections of certain interests we take. We can say, for example, that while there are rudiments of her later feminist critique in *A Change of World* and in *The Diamond Cutter and Other Poems*,[1] these works are principally those of the woman writing without feminism, the speaker who, in pretending to be neither male nor female or in filtering her experience through male personae, adopts the (discursively assigned) position typically reserved for the subject as generic masculine speaker. At issue here, however, is not the discursive position per se, a position, as I have suggested in my discussions of Gordimer and Williams, for example, in the sentence, in culture, reserved for woman to this day. *Snapshots of a Daughter-in-Law: Poems, 1954–1962* demonstrates this point more clearly as Rich begins a self-conscious examination of her socially and linguistically assigned position as woman through a process of feminist consciousness-raising designed to explore the dimensions of the female self in culture (e.g., "The Loser" and "A Marriage in the Sixties"). This volume, as indicated in the title poem, presents the poet's effort to (re)figure a sense of the "woman" in culture. Even here, Rich notes later, "I hadn't found the courage yet to do without authorities, or even to use the pronoun 'I'—the woman in the poem is always 'she' " (*On Lies*, 45). This kind of recognition leads Albert Gelpi to call the volume a "transitional book in Adrienne Rich's development. . . . Her themes—the burden of history, the separateness of individuals, the need for relationship where there is no other transcendence—begin to find their clarifying focus and center: what she is as woman and poet in late-twentieth-century America" (Rich/Gelpi 133). This is, of course, easier said (by the critic) than done (by the poet): critical narratives conceal as they reveal the seams in the story of "progress" toward the position valued.

In "The Roofwalker," for example, Rich illustrates the complexity of self-positioning by blurring the distinction between subject and object, female and male, difference and indifference, as the speaker, like others I have considered thus far, realizes:

> A life I didn't choose
> chose me: even
> my tools are the wrong ones
> for what I have to do. (63)

As for Tayo, whom society assigns the position of the "mixed blood"; for Dessa Rose, whose color brings others to impose a slave identity; or for Rosa Burger, whose family/culture encourages and discourages the adoption of a revolutionary identity, Rich's personae virtually from the outset engage the irresolvable struggle between what is chosen and what is not. In *Snapshots*, Rich enacts a strategic (re)positioning that asks us to construct the personal in a new way; that is, to read and to write woman's personal experience as the political text of a woman socially constructed in/by culture. Paraphrasing Rich's own comment, Myriam Díaz-Diocaretz in *The Transforming Power of Language* aptly describes this collection as marking a shift from "poems *about* experience to poems that *are* experience" (7). Her (re)positioning places the reader in a different relation as well. Neither language ("neither words nor music are her own" [*Snapshots*, 3]) nor history ("Time is male" [*Snapshots* 24]) can be counted upon to articulate this new relationship any more adequately than inherited positions and the relationships between them have been expressed. A measure of Rich's political radicality can be seen in the fact that her critical reception now becomes highly problematic: as Rich explains, "this book was ignored, was written off as being too bitter and personal. Yet I *knew* I had gone beyond in that book. I was very conscious of male critics, then, and it was like flunking a course. . . . But I *knew* I was stronger as a poet, I knew I was stronger in my connection with myself" (*Sourcebook* 107). Rich's resistance, her stubborn pursuit of something "beyond," encompasses at the time a consideration of the aesthetic and thematic shifts inherent in both personal and poetic (re)positioning.

In *Our Last First Poets* Cary Nelson describes the success of Rich's poetry as issuing from the (inter)play between positions—what he calls her "poetic signature" (171): "By playing historical, public themes off against her personal experience, Rich sometimes dramatically possesses the ground of their transactions" (154). Her struggle with the social construction of woman is even more pronounced in *Necessities of Life: Poems, 1962–1965,* where Rich undertakes the long process of reinterpreting women's lives, her own and others, that characterizes much of her later work. To (re)interpret is to (re)figure woman, beginning with her domestic relationships (her place in the production and re-production of culture), as wife ("Like This Together"), daughter ("After Dark"), and mother ("In the Woods"). Her consideration of women's relation to men extends back to her foremothers like Emily Dickinson in " 'I Am in Danger—Sir—'," intertexts for reading the woman poet's relationship to those who determine her interface with the public world of literary production.

The political ramifications of Rich's feminist (re)positioning in and through language become increasingly evident in *Leaflets: Poems 1965–1968* and *The Will to Change.* Just as she (re)figures woman's place, Rich redefines the poet's position in the world as requiring a "masculine . . . singlemindedness." Through her reading of Dickinson, of Bradstreet in "The Tensions of Anne Bradstreet" (1966), and of Eleanor Ross Taylor in "Woman Observing, Preserving, Conspiring, Surviving" (1972), essays later collected in *On Lies, Secrets and Silence,* Rich studies herself as poet, lending credence to Barthes's observation that "In the *exposé,* more aptly named than we tend to think, it is not knowledge which is exposed, it is the subject (who exposes him[her]self to all sorts of painful adventures)" (*Image* 194). Exploring her personal experience, the poet plumbs her feelings, preparing to uncover (ex-pose) their political dimensions. She examines the personal implications of the public world as it presents itself in the death of a revolutionary ("To Frantz Fanon"), and the artistic implications of changing position—a resistance to conformity that desires to make words change us ("Implosions" 42), noting that "Every existence speaks a language of its own" (*Leaflets* 68). The smooth lines of the poem break open, admitting uncertainty and violation, as in "Nightbreak" where the figurations of the poet's body and the bombed villages of Vietnam simultaneously coalesce as they are devastated. This vision seeks a new language (Identity) and an altered form (relationship) to mark its way through the ruptured landscape and the female body, both at odds with (in) their situations. Breaking with tradition to signal the breaks in tradition, Rich's style becomes more experimental, and, as Wendy Martin notes, "the spaces between the words [become] as significant as the words themselves" (186). The function of the poet, the woman, the feminist fuse in the imaginative and pragmatic quest to determine "how we can use what we have / to invent what we need" ("Leaflets" 56) as she tries "to drive a tradition up against the wall" ("Ghazals" ii, 62).

In *The Will to Change*, Rich deepens and particularizes her understanding of the relationship between the aesthetic, personal, and political dimensions of experience. In lines that characterize this volume in their refusal to marginalize the political, she writes: *"The moment when a feeling enters the body /* is political" ("The Blue Ghazals" 24). It grows politically and artistically necessary to determine what it means to "speak as a woman." In "Planetarium," for example, she writes, "I am an instrument in the shape / of a woman," and aligns herself with Caroline Herschel, the astronomer—"A woman in the shape of a monster / a monster in the shape of a woman" (13–14). Critical (re)vision gains a more radical function in the scene of writing: "I tear up answers / I once gave . . ." ("Letters: March 1969" 31). Like her subject, the poet persona transgresses boundaries, forbidden separations of outer and inner space, of the artistic and the political, the political and the personal in moves recalling Derrida's ironic pronouncement in "The Law of Genre": "As soon as genre [gender] announces itself, one must respect a norm, one must not cross a line of demarcation, one must not risk impurity, anomaly, or monstrosity" (203). Through these border crossings and (as) transgressions, which of course one is always risking, Derrida suggests precisely what is at stake in Rich's revolutionary texts.

"Identity" requires demarcation, the setting apart of an individual self, while relationship demands transgressions, but the arbitrary and provisional (rather than intrinsic and essential) nature of the "territories" makes such a revisionary project more problematic than we sometimes care to acknowledge. The radical and monstrous violations that Rich commits in the interest of poetry and feminism are evident in her poetic language and structure, as in "The Burning of Paper instead of Children," where sections of prose frame and interrupt passages of poetry. Except for lineation, one genre is indistinguishable from the other. Rich gives us a study of oppression and language in which the speaker observes: " 'to hear a mother say she do not have money to buy food for her children and to see a child without cloth it will make tears in your eyes' " (16). The poem itself calls attention to this passage, which it describes as

> (the fracture of order
> the repair of speech
> to overcome this suffering)(16).

Rendering a material (ortho/graphic) representation of one of her final comments, "A language is a map of our failures" (18), the poem (re)presents the tension of Rich's most frequently cited lines:

> this is the oppressor's language
> yet I need it to talk to you (*Will* 16).

She engages the irresolvable dilemma of positioning, the paradox within language and culture of the speaker in the margins who realizes how language, necessarily in/of "the center" and "tradition," both liberates and entraps, or as Barthes puts it, "language is always a matter of force, to speak is to exercise a will for power; in the realm of speech there is no innocence, no safety" (*Image* 192). The terrain grows more treacherous. Rich expresses her aim as "the relief of the body / and the reconstruction of the mind" (*Will* 14)—a subject which receives deliberate consideration in her landmark essay "When We Dead Awaken: Writing as Re-Vision" (1971). Her often-cited definition of "re-vision" still informs much of the best work in feminist criticism: "Re-vision—the act of looking back, of seeing with fresh eyes, of entering an old text from a new critical direction—is for women more than a chapter in cultural history: it is an act of survival" (*On Lies* 35).

Rich extends her consideration of categorical violation through transgressions of gender in *Diving into the Wreck* (1973), where, in "The Phenomenology of Anger," she writes:

> Every act of becoming conscious
> (it says here in this book)
> is an unnatural act (31).

Men are figured as adulterers, destroyers, murderers of babies, rapists, and women are their (unwitting) accomplices. Similarly, in the essay "Caryatid: Two Columns" (1973), Rich connects the violence in southeast Asia with sexual violence at home: "Rape has always been a part of war" (*On Lies* 114). Women make only the most tentative gestures of solidarity and support, fashioning garments, deconstructing and reconstructing their materiality as a metaphor for the fabric of women's lives. The exercise of male power creates a world no better than "scarred volcanic rock" (*Diving* 12), and woman's psyche is imaged as somehow inaccessible, a huge lock without a key (6). Women are "outside the frame of his dream" (12), looking for ways to articulate their need and their anger, to intersect with the discursive structure that writes them and the world they inhabit. To (re)write both of them demands that the poet (re)frame the "American dream."

Playing with the law of gender, Rich frequently presents herself as another kind of half-breed—the androgyne (19), the mermaid and merman of "Diving into the Wreck": "I am she: I am he" (19). This figure, commonly used to represent the artist, assumes new significance in the polarized context of sexual opposition, anger, and devastation. The androgyne suggests, on the one hand, the poet's complicity, and on the other, her difference from the tradition of masculine poets and social prescriptions for women. Rich's androgyne signifies the effects of exclusion and repression—being "outside" the frame—needed for the "dead language" to do its work:

> if they ask me my identity
> what can I say but
> I am the androgyne
> I am the living mind you fail to describe
> in your dead language
> the lost noun, the verb surviving
> only in the infinitive (19)

Through "woman" as a "lost noun" projected in the infinitive space, the "to (be)come," Rich articulates the rift between the language of things and the meaning of things in their essence, the effect of which suggests an attempt to rewrite the antithetical, the contradictory—subject/object, masculine/feminine, self/other, inside/outside (see Martin 191). But a language of the rift is a language about the woman poet's struggle with the signifying capacity of language—what, as Spillers helps us to see with respect to racism, its lexicon, syntax, and grammar both permit and refuse.

The political and artistic aim of her scorching anger is purification, to burn away the enemy's masks, words, lies

> leaving him in a new
> world; a changed
> man (29).

Again, the enemy is figured as masculine, suggesting the power of oppositional logic. At the same time, Rich represents her u-topic desire, not by means of separatism or the destruction of men but in terms of harmonious life in a lush, green world of women and men, in a state of peaceful human/ecological integration: "each with its own pattern— / a conspiracy to coexist" (*Diving* 30). Critics interested in Rich as a theorist have paid considerable attention to this poem. Farwell describes its linking of male and female principles as the formation of "an ethical situation . . . which depends not on the use or manipulation of the other but on a communal relationship of equal interaction" (195). Through an examination of "the position of the narrative voice in relation to its subject matter and its audience," Flowers explores the emergence of the androgyne figure in Rich's work up to 1974, to the point of its culmination in what she calls the "communal I," a collective (feminist) women's voice (32). But what remains unremarked is how Rich negotiates the tension between the exclusion of the masculine which the collectivity of women requires for the construction of its singular identity and the more pragmatic need for a nonetheless u-topic negotiated coexistence.

The development of Rich's feminist and lesbian/feminist aesthetic in the 1970s, beginning more clearly with *The Dream of a Common Language,* opens new possibilities for feminist criticism at the same time that it alienates some of her earlier critics and supporters who, as Díaz-Diocaretz notes, now dismiss her "for being too polemical, a feminist, or lesbian" (*Transforming* 17). Díaz-Diocaretz explains that this "need to push language relentlessly beyond the limits of patriarchy" asks us to refuse to see it as "a neutral medium. Writing and language must be the space and the instruments to shape an ideology that only begins to be reified and named" (18). Helen Vendler, displaying her own resistance to Rich's feminist work, complains about "the incrimination of all men in the encapsulation of brothers and fathers in the portrait of this rapist super-cop" in the poem "Rape." She finds Rich's reversal of the stereotype unfair, "a deliberate refusal of the modulations of intelligence in favor of an annulling and untenable propaganda, a grisly indictment, a fictitious and mechanical drama denying the simple fact of possible decency" (243).[2] In a sense Vendler's objection parallels the point I just made concerning Rich's inability or unwillingness at this time to move beyond the oppositional logic of the sex/power/knowledge nexus of language. The important difference between my observation and Vendler's complaints is that she (the "other" critic) refuses to perceive the political importance of the reversal Rich enacts. After all, what is this force of "intelligence" or reason that mediates the unreason of anger and passion? And how can the reversal of power relationships ever be "decent"? Reinscribing the dominant hierarchy of sexual politics, Vendler prefers to defend the good father, brother, and cop, reminding us that "The truth of feeling ('I felt this way, I wrote it down') has never been coterminous with the truth of art" (243). Instead of pursuing these obscure "truths," she uncritically espouses mastery, outcry mediated by analysis (247), or "the attempt at the conquering of experience which is the ground of the aesthetic" (248). What upsets Vendler is Rich's refusal to engage in a disciplining of the heart in the form(s) of tradition which offers to recuperate woman, to give the good girl her "place." In spite of her resistances, Vendler's commitment to tradition is so strong that, having jettisoned Rich's "recent prose propaganda" (249), she still represents the poet's work to this point, despite its challenges and transformations, in terms of an unbreached continuity[3]—"no betrayal of continuity in these later books"—a tradition of mastery according to which all of us have been appropriately mastered (259, 262). Vendler's judgment and her automatic defense of the fathers underscore the very purpose of Rich's feminist critique and her desire to forge an/ other discourse for/as feminist writing; this is an issue, a difference in reading and political positioning, that I will return to later in the form of a constructed debate between two of Rich's critics, Jan Montefiore and Maggie Humm.

The similarly hostile responses from nonfeminist critics and readers, Vendler included, provoked by Rich's *Of Woman Born* suggest that what is at stake is not so simply the presumed aesthetic shortcomings of polemical or didactic poetry but the intent of the underlying polemic. The volume's considerations, begun in a review essay, "The Anti-Feminist Woman" (1972), clarify Rich's views on women's "place" in patriarchal culture, what it is that she wishes to renounce. As the subtitle suggests, she attempts a tricky differentiation between *Motherhood as Experience and Institution.* Her audience is not always able or willing to engage this subtle difference, when read in the context of her strong indictment of patriarchy, which she defines as "the power of the fathers: a familial-social, ideological, political system in which men—by force, direct pressure, or through ritual, tradition, law, and language, customs, etiquette, education, and the division of labor, determine what part women shall or shall not play, and in which the female is everywhere subsumed under the male" (57). Positioned there, women's bodies and their (re)productive capacities can be read as the locus of socially constructed regulative technologies.

The distinctions between experience and institutional effects pose problems for feminist criticism because the understanding of one cannot be neatly separated from the other. In its public form, motherhood, woman's socially preeminent role, exists under the control of men and is superimposed upon "the *potential relationship* of any woman to her powers of reproduction and to children" (13). Experienced in this form, it is difficult to separate the alienating effect of woman's "place" in social institutions from the "actual fact" (experience) of woman as mother. Rich provides one of the early feminist explorations of how woman's identity is figured, that is, produced and socially represented, in Western culture. When she talks about her own transformation at twenty-five, she imagined that "new self" as male—"independent, astutely willing, original" (193). Through feminist analysis, she struggles to separate these and other desirable properties from their (en)gendered (em)bodiment in language so that one's (biological) "identity" as a woman and one's (social/discursive) potential for positive (re)presentation are no longer antithetical captives of gender opposition. Rich nonetheless resists biologistic essentialism, anti-intellectualism, and separatism—all of which she has been accused of advocating. Here and elsewhere she focuses on a particular form of social transformation which she claims for radical feminism; citing Mary Daly, Rich maintains that radical feminism "alone opens up human consciousness adequately to the desire for non-hierarchal, nonoppressive society" (80). Still caught up in an exclusionary logic, Rich confronts the challenge of constructing (as) a displacement, side-stepping the claim she wants to make for radical feminism's singular access to the social truth.

Continuing to refine her notion of a feminist poetics, Rich characterizes "the true nature of poetry" as "The drive / to connect. The dream of a common language" (*Dream* 7) so that the personal, the political, and the aesthetic share a common purpose in language. As she frees herself *"of the hunter, the trapper / the wardens of the mind—"* (*Dream* 8), she expands her image of the poet to include the mother "dumb / with loneliness" (15) in whom Rich recognizes her own trajectory of escape. Probing the limits, the "Cartographies of Silence," knowing that "Language cannot do everything—" (19), she imagines a poetics of silence, struggling at the perimeter, marking its opposite—sound, but returning always

> . . . to the concrete and everlasting world
> what in fact I keep choosing
>
> are these words, these whispers, conversations
> from which time after time the truth breaks moist and green (20).

Rich's writings which explore the force of woman's anger and alienation, culminating in *Diving into the Wreck* and *Of Woman Born*, are supplanted more and more with explicitly lesbian works concerned with issues of possibility and connectedness between women. As Díaz-Diocaretz elaborates, "Rich—speaking from her lesbian/feminist position—is no longer reacting predominantly against the world of patriarchy, but is acting towards the meaning and complexities of bonds and alliances among women, moving into the nurturing world these relationships can create. If man exists in this new type of discourse, it is only incidentally, as a distant presence, as an outsider to this woman's world, or as a transgressor, and, ironically, as a deterritorialized being" (*Transforming* 22). Through the figure of the lesbian and lesbian relationship, as Joanne Feit Diehl notes, Rich, "the woman poet," opens "the possibility of escaping the anxieties of male-dominated poetic influence" (98). This view, while comforting to the poet, critic, and social activist, is however too simple. How it is appre-hended or (re)cognized determines to a degree the kind of accounting Rich's critics give of her work.

The poet looks for sources of (re)constructive power in women like Marie Curie ("Power"), and in relationships between women in "Paula Becker to Clara Westhoff," with her own sister in "Sibling Mysteries," and with the women mountain climbers united by "*A cable of blue fire*," refusing "*to settle for less*" than the realization of their dream (6) in "Phantasia for Elvira Shatayev." Survival depends literally upon connectedness: "Until we find each other, we are alone" (14). As Caruthers points out, this "Lesbian *civitas*" of Rich's later work is "predicated upon familiarity and likeness, rather than oppositions" (304). However as a theorist Rich invokes no simple, romantic notion of woman as biological monolithic entity; the ideology of sameness or likeness receives as rigorous a critique as that of difference. In a move that Caruthers calls a rejection of "the logic of opposition and concomitant logics of dominance and submission, merging and tran-scendence" (304), Rich (re)figures relationships with men in "Natural Resources." It is as though the poet returns to set the record straight. What woman wants is "The phantom of the man-who-would-under-stand, / the lost brother, the twin—" (62), not the rapist, but "the comrade / twin": "merely a fellow-creature / with natural resources equal to our own" (62). She (re)signs other possibilities designated as "humanism" and "androgyny," words too shallow to express wom-an's difference in relationship to men, to other women, and to herself. Withholding these comfortable props, she forces the reader to engage her work as feminist, just as she enlists the reader's participation in (re)figuring women and sociopolitical relations. She (re)writes the (un)written (of) tradition and continuity, casting her lot with "the raging stoic grandmothers," the nurturers and conservators of value

> who age after age, perversely,
> with no extraordinary power,
> reconstitute the world (67).

Reconstituting the world as word, Rich wants to write an intelligent love which refuses what she sees as the heterosexist division of love and action, itself marked by an essential arbitrariness as the "natural" (unbalanced) figure for human relationship which few of her critics want to engage.

When the sphere of Rich's political involvement broadens, her analysis sharpens, as demonstrated in the poem "Hunger," dedicated to Audre Lorde. Taking "the politics of hunger" as her subject, Rich exposes the horizontal hostility articulated in the hierarchicization of suffering that patriarchal society promotes as a deterrent to the solidarity of oppressed peoples:

> The decision to feed the world
> is the real decision. No revolution
> has chosen it. For that choice requires
> that women shall be free. (13)

Perhaps the suggestion that the freedom of women as a group will tip the (in)balance of world decision in a life-preserving direction reflects a naive, partisan, even essentializing view, but the same logic (the logic of the same) also dictates that intervention in the balance of power (as a no-power/all-power in/balance) will demand a rewriting of relation, distribution, and production.

Writing at the edge, where none of our rehearsed performances can be trusted, Rich questions the familiar forms, the "oratory, formulas, choruses, laments" (75). She searches for what does not lie, like something she feels in the eyes of the lioness. Using the "oppressor's language," because she needs to talk to us, because it is her language as well, Rich harbors no illusions about the lesbian feminist's, or anyone else's, ability to escape the patriarchal province of language: "Poetry never stood a chance / of standing outside history" (*Fact* 325). As Díaz-Diocaretz observes, "we cannot deny that writing poetry that is essentially feminist in orientation means being part of the struggle for the images that will express a single consciousness, by means of the word which 'can never free itself from the dominion of the contexts of which it has been part' (Bakhtin)" (*Transforming* 50). This "new" language of the disinherited, the undisciplined cry of the heart, is not really new in human and sociopolitical terms: "in fact we were always like this, / rootless, dismembered: knowing it makes the difference" (75). What *is* new is the process of trying to articulate (an/other kind of disciplining) the cry in a form which politicizes rather than recuperates or represses the disinherited. The knowledge that makes a difference is a knowledge of difference earned, in Rich's case, through her lesbian/feminist repositioning. As "Transcendental Etude" demonstrates most brilliantly, she returns repeatedly to material things—milkweed skeins, petunia petals, the feather of a finch—and to concrete gestures—composing valued objects on the scrub board—to reorient herself, to test out what matters, as a material antidote to "the arguments and jargon" that quickly fill a room and that we mistake for signification and signs of our relatedness. The representation of the material realities of women's lives, as they are (textually) remembered, preserved, examined, and addressed, asks the writer and reader to (re)orient themselves politically.

The concerns of her collection of essays, *On Lies, Secrets, and Silence: Selected Prose 1966–1978*, overlap and reinforce those expressed in the poetry written during the same period. The introduction to the volume reveals a writer conscious of her position as a white lesbian/feminist living in the United States. The purpose of her work at this time is "to define a female consciousness which is political, aesthetic, and erotic, and which refuses to be included or contained in the culture of passivity" (18). While she continues the task of reclamation or repossession of her sources and foremothers, as in "Vesuvius at Home: The Poetry of Emily Dickinson (1975)," she sharpens her articulation of the goal of a feminist critique: to achieve "an end to male privilege and a changed relationship between the sexes" (153). This goal emerges as her response to the need for a new ethics to supplant the scandalous lies of the sociopolitical contract and the common lies we tell in speech and silence. The notion of replacing the old with a new ethics implies that there is a "truth" that can be spoken; Rich, however, resists this presumptive move, maintaining in her essay "Women and Honor: Some Notes on Lying (1975)" that "There is no 'the truth,' 'a truth'—truth is not one thing, or even a system. It is an increasing complexity" (187). Throughout these essays she passes over the doctrinaire solution, "for certainty even at the cost of honesty, for an analysis which, once given, need not be reexamined" (193). She speaks in favor of an expanded rather than a reduced complexity, a point that is exemplified in "Power and Danger: Works of a Common Woman (1977)," where Rich pursues the questions of the political poem, the politics of poetics, and the poetics of politics, through a discussion of Judy Grahn's work. Uniting two strains in her own writing—the poems of lesbian love and of politics—Rich claims "powerlessness and power" as textuality's common ground: "No true political poetry can be written with propaganda as an aim, to persuade others 'out there' of some atrocity or injustice" (251). The power of the love poem, like that of the political poem, resides in the turn it effects: how the poet creates a relationship to experience, or how the artistic and the political come together through the poet-in-the-poem (the woman as speaking subject) and her relation to the poem in tradition (the lesbian artist).

Rich's rejection of the political tendency as determinative of value, like her earlier refusal to rest securely in her aesthetic accomplishment, or artistic tendency, points toward Benjamin's more complex view of indissolubly linked features requiring that the reader, no longer "out there," discover her or his own (rewritten) means of producing the poems' meanings.

Seeking "a profound transformation of world society and of human relationships," Rich focuses ever more insistently on the (re)figuration of sociopolitical contexts. The positive construction of relationships between women reaches its fullest elaboration in *Twenty-One Love Poems*, which was first published separately in 1976, not by Norton, her usual publisher, but by a women's press—a gesture which can perhaps be read as a statement about Rich's own relation to literary production. Two years later, these poems are included in *The Dream of a Common Language: Poems 1974–1977*, a return to Norton, not in a countermanding gesture but as an insertion of the revolutionary within the space of the tradition(al). Testing feminism's radical potential and stretching the limits of discourse, Rich increases her commitment to writing lesbianism as the unspeakable, the unwritten text of women's lives, because "what has been kept unspoken, therefore *unspeakable*, in us is what is most threatening to the patriarchal order in which men control, first women, then all who can be defined and exploited as 'other' " (308). The lesbian (black and white) and the black (woman and man) as the repressed "Other" are the "beyond" of sex and race with whom heterosexual and white women respectively must form solidarity. As such, they provide the inevitable subjects (as material and, in the case primarily of the white lesbian, as speaker) of Rich's revolutionary poetry and politics.

As Rich's work becomes more explicitly radical, the issues of masculine exclusion and culpability, feminist separatism and identity, constitute a battleground for contemporary feminist critical responses. In "Notes for a Magazine: What Does Separatism Mean?" she reverses the negative judgments of exclusion to construe separation as a positive gesture of claiming "one's identity and community as an act of resistance" (86), but for Rich separatism finally is as much an escape from the engagement with difference as it is a liberating move. In a note to the "Foreword" in *Blood, Bread, and Poetry: Selected Prose 1979–1985*, she offers her most direct position statement: "At no time have I ever defined myself as, or considered myself, a lesbian separatist. I have worked with self-defined separatists and have recognized the importance of separatism as grounding and strategy. I have opposed it as a pressure to conformity and where it seemed to derive from biological determinism. The necessity for autonomous women's groups still seems obvious to me" (viii, n. 1). The essays collected in the volume reflect these views, and in fact gain their radical potential through the writer's commitment to forging larger coalitions. By writing alliances, Rich attempts to con/script others, to impose on us the task of co-authoring a new sociopolitical discourse. The most explosive of these gestures occurs in "Compulsory Heterosexuality and Lesbian Existence" (1980).

In this essay, Rich performs what I regard, after Brecht, as an *Umfunktionierung*, or a functional transformation that provides the mechanism for the startling effect of the Brechtian *gestus* in which the reader (audience) is asked to become a producer of (re)functioned sociopolitical institutions (see Benjamin 228). She accomplishes this through the unsettling move of plotting all women's lives on a "lesbian continuum," thereby stripping those sub/scribing to a socially "compulsory heterosexuality" of their unexamined position as exemplars of "*the* natural emotional and sensual inclination for women" (56). The subversive effects of this (re)writing are several. In a disturbing reversal, the lesbian is publicly, unabashedly figured as the "bottom line," the indicial feature or common thread in women's lives. Just as Rich, who eventually publishes her lesbian love poems with Norton, places lesbian texts in the place of tradition, the lesbian of the continuum is inserted, takes (a) place, in tradition. And the heterosexual woman is shaken from her position of privilege and con/scripted into the proscribed, socially reprehensible place of the lesbian as "deviant," "abhorrent," or simply "invisible" (26). Heterosexual women who want to preserve an identity of privilege and lesbian women, interested, according to the same logic, in maintaining "pure" identity "to regulate and control passages into and out of the lesbian community" (Zita in Ferguson, Zita, and Addelson 164), are (dis)placed through Rich's daring repositioning with respect to the way in which the dominant ideology constructs heterosexuality, as a sociopolitical institution.[4] In effect, we are all (textually) alienated from the conditions with/in which we live.[5]

Though frequently read as such, this essay is not about "compulsory lesbianism," for, indeed, who might compel women to adopt a "lesbian position"? How might lesbianism, in its own right, be written as a political institution? Indeed, the figure would not have such force had Rich presented it as a "heterosexual continuum" or an "androgyny scale." Through the figure of the "lesbian continuum," Rich suggests a range of experiences that any woman may have, regardless of how she identifies herself, whether or not she claims the name "lesbian."

In doing so, Rich positions us in a critical relation analogous to what Benjamin describes as "the bourgeois apparatus of production and publication [that] can assimilate astonishing quantities of revolutionary themes, indeed, can propagate them without calling its own existence, and the existence of the class that owns it, seriously into question" (229). Through the "lesbian continuum," doubtless a problematic figure, as are all figures of a problematic, Rich's revolutionary performance eludes assimilation and foregrounds critical examination as it positions women and their past experiences in relation to one another rather than, or at least in addition to, their relationships with men. Trying to move "beyond" the conventional binary oppositions, rather than simply negating them, Rich (re)figures lesbianism and heterosexuality along the continuum's subversive relational structure which connects women in their difference, asks each woman to identify the differences within herself, and relates one to another.

Earlier I made the point that Rich's work has served as an arena for conflicting feminist critical arguments. Any writer who has given us so much writing is a likely target or at least offers a ready supply of words that can be enlisted in the service of critical disputes. Two recent works exemplify the divergent approaches of the moment: Jan Montefiore's *Feminism and Poetry: Language, Experience, Identity in Women's Writing* and Maggie Humm's *Feminist Criticism: Women as Contemporary Critics*. Montefiore, making an argument against what she sees as a narrow essentialism in radical feminist poetry, claims that Rich holds to the problematic "assumption that the woman's tradition is the articulation of woman-centred experience" (60) and is distinct from masculine tradition. To further her thesis, and based only on a few convenient examples, Montefiore constructs a monolithic picture of Rich's ideas, erasing the complex contradictions that characterize her art. Discussing "Compulsory Heterosexuality and Lesbian Existence," Montefiore writes that "Adrienne Rich's claim that lesbian feminism represents a primordial female authenticity replicated in all woman-identified relationships is a piece of thoroughly monolithic essentialism" (72–73). If Rich maintained such an unequivocal view concerning the lesbian's privileged access to authenticity, Montefiore would certainly be justified in her criticism, but the critic rather carelessly sweeps Rich up in her broad net, along with a number of poets, in order to argue that subject matter rather than style or tradition differentiates lesbian poets from others. Montefiore's charges of essentialism are uncomfortably independent of evidence and persuasive argument. Instead, she asserts a reading of the Rich she wants as one who insists "on the ideal of female identity as a seamless unity," demonstrating in "naively literal terms" (138) "a Romantic literal-mindedness" (138). Maggie Humm, discussing many of the same texts, works toward very different ends. Montefiore, on the one hand, reads Rich's *Twenty-One Love Poems* as feminist only on the basis of "their subject matter and Rich's acknowledged public identity as feminist" (166);[6] Humm, on the other hand, reads them as "describing a semiotic of eroticism" which is related to Rich's "critical concept of difference as a dynamic force" (195). Humm exercises considerable caution in her approach, refusing to fault Rich for her nonalliance with the post-modernists favoring ambiguity (though post-modernism has produced an intellectual drift, I would argue, the traces of which can be read in many of Rich's texts) and denying her relation to American romantics with their detachment from social action: "Her position, as we have seen, is inseparably bound up with her feminism, where poems are politics" (196). In Humm's reading, difference abounds.

My point about Montefiore's book (which raises some worthwhile issues) is a simple one—not that there is one reading for Rich's work but rather that there is, perhaps, a certain protocol for all reading, which is that careful attention to the texts is expected of every reader. A writer like Rich whose thematic concerns alone have focused so unrelentingly on the complexities and ambiguities of human language (and) experience puts us on notice. Contra/dictions characterize her life and work; they preoccupy her still, as the title of the third section of *Your Native Land, Your Life* suggests: "Contradictions: Tracking Poems." Rich summarizes her perplexity in the essay "Split at the Root," where she (re)presents herself as "The middle-class white girl taught to trade obedience for privilege. The Jewish lesbian raised to be a heterosexual gentile. The woman who first heard oppression named and analyzed in the Black Civil Rights struggle. The woman with three sons, the feminist who hates male violence. The woman limping with a cane, the woman who has stopped bleeding are also accountable. The poet who knows that beautiful language can lie, that the oppressor's language sometimes sounds beautiful. The woman trying, as part of her resistance, to clean up her act" (*Blood* 123). These tensions are not easily reduced to a monolithic or single(simple)-minded vision, and efforts to do so tend to suggest more about our own anxieties and interests than hers.

Also deserving of mention is another related failure to read the lessons of Rich's texts. It would seem, in the abstract, that her long-standing, often-expressed desire for a nonoppressive, nonhierarchical society of negotiated coexistence could not be easily (dis)missed by "liberal" and radical readers. Yet her work is frequently dismissed in critical and academic circles, or she is represented as a poet whose work stopped with the now somewhat-less-threatening *Diving into the Wreck*. On charges of essentialism and separatism respectively, post-structuralist critics and creative writers in academic institutions have forged a curious coalition as they line up behind Vendler in their resistance to reading Rich. What these readers reject, if we can even for a moment take Rich at her word, is her u-topic desire for women and men to relate as understanding "comrade/twins" in a radically (trans)formed structure of equals—a writing some refuse to read.

To figure the "beyond" of sociopolitical organization and relationship requires a "quantum leap," "a leap of the imagination" (*Lies* 271), "beyond" the oppositions the phallogocentric analytical method uses to produce heterosexism, racial dominance, and class oppression masquerading as knowledge. By looking "beneath what is apparent for what has been simultaneously true, though unseen" (299), a method she claims for radical feminism, Rich wants to (dis)place the opposition of the One and the Other, white/black, rich/poor, of man's privilege and woman's "place," in favor of a something "otherwise" and "elsewhere." The separation from the other is a separation within the self, requiring us to undertake multiple, unending negotiations with the logic of identity. As early as "When We Dead Awaken," Rich described the transformative capacity of the imagination in terms of its power to undo conventional oppositions: "You have to be free to play around with the notion that day might be night, love might be hate; nothing can be too sacred for the imagination to turn into its opposite or to call experimentally by another name" (*Lies* 43). She is not talking about a reversal where women dominate men, blacks victimize whites, the homeless dispossess the possessed, or lesbians take over the world. Nor is she urging appropriation where the differences between black and white women are eliminated through "color-blindness," which she insists is not the opposite of racism (although perhaps it is, in terms of the constricting oppositional mechanics of racist grammar) but is instead "a form of naivete and moral stupidity" (300) through which whites solipsistically deny the particularity of black experience.[7]

The poems collected in *A Wild Patience Has Taken Me This Far: Poems 1978–1981* and *Your Native Land, Your Life* demonstrate how increasingly difficult it is to write beyond this point, that is, to manipulate language in order to negotiate the constraints of the metalogic. Perhaps no one has tried so hard for so long as Rich has. "The Images," for example, explicitly undertakes the problem of (re)figuring "woman," given the realization that "no-man's-land does not exist"

(*Wild* 4), that separatism will neither (re)form nor displace the system of opposition. Only in the private world of intimate physical love is the speaker re-membered, fulfilling her need to assemble an alternative view of herself within the context of "the war of the images" (*Wild* 5). She reconsiders the split self again in "Integrity," where, like the spider, who brings to mind the powerful, mythic spider-grandmother, she spins and weaves simultaneously. In this light, Martin notes Rich's reliance on oxymorons to yoke the oppositional terms, to make them one again, just as women and the spaces they inhabit are fused (223). Through her struggle with the word, the poet tests the limits of a singular meaning and a unicentered identity for woman and culture.

Rich writes her own account of "Culture and Anarchy," conspicuously stealing her title from Arnold and positioning herself at once in the culture of nineteenth-century women writers and in the anarchy of nature in August. She juxtaposes natural wildness with the oppressively orderly, unnatural constructions of culture (the tradition of continuity without rupture) by permitting the intertexts of feminism—Susan B. Anthony, Jane Addams, Elizabeth Barrett, Ida Husted Harper, Elizabeth Cady Stanton—to break open her text. The letters blur as THE HISTORY OF WOMAN SUFFRAGE is transmuted into THE HISTORY OF HUMAN SUFFERING. Exposing the price of order, Rich presents a litany of the omissions cultural tradition needs to construct itself. "For Julia in Nebraska" continues the accumulation of intertexts with the lesbian writer Willa Cather "whose letters were burnt in shame" (*Wild* 17), analogous to the mute historical marker whose silence lies, concealing the "broken treaties, Indian blood / women wiped out in childbirths, massacres" (17) in the "American" desire to construct a narrative celebration of the frontiersman's "heroic conquest." This history is a pictograph, "neither your script nor mine," that asks for (re)interpretation.

Rich's search for a method that will take her out of the metalogical trap is well illustrated in "What Is Possible." The speaker exposes the path she chooses over and over in her poetry as a means of questioning oppositional thinking and of displaying analytical method with a truth as "true" as planetary motion. She sidesteps the "abstract and pure" (*Wild* 24), "knowing better than the poem she reads," but also "knowing through the poem" (25). She confounds the interior and the exterior, private and public. Figuring the interior as the "beyond" of an intimacy withheld from public discourse, she positions her speaker inside a house, surrounded by the killing wind of winter. At the same time, the speaker claims she could know what is "beyond" if only the mind were ever as simple as "a swept interior" and deciphering were as clear as "a comb passing through hair beside a window" (24).

The poem creates the sense that these places and gestures have a "truthfulness" that writing or (as) analysis never does or can have, and yet such concrete manifestations of life are not really interpretable either, irresolutely stubborn as they are in the silent immanental materiality of event and the elusive significance of affect until they enter the inescapably limiting and orderly (unnatural) scene of language. In the most troublesome way, they are always already written. Such is the paradox of immanence: that properties appear to reside in the thing itself while they are effects of mind, one's subjectivity acting in and constructed by language. In "The Spirit of Place," Rich continues her struggle with the wor(l)d "as it is," as it has been (re)presented, as it might be. She unsettles identity, just as knowledge itself. There is always a part of us "out beyond ourselves / knowing knowing knowing" (45)—but what that is—the identity, the knowledge—is never fully articulated, ever returning to (in)form or motivate our struggles with language and action. She locates the text of the wor(l)d "as it is" with the repressed and victimized of history, the unspeakable and silent "Other" whose text "on a pure night" remains to be read. A perspective on the construction of knowledge, other than the view of it as a conclusive accumulation of logical and analytical detail, is at work in these poems. Instead, we are asked to engage the other woman, to look life in the face, in the eyes—to see and feel it: "look at her closely if you dare" (57), hoping somehow that the way we (re)write the wor(l)d will allow us to see her, and it to write us with a difference.

Aware of the problematic nature of her project, Rich explicitly takes up the question of framing, what is seen under what circumstances, how self-positioning entails a frame of vision. In "Frame" the speaker regards another woman's victimization as she constructs her. Rich reiterates the refrain of her own self-positioning: "*I am standing all this time / just beyond the frame, trying to see*" (46). Similarly, *Sources*, published as a chapbook in 1983 and reprinted as the first section of *Your Native Land, Your Life*, explores the question of the subject position in terms of who one is and where one stands, the conundrum, she claims, of all her poems: "There is a *whom*, a *where* / that is not chosen that is given and sometimes falsely given" (*Your* 6). In this beautiful and very personal poem, Rich attempts to (re)view as she (re)constructs her history. The reflective anger of the poem belongs to one who grieves for what is lost; in fact the volume reverberates with echoes of the lesbian poet Elizabeth Bishop, particularly her "One Art," which provides the occasion for the poem, "It's true, these last few years I've lived" (98). Rich cannot take comfort in the knowledge

175

of the common things she can name: "there is no finite knowing, no such rest" (27). She ends the poem, but not the quest, with a reflection on a line from Gordimer's *Burger's Daughter*: "When I speak of an end to suffering I don't mean anesthesia. I mean knowing the world, and my place in it, not in order to stare with bitterness or detachment, but as a powerful and womanly series of choices" (27; see note, 113). The poems seem to respond to the question "What can I see from here?" This is not a new question, as evidenced by the title poem and epigraph from the collection *The Fact of a Doorframe: Poems Selected and New 1950–1984*. The self-reflexive poem from 1974 presents poetry as support, method, and view—"violent, arcane, common, / hewn of the commonest living substance" (iv). The frame, as a structure of figuration, is both inside and outside, the condition for seeing and part of what is seen.

Rich defuses polarization, particularly the "we"/"they" opposition that marks some feminist criticism, by accepting her own position with respect to her country's history: "What if I told you home / is this continent of the homeless" (*Fact* 323), a country which suppresses diasporas, refugees, taboo languages, the "trails of tears." In "North American Time," the title poem of the middle section of *Your Native Land, Your Life*, the poet suggests that there is no escaping our position, where we stand literally and metaphorically:

> Everything we write
> will be used against us
> or against those we love. (33)

There is no hope of escaping history through language, because even if we were to move, change positions, "our words stand." The poem signals a renewed commitment to global accountability, an idea which gains importance in the essays of *Blood, Bread, and Poetry: Selected Prose, 1979–1985*. In the title essay, "Blood, Bread and Poetry: The Location of the Poet," Rich begins a line of inquiry which she extends further in "Notes toward a Politics of Location." Beginning with a need to understand how she is affected by "*location*" as a lesbian feminist poet and writer in the United States, Rich acknowledges in the later essay the ways in which her position in this country entails a particular perspectival politics. Derrida in *The Truth in Painting* describes the seductive operation of the fragily constructed frame in relation to philosophical speculation as a particular kind of narrative discourse: "But what has produced and manipulated the frame puts everything to work in order to efface the frame effect, most often by naturalizing it to infinity, in the hands of God"(73). Consequently, we might say that what bothers Rich most about location and the frame's effect are the assumptions of centrism and forgetfulness implicit as well in Derrida's critique. To understand the politics of location, she begins with her body, which determines by sex and color "the places it has taken me, the places it has not let me go" (*Blood* 216). Rich is disarmingly self-critical, of her ideas and of the process of writing: "I wrote a sentence just now and x'd it out. In it I said that women have always understood the struggle against free-floating abstraction. . . . I don't want to write that kind of sentence now, the sentence that begins, 'Women have always . . .' . . . If we have learned anything, in these years of late twentieth century feminism, it's that that 'always' blots out what we really need to know: when, where and under what conditions has the statement been true?" (214). The application of such self-scrutinizing questions produces a challenge to the construction of feminist theory today. Rich's texts do more than present lesbian/feminist polemics; in their unrelenting insistence on the inextricable relation between form and content, one person and another, they perform their (re)visionary revolutions in the letter. In this sense, she lives up to the terms of Benjamin's eloquent description of the "author as producer," the intellectual as revolutionary: "*An author who teaches writers nothing, teaches no one.* What matters, therefore, is the exemplary character of production, which is able first to induce other producers to produce, and second to put an improved apparatus as their disposal. And this apparatus is better the more consumers it is able to turn into producers—that is, readers and spectators into collaborators" (233).

Struggling with feminism's definition of theory, Rich asks if it is "something made only by white women and only by women acknowledged as writers?" (*Blood* 219). As I have suggested in previous chapters, feminist critical theory certainly acts at times as though this were true. From her position in Nicaragua, the site of the earlier essay on location, Rich recognizes the inescapable importance of her position in North America to her perspective on identity and value. She opposes the oppositions, "the climate of an enormous either/or" (221), which masquerade in a politics of absolute choice. In several (de)centering moves, Rich unsettles Feminist Identity, questioning the pronoun of individual identity, "I," as well as the comfortable "we" of collective presumption. She no longer believes "that the white eye sees from the center" (226). In her summary of what white North American feminists in the United States have been told about the "other woman," Rich poses for herself and her readers some of feminist criticism's most pressing questions as it tries to escape the tyranny of Feminism, the proper name. Citing the resistance of women in South Africa, Lebanon, and Peru, Rich questions the view of White Feminism that this other woman's ideas "are not real ideas" and "that only when a white mind formulates is the formulation to be taken seriously" (230). She concludes with a difficult challenge to the perils of abstract theorizing: "Once again: who is we?" Similarly, she ends the series of contradiction poems (if we can say that there is an end to such poems for Rich) with the caution: "O you who love clear edges / more than anything   watch the edges that blur" (*Your* 111).

The terms of a writing practice, though not the answer, are evident by now, although even those may blur before our eyes. Radhakrishnan's description of a (de)centered, nonauthoritarian practice as "an a-categorical heterogeneity that finds its 'self-expression' through the breakdown of the 'categorical' " ("Ethnic" 217) articulates an interest for feminist criticism that applies specifically to Rich's project. In "Blood, Bread, and Poetry" Rich considers what is at stake in any effort at (re)figuration. She reflects on a comment from James Baldwin: "Any real change implies the breakup of the world as one has always known it, the loss of all that gave one an identity, the end of safety" (*Blood* 176). The threat of the coalescence of the political and the aesthetic rests in the power of language to destroy as it creates: the work of any (re)writing. Although we can understand in addition why the institution of literature, like any sociopolitical body with a stake in its perpetuation and preservation, writes so unceasingly against this powerful union of the political and the artistic, we can also recognize how an institution's life issues from the vitality associated with change and the "new."

In "Virginia 1906," Rich asks of her persona, "How does she keep from dreaming the old dreams?" (*Your* 43) By reiterating this question, which she and others have written and (re)written, Rich focuses our attention on what matters most in feminist work. The answer, her reader feels certain, will not result from abstraction floating free from the material reality of women's particular relationships within culture. As Rich explains in "Notes toward a Politics of Location," "Theory— the seeing of patterns, showing the forest as well as the trees—theory can be a dew that rises from the earth and collects in the rain cloud and returns to earth over and over. But if it doesn't smell of the earth, it isn't good for the earth" (*Blood* 213–14). But I do not take this as a writing which favors experience over theory; rather, I read it as the writer's challenge to those of us, including herself, who are theorizing feminism. Through some metaphorical side step or quantum leap, feminist theory, like rain when it comes back down, must smell of the earth. Rich's global phase, a looking "beyond" what she calls "North American Tunnel Vision," (re)presents an agenda of magnitude and urgency for Rich, feminist critical theorists, and readers in the decades ahead. The revolutionary political and artistic force of Rich's work is that she tracks the contradictions and, doing so, holds us to these fundamental questions concerning one's position in relation to the world of production which the text of feminism must engage if it is to write itself. Through her resistance to the easy course, she gives us an improved apparatus—texts which suggest methods, though not answers, and an improved politics which requires our involvement as critical producers if we are ever to speak of global feminism and to write (it) in other ways.

CHAPTER EIGHT

Ex/Positions

In writing, I am always in "position"—the place in the sentence of the speaking/writing subject and in the network of texts, in the social context. I am the subject of my sentence, just as I say that the subject is feminism(s), other writers, other texts. Here I am looking for a last chance to re(as)sign my position, to speak *ex*-position(s), without a controlling interest in my subject. What could I say that might help my text go off, not along its coded pathways, its chapters, divisions, and arguments, but along some unexpected routes, metonymic by-ways, unplanned and even unwanted, but often too as gratifying as surprise? This tension inhabits and ex/tends con/clusion.

There is without question an argument and a plan here, insisting on a certain recognition. Because particular ideas, settling and unsettling, identity and (non)identity, negotiation and (non)relationship, are my interests, they warrant repetition. Again and again I circle around the desire for both an acknowledgment and an irresolution of the (ex)tensions that necessarily inhabit the positing of identity and relationship, whether we are speaking psychically, socially, politically, or intellectually. The subject must or at least wants to speak, and she does so with the full arbitrariness and inevitability of assuming a position in a structure of relations that simultaneously composes and (dis)composes herself and others.

There is no end to this process of composing and being composed, figuring and being figured, whether we look to representations in the discursive economy or in the sociopolitical context. We are always (being) represented and representing ("being"). Such an endless (re)-figuration characterizes the project of the speaker who speaks ("I"), the one spoken of ("who is 'she' "), the movement feminists are constructing ("feminism[s] is"), and the critical work in which we engage ("feminist literary criticism is").

The drama of and desire for polyvocal, polylocal feminism(s) set in motion in my first chapter finds reinforcement through the production, analysis, and disturbance that comes to us through multiple, simultaneous figures—Silko's "mixed blood," Gordimer's radical white subject, Duras's shifting other, Rich's lesbian woman, Williams's revolutionary black woman, Menchu's (non)feminist feminism. Acknowledged disturbances in the categorical field offered by such figures challenge the identity positions of the differences inhabiting and composing our subject positions and our relationships. They form the ground upon which the respect that coalitions and alliances require, if they are to exist, can and, in my view, must be negotiated, not once and for all, but repeatedly as positions shift, slide, and are figured (out) and re-figured once again.

The project of (re)figuring feminist criticism asks for negotiations with the obstacles, work in/on the borders and borderlands, as a calculation of interest against the odds—our inability to write "feminism," "race," "lesbianism," "revolution," "identity." But the greater the odds, the greater the chance of a return, producing a richness of textuality, a stunning brilliance in the particularities of struggle, tensions, and (ex)tensions. As such, then, feminist criticism asks us to say yes to writing the struggles to (trans)form, to (re)write, to escape the (meta)logic. Yes to tensions and struggle; yes to more writing.

Of necessity every text, as a trajectory of desire and/in language, explodes its borders to write other unarticulated but nonetheless (im)-pertinent relations. How could it not disperse itself in that way, as the reader, at times a subject spoken of, assumes the position of the subject who speaks? In this resides the hope as well as the fear of every writer, of every revolutionary movement: never to be "used" (up), in the interest of being (ex)tended and promoting the u-topic "out of place." The question for us, then, is always more. What is the excess of/in feminist literary criticism? Can we read it? What does it say about what we have been saying to each other? What is (un)spoken in the name of Feminist Literary Criticism?

In *The Aerial Letter*, Nicole Brossard writes, "I say that the text begins here. At the hole, this place that fulfills, overfills me, because it is my *intention*, a happy tension which makes me let go like matter in expansion (and here there is no centre, no axis, and this is in no way chaos). This is the opening (thought, the boundless activity of the body, often comes of it)" (63). Writing is (like) a passionate affair of and in in/tentions and ex/tensions. The (re)figuring of feminism(s) and feminist literary criticism is a form of love, contestatory workings out—in Barthes's sense of the figure as a juxtaposition of the gymnastic and the choreo/graphic, in which the rhetorical form figures as *schema:*

"The figure is the lover at work" (*Lover's* 4)—in the sexual/textual body of desire, what we want to be and to become. A dance. An exercise. A play. A pleasure.

By "Ex/Positions" the generative capacity is provided for, protecting future re-figurings, resisting reification and exclusion. But this is not a narrative of progress, of beginning, middle, and end—where Silko's "mixed blood" is ultimately (trans)formed into Rich's lesbian figure. Discontinuity coexists with continuity—apartheid/U.S.A.— one view depending on, inextricably joined with, the other. It is rather a matter of accumulation, the acknowledgment of abundance at work within the subject (woman, feminism[s], feminist literary criticism) and between subjects. I want no end to this text of feminism(s). Without end, a text refuses itself as a system of speculation to which post-scripts and appendices may be added. In the beginning was no conclusion; in the end no summation, no supplement, post-script, to the already-written (Derrida, *Dissemination* 27–28)—just more beginning(s), as one text gives way to another in the play of process, of (dis)placement (Kamuf, "Replacing"). So the post-script is not after writing but more writing. After no-"thing," but obviously after some-thing, some writing, pursuing its subjects of Identity and relationship with(in)/for feminism(s), feminist literary criticism, woman. Here is a text offered in the interest of the copiousness, the capaciousness and capacity, of feminist writing (Parker). I am in mind of Cixous's "More body, hence more writing" (886). So today I am writing here in a kind of for(e)play of anticipation, in the incalculable interest in and of the more to come.

Notes

1. In this light it is interesting to compare even superficially the contents of two recent anthologies of feminist criticism: *The New Feminist Criticism*, ed. Elaine Showalter, and *The (M)other Tongue*, ed. Shirley Nelson Garner, Claire Kahane, and Madelon Sprengnether. These two collections, arriving within a few weeks of one another, have in common only one author (Annette Kolodny) and the same essay by her ("A Map for Misreading: Or, Gender and the Interpretation of Literary Texts"). The Showalter anthology, despite the claim of the title, has nothing to do with "new" feminist criticism. The contention is unnecessary, since its real function, to make available old and venerable ("classic" or "canonical") feminist essays, makes it useful enough. Other comparisons might be made: the Showalter anthology contains essays written by women only; the Garner, Kahane, and Sprengnether anthology contains no essays by or about black or Hispanic women or women of color.

2. The debate on pluralism is an extended one which bears more consideration than I can give it here. For a fuller discussion, see chap. 8 of my *Crossing the Double-Cross: The Practice of Feminist Criticism*; Laurie Finke offers a good summary of the issue (256–58). Spivak's observation on the limits of pluralism warrants repeating: "Pluralism is the method employed by the *central* authorities to neutralize opposition by seeming to accept it" (Marcus, "Storming the Toolshed" 218n). I am also grateful to my colleague Stephen Karatheodoris for calling to my attention Herbert Marcuse's "Repressive Tolerance." Marcuse differentiates between "repressive tolerance," the posture of critical pluralism, and "liberating" or "discriminating" tolerance which requires "intolerance against movements from the Right" (109). This discrimination is necessary, he argues, because the sociopolitical and economic structures are such that "equality of tolerance" is not practiced.

3. For an elaboration of this general point, see Alice Jardine's chapter, "Crisis in Legitimation: Crossing the Great Voids,"in *Gynesis* 65–87.

4. In "Towards a Feminist Poetics," Showalter quips: "Feminist criticism

183

cannot go around forever in men's ill-fitting hand-me-downs, the Annie Hall of English studies" (37).

5. For elaboration of this term, see Jacques Derrida's *Dissemination*.

6. In addition to Laurie Finke's review of the *Tulsa Studies* issue, articles by Linda Alcoff (*Signs* 13 [1988]) and Mary Poovey (*Feminist Studies* 14 [Spring 1988]) provide lucid accounts of the tensions between feminist criticism and deconstruction. Judith Newton's essay "History as Usual? Feminism and the 'New Historicism' " is also of interest here.

7. For varied discussions of this question, see *Men in Feminism*.

8. Terry Eagleton, in *Against the Grain*, provides a useful explanation of iterability: "The person who uses the same privately invented sign each time an experience comes up has grasped the point that signs, to be signs at all, must be in Derrida's term 'iterable,' but not the point that it is just this iterability which fissures their self-identity--that since there is no 'pure' repetition, the question of what counts as difference or identity is a social question to be contended over within discourse and forms of life, not a problem resolvable by 'experience' " (102).

CHAPTER TWO

1. See, for example, review essays by Zagarell and Robinson in *Tulsa Studies in Women's Literature* 5 (1986): 273–303.

2. These few occasional references only begin to suggest the range and power of Smith's carefully conceived and complexly argued work.

3. In his essay, "Post-Structuralism and Oral Literature," Arnold Krupat notes concerning this same passage that it has been "the dream of Western social science and philosophy" to use language so that there can be no mistakes, achieved through a reliance "upon a 'signified-based theory of meaning.' Here, Silko attributes such a dream to a representative of a non-Western tradition. (This dream, let me say all too quickly here, may not be Silko's, for her novel shows that there may be more to efficacious storytelling than what Ku'oosh can imagine" [117–18].)

CHAPTER THREE

1. I want to express my gratitude to Abdul JanMohamed for his thoughtful response (Modern Language Association convention, Dec. 27, 1989) to a shorter version of this chapter. While our interests diverge and my views should not be (mis)taken for his, this latest version of my thoughts on Gordimer's novel has benefited from his generous comments.

2. I am indebted to Alice Parker for this and other observations concerning points made here.

3. R. Radhakrishnan wrote "Negotiating Subject Positions in an Uneven World" as a response to a shorter version of this chapter. Both of our essays appear in *Feminism and Institutions*, edited by Linda Kauffman. His

analysis of the problems raised here has helped me to rethink certain points. I am grateful to him for this and other work he has done, and to Linda Kauffman for envisioning the project that brought our texts together.

4. See Newman, *Nadine Gordimer*.

CHAPTER FOUR

1. The translations of Marini's *Territoires* are mine.

2. It is worth noting a significant refrain from the 1988 U.S. presidential campaign: "What does Jesse [Jackson] want?"

3. There is a sense too in which Duras's life can be read as a simultaneous inscription of these two interlocking terms; see Yann Andréa's *M.D.*

4. The collection, *The Purloined Poe: Lacan, Derrida, and Psychoanalytic Reading*, offers many provocative explorations of the question of the purloined letter.

CHAPTER FIVE

1. I use the terms *Indian* and *indigenous* for the moment, taking note of Rigoberta Menchu's observation that these names were attributed to groups of people by the European colonialists, and her injunction that they be used only until the actual groups being referred to choose their own terms (*We Continue Forever*, cover note).

2. The 31 January Popular Front group formed to commemorate the massacre of Quiché Indians who, in an effort to seek relief for their exploitation, had occupied the Spanish embassy in Cuidad, Guatemala.

CHAPTER SIX

1. Bell Hooks, in *Ain't I a Woman*, provides a useful starting point for her sensitive, probing treatment of the relationship between black and white women in the context of feminism.

2. See, for example, Lorde's "Grenada Revisited: An Interim Report," in *Sister Outsider* 176–90, and "Apartheid U.S.A." in *A Burst of Light* 27–38, and Walker's " 'Nobody Was Supposed to Survive': The MOVE Massacre" in *Living by the Word* 153–62.

3. There is more at stake here than simply the sex of the black respondents. The comments of Killens and Harding, for example, demand that black women writers present a response to their response. Harding claims that Styron writes his travesty-story because "we have allowed it, and we who are black must be men enough to admit that bitter fact" (32). Worse still is Killens's sexist fantasy that *The Confessions of Nat Turner* is a hoax against the American reading public that those readers "dearly loved. . . . Like a whore being brutally ravished and loving every masochistic minute of it" (34).

4. Spillers's illuminating analysis shows us the African-American slave

woman dispossessed and possessed, misread and mis/assigned: "Even though we are not even talking about *any* of the matriarchal features of social production/reproduction—matrifocality, matrilinearity, matriarchy—when we speak of the enslaved person, we perceive that the dominant culture, in a fatal misunderstanding, assigns a matriarchist value where it does not belong; actually *misnames* the power of the female regarding the enslaved community. Such naming is false because the female could not, in fact, claim her child, and false, once again, because 'motherhood' is not perceived in the prevailing social climate as a legitimate procedure of cultural inheritance" ("Mama's" 80).

5. Benston notes the importance of the combined practice of writing and unwriting among blacks freed from enslavement: "The *unnaming* of the immediate past ('Hatcher's John,' etc.) was reinforced by the insertion of a mysterious initial, a symbol of the long-acknowledged, nascent selfhood that had survived and transcended slavery. On the other hand, the association with tropes of American heroism ('Lincoln,' 'Sherman,' etc.) was also an act of *naming*, a staging of self in relation to a specific context of revolutionary affirmation" (153).

Throughout the novel, various characters, Ruth and Nehemiah in particular, have referred to Dessa as Odessa. Anthony Appiah, commenting on Sunday O. Anozie's name, makes an interesting observation concerning the fugitive "O." Appiah remarks that in the name Sunday O. Anozie, the Sunday Christian and the Ibo family names come together. Appiah writes that perhaps "the 'O' which mediates between the names is a zero, an absence, a nothing— the nothing, in fact, which joins Africa and Europe together" (127). In the case of (O)Dessa Rose, we might wonder if the "O" stands for something rather than nothing, an excess of slavery, which the subject sheds in the production of an identity beyond slavery, what Radhakrishnan calls a "pre-post-erous" identity ("Ethnic" 220).

Sharon Devaney-Lovinguth's unpublished paper on naming in *Dessa Rose* has also been helpful to my analysis.

6. See Radhakrishnan's careful elaboration of ethnic positionality in "Ethnic Identity and Post-Structuralist Différance."

CHAPTER SEVEN

1. See Deborah Pope's discussion (116–30).

2. Frances Justina Strong, in an unpublished essay, traces the relationship between Rich and Vendler as the latter in 1973 recounts the course from affection in 1951—"someone my age was writing down my life . . . a twin: I had not known till then how much I had wanted a contemporary and a woman as a speaking voice of life" (237)—to disaffection upon the publication of *Diving into the Wreck* (1973) where the danger is no longer contained, rebellion no longer capitulates or loses to tradition, and the "poems which played with fire" also burned (238).

Notes

3. See Robert Miklitsch's excellent assessment of Vendler's criticism and her insistence on "history-as-continuity" over "history-as-discontinuity" (32).

4. Humm, in her discussion of the essay, makes the useful observation that Rich fails to direct our attention to the ways in which lesbian relations may also be distorted by power differentials (193).

5. Rich's essay has elicited diverse reactions from the feminist community, although no one has undertaken an examination of this interchange; see Ann Ferguson, Jacquelyn N. Zita, and Kathryn Pyne Addelson, "On 'Compulsory Heterosexuality and Lesbian Existence': Defining the Issues," and the exchange of letters between Rich and Ann Snitow, Christine Stansell, and Sharon Thompson in Rich, *Blood, Bread, and Poetry* 68–75.

6. See also Myriam Díaz-Diocaretz's discussion in *Translating Poetic Discourse* 49–51, passim.

7. Celia Kitzinger presents a parallel argument concerning the depoliticization of lesbianism through the appropriation of difference in the social scientific discourse of life-style choice, sameness, and personal "empowerment."

Bibliography

Alcoff, Linda. "Cultural Feminism versus Post-Structuralism: The Identity Crisis in Feminist Theory." *Signs* 13 (1988): 419–36.

Allen, Paula Gunn. *The Sacred Hoop: Recovering the Feminine in American Indian Tradition*. Boston: Beacon Press, 1986.

———. "This Wilderness in My Blood: Spiritual Foundations of the Poetry of Five American Indian Women." In *Coyote Was Here: Essays on Contemporary Native American Literary and Political Mobilization*. Edited by Bo Scholer. Aarhus, Denmark: SEKLOS, 1984: 95–115.

Andréa, Yann. *M.D.* Paris: Les Editions de Minuit, 1983.

Anzaldua, Gloria. *Borderlands: La Frontera: The New Mestiza*. San Francisco: Spinsters, 1987.

Appiah, Anthony. "Strictures on Structures: The Prospects for a Structuralist Poetics of African Fiction." In *Black Literature and Literary Theory*. Edited by Henry Louis Gates, Jr. New York: Methuen, 1984: 127–50.

Aptheker, Herbert. *American Negro Slave Revolts*. 1948; New York: International Pubs., 1970.

Auden, W. H. "Foreword" to *A Change of World: Adrienne Rich's Poetry*. Edited by Barbara Charlesworth Gelpi and Albert Gelpi. New York: W. W. Norton, 1975: 125–27.

Auerbach, Nina. "Why Communities of Women Aren't Enough." *Tulsa Studies in Women's Literature* 3 (1984): 153–57.

Barthes, Roland. *A Lover's Discourse: Fragments*. Trans. Richard Howard. New York: Hill and Wang, 1978.

———. *Image-Music-Text*. Trans. Stephen Heath. New York: Hill and Wang, 1977.

Baudrillard, Jean. *For a Critique of the Political Economy of the Sign*. Trans. Charles Levin. St. Louis: Telos Press, 1981.

———. *The Mirror of Production*. Trans. Mark Poster. St. Louis: Telos Press, 1975.

Baym, Nina. "The Madwoman and Her Languages: Why I Don't Do Feminist Literary Theory." *Tulsa Studies in Women's Literature* 3 (1984): 45–60.

Bibliography

Benjamin, Walter. "The Author as Producer." In *Reflections: Essays, Aphorisms, Autobiographical Writings*. Edited by Peter Demetz. Trans. Edmund Jephcott. New York: Harcourt, Brace, Jovanovich, 1978: 220–38.

Bennett, Lerone, Jr. "Nat's Last White Man." In *William Styron's Nat Turner: Ten Black Writers Respond*. Edited by John Henrik Clarke. Boston: Beacon Press, 1968: 3–16.

Benstock, Shari. "Beyond the Reaches of Feminist Criticism: A Letter from Paris." *Tulsa Studies in Women's Literature* 3 (1984): 5–27.

Benston, Kimberly W. "I Yam What I Am: The Topos of Un(naming) in Afro-American Literature." In *Black Literature and Literary Theory*. Edited by Henry Louis Gates, Jr. New York: Methuen, 1984: 151–72.

Bhabha, Homi K. "Difference, Discrimination and the Discourse of Colonialism." In *The Politics of Theory*. Edited by Francis Barker et al. Colchester: Univ. of Essex Press, 1983: 194–211.

Bishop, Elizabeth. "One Art." In *Geography III*. New York: Farrar, Straus and Giroux, 1976: 40–41.

Boyers, Robert. "Public and Private: On *Burger's Daughter*." *Salmagundi* 62 (Winter 1984): 62–93.

Breytenbach, Breyten. *The True Confessions of an Albino Terrorist*. London: Faber and Faber, 1984.

Brossard, Nicole. *The Aerial Letter*. Toronto: Women's Press, 1988.

———. *L'Amèr ou Le chapitre effrité*. Montreal: l'Hexagone, 1977.

Carby, Hazel. *Reconstructing Womanhood: The Emergence of the Afro-American Woman Novelist*. New York: Oxford Univ. Press, 1987.

Caruthers, Mary J. "The Re-Vision of the Muse: Adrienne Rich, Audre Lorde, Judy Grahn, Olga Broumas." *Hudson Review* 36 (1983): 293–322.

Certeau, Michel de. *Heterologies: Discourse on the Other*. Trans. Brian Massumi. Minneapolis: Univ. of Minnesota Press, 1985.

Chungara, Domitila Barrios de, with Moema Viezzer. *Let Me Speak! Testimony of Domitila, a Woman of the Bolivian Mines*. New York: Monthly Review Press, 1978.

Cixous, Hélène. "The Laugh of the Medusa." Trans. Keith Cohen and Paula Cohen. *Signs* 1 (1976): 875–93.

Clifton, Lucille. *Generations: A Memoir*. New York: Random House, 1976.

Clingman, Stephen. *The Novels of Nadine Gordimer: History from the Inside*. London: Allen & Unwin, 1986.

Conjuring: Black Women, Fiction, and Literary Tradition. Edited by Marjorie Pryse and Hortense J. Spillers. Bloomington: Indiana Univ. Press, 1985.

Cooke, John. *The Novels of Nadine Gordimer: Private Lives/Public Landscapes*. Baton Rouge: Louisiana State Univ. Press, 1985.

Davenport, Doris. "The Pathology of Racism: A Conversation with Third World Women." In *This Bridge Called My Back: Writings by Radical Women of Color*. Edited by Cherrie Moraga and Gloria Anzaldua. Watertown, Mass.: Persephone Press, 1981: 85–90.

Davis, Angela Y. "The Black Woman's Role in the Community of Slaves." *Black Scholar* 3 (1971): 2–15.

Deleuze, Gilles, and Michel Foucault. "Intellectuals and Power." In *Language, Counter-Memory, Practice: Selected Essays and Interviews*. Edited by Donald F. Bouchard. Trans. Donald F. Bouchard and Sherry Simon. Ithaca: Cornell Univ. Press, 1977: 205–17.

Deleuze, Gilles, and Felix Guattari. *Kafka: Toward a Minor Literature*. Trans. Dana Polan. Minneapolis: Univ. of Minnesota Press, 1986.

Derrida, Jacques. "But, beyond . . . (Open Letter to Anne McClintock and Rob Nixon)." *Critical Inquiry* 13 (1986): 155–70.

———. *Dissemination*. Trans. Barbara Johnson. Chicago: Univ. of Chicago Press, 1981.

———. "The Law of Genre." *Glyph 7*. Baltimore: The Johns Hopkins Univ. Press, 1980: 202–29.

———. *The Post Card: From Socrates to Freud and Beyond*. Trans. Alan Bass. Chicago: Univ. of Chicago Press, 1987.

———. "Racism's Last Word." *Critical Inquiry* 12 (1985): 290–99.

———. *Spurs/Eperons*. Trans. Barbara Harlow. Chicago: Univ. of Chicago Press, 1979.

———. *The Truth in Painting*. Trans. Geoff Bennington and Ian McLeod. Chicago: Univ. of Chicago Press, 1987.

———. "Women in the Beehive: A Seminar with Jacques Derrida." In *Men in Feminism*. Edited by Alice Jardine and Paul Smith. New York: Methuen, 1987: 189–203.

———. *Writing and Difference*. Trans. Alan Bass. Chicago: Univ. of Chicago Press, 1978.

Derrida, Jacques, James Creech, Peggy Kamuf, and Jane Todd. "Deconstruction in America: An Interview with Jacques Derrida." *Critical Exchange* 17 (1985): 1–33.

Derrida, Jacques, and Christie V. McDonald. "Choreographics." *Diacritics* 12 (1982): 66–76.

Devaney-Lovinguth, Sharon. Unpublished paper on *Dessa Rose*. Presented at South Atlantic Modern Language Association convention, November 1988.

Díaz-Diocaretz, Myriam. *The Transforming Power of Language: The Poetry of Adrienne Rich*. Utrecht: Hes Publishers, 1984.

———. *Translating Poetic Discourse: Questions on Feminist Strategies in Adrienne Rich*. Philadelphia: John Benjamins Pub. Co., 1985.

Diehl, Joanne Feit. " 'Cartographies of Silence': Rich's *Common Language* and the Woman Poet." In *Reading Adrienne Rich: Reviews and Re-Vision, 1951–81*. Edited by Jane Roberta Cooper. Ann Arbor: Univ. of Michigan Press, 1984: 91–110.

Duras, Marguerite. *The Lover*. Trans. Barbara Bray. 1984; New York: Pantheon, 1985.

———. *The Ravishing of Lol Stein*. Trans. Richard Seaver. 1964; New York: Pantheon, 1966.

———. *The Sea Wall*. Trans. Herma Briffault. 1950; New York: Farrar, Straus and Giroux, 1985.

Bibliography

———. *The Vice-Consul.* Trans. Eileen Ellenbogen. New York: Pantheon, 1968.

Duyfhuizen, Bernard. "Review Essay: Deconstruction and Feminist Literary Theory." *Tulsa Studies in Women's Literature* 3 (1984): 159–67.

Eagleton, Terry. *Against the Grain: Essays 1975–1985.* London: Verso, 1986.

———. *Literary Theory: An Introduction.* Minneapolis: Univ. of Minnesota Press, 1985.

Ellison, Ralph. *Shadow and Act.* New York: New American Library, 1966.

Erlande-Brandenburg, Alain. *The Lady and the Unicorn/La Dame a la Licorne.* Paris: Editions de la Réunion des Musées Nationaux, 1979.

Evans, Martha Noel. *Masks of Tradition: Women and the Politics of Writing in Twentieth-Century France.* Ithaca: Cornell Univ. Press, 1987.

Farwell, Marilyn R. "Adrienne Rich and an Organic Feminist Criticism." *College English* 39 (1977): 191–203.

Felman, Shoshana. *Jacques Lacan and the Adventure of Insight: Psychoanalysis in Contemporary Culture.* Cambridge: Harvard Univ. Press, 1987.

———. "Women and Madness: The Critical Phallacy." *Diacritics* 5 (1975): 2–10.

Feminism and Institutions: Dialogues on Feminist Theory. Edited by Linda Kauffman. London: Basil Blackwell, 1989.

Feminist Criticism and Social Change: Sex, Class, and Race in Literature and Culture. Edited by Judith Newton and Deborah Rosenfelt. New York: Methuen Press, 1985.

Feminist Issues in Literary Scholarship. Edited by Shari Benstock. Bloomington: Indiana Univ. Press, 1987.

Feminist Studies/Critical Studies. Edited by Teresa de Lauretis. Bloomington: Indiana Univ. Press, 1986.

Ferguson, Anne, Jacquelyn N. Zita, and Kathryn Pyne Addelson. "On 'Compulsory Heterosexuality and Lesbian Existence': Defining the Issues." In *Feminist Theory: A Critique of Ideology.* Edited by Nannerl O. Keohane, Michele Z. Rosaldo, and Barbara C. Gelpi. Chicago: Univ. of Chicago Press, 1982: 147–88.

Finke, Laurie. "The Rhetoric of Marginality: Why I Do Feminist Theory." *Tulsa Studies in Women's Literature* 5 (1986): 251–72.

Firestone, Shulamith. *The Dialectic of Sex: A Case for Feminist Revolution.* New York: Bantam, 1970.

Flowers, Betty S. "The 'I' in Adrienne Rich: Individuation and the Androgyne Archetype." In *Theory and Practice of Feminist Literary Criticism.* Edited by Gabriela Mora and Karen S. Van Hooft. Ypsilanti, Mich.: Bilingual Press, 1982: 14–35.

Foucault, Michel. *The Archaeology of Knowledge and the Discourse on Language.* Trans. A. M. Sheridan Smith. New York: Harper Colophon, 1972.

———. *The History of Sexuality.* Volume 1: *An Introduction.* Trans. Robert Hurley. New York: Random House, 1980.

———. *Power/Knowledge: Selected Interviews and Other Writings, 1972–1977.* Trans. Colin Gordon et al. Edited by Colin Gordon. New York: Pantheon, 1980.

Foucault, Michel, and Gilles Deleuze, "Intellectuals and Power." In *Language, Counter-Memory, Practice*. Edited by Donald F. Bouchard. Ithaca: Cornell Univ. Press, 1977: 205–17.

Gallop, Jane. "Critical Response--Writing and Sexual Difference: The Difference Within." In *Writing and Sexual Difference*. Edited by Elizabeth Abel. Chicago: Univ. of Chicago Press, 1982: 283–90.

———. *The Daughter's Seduction: Feminism and Psychoanalysis*. Ithaca: Cornell Univ. Press, 1982.

———. *Thinking through the Body*. New York: Columbia Univ. Press, 1988.

Gates, Henry Louis, Jr. *Figures in Black: Words, Signs, and the "Racial" Self*. New York: Oxford Univ. Press, 1987.

———. "Writing 'Race' and the Difference It Makes." *Critical Inquiry* 12 (1985): 1–20.

Genette, Gérard. *Figures of Literary Discourse*. Trans. Alan Sheridan. Intro. Marie-Rose Logan. New York: Columbia Univ. Press, 1982.

Giddings, Paula. *When and Where I Enter: The Impact of Black Women on Race and Sex in America*. New York: Bantam, 1984.

Gordimer, Nadine. "Art and the State in South Africa." *The Nation* 237, 21 (Dec. 24, 1983): 657–61.

———. *Burger's Daughter*. New York: Viking Press, 1979.

———. "The Clash." (With Diana Cooper-Clark.) *London Magazine*, n.s. 22, 11 (Feb. 1983): 45–59.

———. "A Conversation with Nadine Gordimer." (With Robert Boyers, Clark Blaise, Terence Diggory, and Jordan Elgrably.) *Salmagundi* 62 (1984): 3–31.

———. "The Essential Gesture: Writers and Responsibility." *Granta* 15 (1985): 45–59.

———. *A Guest of Honour*. New York: Viking Press, 1970.

———. "Interview with Nadine Gordimer." (With Stephen Gray.) *Contemporary Literature* 22 (1981): 263–71.

———. *The Late Bourgeois World*. 1966; Middlesex: Penguin, 1986.

———. "Letter from South Africa." *New York Review of Books*, Dec. 9, 1976: 3–10.

———. *A Sport of Nature*. New York: Knopf, 1987.

———. "A Story for This Place and Time: An Interview with Nadine Gordimer about *Burger's Daughter*." (With Susan Gardner.) *Kunapipi* 3 (1981): 99–112.

———. *What Happened to Burger's Daughter or How South African Censorship Works*. Emmarentia, S.A.: Taurus, 1980.

———. "Where Do Whites Fit In?" *Twentieth Century* 65 (1959): 326–31.

———. *A World of Strangers*. 1958; New York: Penguin, 1984.

Guatemala in Rebellion: Unfinished History. Edited by Jonathan L. Fried, Marvin E. Gettleman, Deborah T. Levenson, and Nancy Peckenham. New York: Grove Press, 1983.

Guillaumin, Colette. "Women and Theories about Society: The Effects on Theory of the Anger of the Oppressed." *Feminist Issues* 4 (1984): 23–39.

Harding, Vincent. "You've Taken My Nat and Gone." In *William Styron's Nat*

Bibliography

Turner: Ten Black Writers Respond. Edited by John Henrik Clarke. Boston: Beacon Press, 1968: 23–33.

Homans, Margaret. *Women Writers and Poetic Identity: Dorothy Wordsworth, Emily Brontë, and Emily Dickinson.* Princeton: Princeton Univ. Press, 1980.

Hooks, Bell. *Ain't I a Woman: Black Women and Feminism.* Boston: South End Press, 1981.

Humm, Maggie. *Feminist Criticism: Women as Contemporary Critics.* New York: St. Martin's Press, 1986.

Hurwitt, Jannika. "The Art of Fiction LXXVII: Nadine Gordimer." *Paris Review* 78 (1983): 83–127.

Hyde, Lewis. *The Gift: Imagination and the Erotic Life of Property.* New York: Vintage, 1979.

Jaggar, Alison M. *Feminist Politics and Human Nature.* Sussex: Rowman & Allenheld, 1983.

JanMohamed, Abdul R. *Manichean Aesthetics: The Politics of Literature in Colonial Africa.* Amherst: Univ. of Massachusetts Press, 1983.

Jardine, Alice A. *Gynesis: Configurations of Woman and Modernity.* Ithaca: Cornell Univ. Press, 1985.

Johnson, Barbara. *A World of Difference.* Baltimore: The Johns Hopkins Univ. Press, 1987.

Juana and Lucia. "Indian Women in the Revolution Speak." In *Guatemala in Rebellion: Unfinished History.* Edited by Jonathan L. Fried, Marvin E. Gettleman, Deborah T. Levenson, and Nancy Peckenham. New York: Grove Press, 1983: 284–387.

Kafka, Franz. "Before the Law." In *The Penal Colony: Stories and Short Pieces.* New York: Schocken Books, 1961: 148–50.

Kamuf, Peggy. "Femmeninism." In *Men in Feminism.* Edited by Alice Jardine and Paul Smith. New York: Methuen, 1987: 78–84.

———. "Replacing Feminist Criticism." *Diacritics* 12 (1982): 42–47.

———. *Signature Pieces: On the Institution of Authorship.* Ithaca: Cornell Univ. Press, 1988.

Kaplan, Caren. "Deterritorializations: The Rewriting of Home and Exile in Western Feminist Discourse." *Cultural Critique* 6 (1987): 187–98.

Kauffman, Linda S. *Discourses of Desire: Gender, Genre, and Epistolary Fictions.* Ithaca: Cornell Univ. Press, 1986.

Killens, John Oliver. "The Confessions of Willie Styron." In *William Styron's Nat Turner: Ten Black Writers Respond.* Edited by John Henrik Clarke. Boston: Beacon Press, 1968: 34–44.

Kitzinger, Celia. *The Social Construction of Lesbianism.* London: SAGE Publications, 1987.

Kolodny, Annette. "The Integrity of Memory: Creating a New Literary History of the United States." *American Literature* 57 (1985): 291–307.

———. "Respectability Is Eroding the Revolutionary Potential of Feminist Criticism." *Chronicle of Higher Education,* May 4, 1988: A52.

Krupat, Arnold. "Criticism and the Canon: Cross-Relations." *Diacritics* 17 (1987): 3–20.

————. "Post-Structuralism and Oral Literature." In *Recovering the Word: Essays on Native American Literature*. Edited by Brian Swann and Arnold Krupat. Berkeley: Univ. of California Press, 1987: 113–48.

Kuzwayo, Ellen. "Foreword." In *Women in South Africa: From the Heart—An Anthology of Stories Written by a New Generation of Writers*. Johannesburg: Seriti sa Sechara, 1988: 1–4.

Lacan, Jacques. *Four Fundamental Concepts of Psycho-Analysis*. Edited by Jacques-Alain Miller. Trans. Alan Sheridan. New York: W. W. Norton, 1981.

————. "Guiding Remarks for a Congress on Feminine Sexuality." In *Feminine Sexuality: Jacques Lacan and the école freudienne [FS]*. Edited by Juliet Mitchell and Jacqueline Rose. Trans. Jacqueline Rose. New York: W. W. Norton, 1985.

————. *Ecrits: A Selection [E]*. Trans. Alan Sheridan. New York: W. W. Norton, 1977.

Larson, Charles R. *American Indian Fiction*. Albuquerque: Univ. of New Mexico Press, 1978.

Lazarus, Neil. "Modernism and Modernity: T. W. Adorno and Contemporary White South African Literature." *Cultural Critique* 5 (1986–87): 131–55.

Lincoln, Kenneth. *Native American Renaissance*. Berkeley: Univ. of California Press, 1983.

Lorde, Audre. "Apartheid U.S.A." In *Burst of Light*. Ithaca: Firebrand Books, 1988: 27–38.

————. "Sadomasochism: Not about Condemnation." (With Susan Leigh Star.) In *Burst of Light*. Ithaca: Firebrand Books, 1988: 11–18.

————. *Sister Outsider: Essays and Speeches*. Trumansburg, N.Y.: Crossing Press, 1984.

Making a Difference: Feminist Literary Criticism. Edited by Gayle Greene and Coppélia Kahn. London: Methuen, 1985.

Mandela, Winnie. *Part of My Soul Went with Him*. Edited by Anne Benjamin. New York: W. W. Norton & Co., 1984.

Marcus, Jane. "Still Practice, A/Wrested Alphabet: Toward a Feminist Aesthetic." *Tulsa Studies in Women's Literature* 3 (1984): 79–97.

————. "Storming the Toolshed." In *Feminist Theory: A Critique of Ideology*. Edited by Nannerl O. Keohane, Michelle Z. Rosaldo, and Barbara C. Gelpi. Chicago: Univ. of Chicago Press, 1982: 217–35.

Marcuse, Herbert. "Repressive Tolerance." In Robert Paul Wolff, Barrington Moore, Jr., and Herbert Marcuse, *A Critique of Repressive Tolerance*. Boston: Beacon Press, 1968: 81–123.

Marini, Marcelle. "Feminism and Literary Criticism: Reflections on the Disciplinary Approach." Trans. Carol Barko. In *Women in Culture and Politics: A Century of Change*. Edited by Judith Friedlander, Blanche Wiesen Cook, Alice Kessler-Harris, and Carroll Smith-Rosenberg. Bloomington: Indiana Univ. Press, 1986: 144–63.

————. *Territoires du féminin avec Marguerite Duras*. Paris: Les Editions de Minuit, 1977.

Bibliography

Martin, Wendy. *American Triptych: Anne Bradstreet, Emily Dickinson, Adrienne Rich.* Chapel Hill: Univ. of North Carolina Press, 1984.

Means, Russell. "The Same Old Song." In *Marxism and Native Americans.* Edited by Ward Churchill. Boston: South End Press, n.d.: 19–33.

Meese, Elizabeth A. *Crossing the Double-Cross: The Practice of Feminist Criticism.* Chapel Hill: Univ. of North Carolina Press, 1986.

Memmi, Albert. *The Colonizer and the Colonized.* Boston: Beacon Press, 1967.

Men in Feminism. Edited by Alice Jardine and Paul Smith. New York: Methuen, 1987.

Menchu, Rigoberta. *Me llamo Rigoberta Menchú y así me nació la conciencia.* Madrid: Siglo Veintiuno Editores, 1985.

———. *I . . . Rigoberta Menchu: An Indian Woman in Guatemala.* Edited by Elisabeth Burgos-Debray. Trans. Ann Wright. London: Verso, 1984.

Menchu, Rigoberta, and Jim Stephens. "Women Are Raising Their Voices." In *We Continue Forever: Sorrow and Strength of Guatemalan Women.* New York: Women's International Resource Exchange, 1983: 50–52.

Miklitsch, Robert. "The Poppies of Practical Criticism: 'Rabbi, Read the Phases of This Difference.' " *Diacritics* 17 (1987): 23–35.

Miller, J. Hillis. "Georges Poulet's 'Criticism of Identification.' " In *The Quest for Imagination.* Edited by O. B. Hardison, Jr. Cleveland: Case Western Univ. Press, 1971: 191–224.

Mohanty, Chandra Talpade. "Under Western Eyes: Feminist Scholarship and Colonial Discourses." *boundary 2* 13 (1984): 333–58.

Mohanty, Chandra Talpade, and Biddy Martin. "Feminist Politics: What's Home Got to Do with It?" In *Feminist Studies/Critical Studies.* Edited by Teresa de Lauretis. Bloomington: Indiana Univ. Press, 1986: 191–212.

Montefiore, Jan. *Feminism and Poetry: Language, Experience, Identity in Women's Writing.* London: Pandora, 1987.

Morrison, Toni. *Tar Baby.* New York: Knopf, 1981.

———. "What the Black Woman Thinks about Women's Lib." *New York Times Magazine,* Aug. 22, 1971: 15+.

The (M)other Tongue: Essays in Feminist Psychoanalytic Interpretation. Edited by Shirley Nelson Garner, Claire Kahane, and Madelon Sprengnether. Ithaca: Cornell Univ. Press, 1985.

Murphy, Carol J. *Alienation and Absence in the Novels of Marguerite Duras.* Lexington, Ky.: French Forum, 1982.

Nelson, Cary. *Our Last First Poets: Vision and History in Contemporary American Poetry.* Urbana: Univ. of Illinois Press, 1981.

The New Feminist Criticism: Essays on Women, Literature, and Theory. Edited by Elaine Showalter. New York: Pantheon, 1985.

Newman, Judie. *Nadine Gordimer.* London: Routledge, 1988.

Newton, Judith. "History as Usual? Feminism and the 'New Historicism.' " *Cultural Critique* 9 (1988): 87–121.

Niatum, Duane. "History in the Colors of Song: A Few Words on Contemporary Native American Poetry." In *Coyote Was Here: Essays on Contemporary*

Native American Literary and Political Mobilization. Edited by Bo Scholer. Aarhus, Denmark: SEKLOS, 1984: 24–34.

Nietzsche, Friedrich. "Truth and Falsity in an Ultramoral Sense." In *The Philosophy of Nietzsche.* Edited by Geoffrey Clive. New York: New American Library, 1965: 503–15.

Norton Anthology of Literature by Women: A Tradition in English. Edited by Sandra M. Gilbert and Susan Gubar. New York: W. W. Norton and Co., 1985.

Organization of the People in Arms. "Eight Years of Silent Organizing." In *Guatemala in Rebellion: Unfinished History.* Edited by Jonathan L. Fried, Marvin E. Gettleman, Deborah T. Levenson, and Nancy Peckenham. New York: Grove Press, 1983: 269–72.

Poovey, Mary. "Feminism and Deconstruction." *Feminist Studies* 14 (1988): 51–65.

Pope, Deborah. *A Separate Vision: Isolation in Contemporary Women's Poetry.* Baton Rouge: Louisiana State Univ. Press, 1984.

Popul Vuh: The Definitive Edition of the Mayan Book of the Dawn of Life and the Glories of Gods and Kings. Trans. Dennis Tedlock. New York: Simon and Schuster, 1985.

The Purloined Poe: Lacan, Derrida, and Psychoanalytic Reading. Edited by John P. Muller and William J. Richardson. Baltimore: The Johns Hopkins Univ. Press, 1988.

Radhakrishnan, R. "Ethnic Identity and Post-Structuralist Différance." *Cultural Critique* 6 (1987): 199–220.

———. "Negotiating Subject Positions in an Uneven World." In *Feminism and Institutions: Dialogues on Feminist Theory.* Edited by Linda Kauffman. London: Basil Blackwell, 1989: 276–90.

———. "The Post-Modern Event and the End of Logocentrism." *boundary 2* 12 (Fall 1983): 33–60.

Randall, Margaret. *Risking a Somersault in the Air: Conversations with Nicaraguan Writers.* San Francisco: Solidarity Publications, 1984.

———. *Sandino's Daughters: Testimonies of Nicaraguan Women in Struggle.* Edited by Lynda Yanz. Toronto: New Star Books, 1981.

Reagon, Bernice Johnson. "Coalition Politics: Turning the Century." In *Home Girls: A Black Feminist Anthology.* Edited by Barbara Smith. New York: Kitchen Table Women of Color Press, 1983: 356–68.

Rich, Adrienne. "Adrienne Rich and Robin Morgan Talk about Poetry and Women's Culture." In *New Women's Survival Sourcebook.* Edited by Kirsten Grimstad and Susan Rennie. New York: Alfred A. Knopf, 1975: 106–11.

———. "The Anti-Feminist Woman (1972)." In *Adrienne Rich's Poetry.* Edited by Barbara Charlesworth Gelpi and Albert Gelpi. New York: W. W. Norton, 1975: 99–105.

———. *Blood, Bread, and Poetry: Selected Prose, 1979–1985.* New York: W. W. Norton, 1986.

———. *A Change of World.* New Haven: Yale Univ. Press, 1951.

———. *The Diamond Cutters and Other Poems.* New York: Harper, 1955.

Bibliography

————. *Diving into the Wreck: Poems, 1971–1972*. New York: Norton, 1973.

————. *The Dream of a Common Language: Poems, 1974–1977*. New York: W. W. Norton, 1978.

————. *The Fact of a Doorframe: Poems Selected and New, 1950–1984*. New York: W. W. Norton, 1984.

————. *Leaflets: Poems, 1965–1968*. New York: W. W. Norton, 1969.

————. *Necessities of Life: Poems, 1962–1965*. New York: W. W. Norton, 1966.

————. "Notes for a Magazine: What Does Separatism Mean?" *Sinister Wisdom* 18 (1981): 83–91.

————. *Of Woman Born*. New York: W. W. Norton, 1976.

————. *On Lies, Secrets, and Silence: Selected Prose 1966–1978*. New York: W. W. Norton, 1979.

————. *Snapshots of a Daughter-in-Law: Poems, 1954–1962*. New York: Harper & Row, 1963.

————. *Sources*. Woodside, Calif.: Heyeck Press, 1983.

————. *Twenty-One Love Poems*. Emeryville, Calif.: Effie's Press, 1976.

————. *A Wild Patience Has Taken Me This Far: Poems, 1978–1981*. New York: W. W. Norton, 1981.

————. *The Will to Change*. New York: W. W. Norton, 1971.

————. *Your Native Land, Your Life: Poems*. New York: W. W. Norton and Co., 1986.

Roberts, Sheila. "Nadine Gordimer's 'Family of Women.' " *Theoria* 60 (1983): 45–57.

Robinson, Lillian S. "Feminist Criticism: How Do We Know When We've Won?" *Tulsa Studies in Women's Literature* 3 (1984): 143–52.

————. "Is There Class in This Text?" *Tulsa Studies in Women's Literature* 5 (1986): 289–302.

————. "Treason Our Text: Feminist Challenges to the Literary Canon." *Tulsa Studies in Women's Literature* 2 (1983): 83–98.

Rose, Jacqueline. *Sexuality in the Field of Vision*. London: Verso, 1986.

Rose, Wendy, and Carol Hunter. "An Interview with Wendy Rose." In *Coyote Was Here: Essays on Contemporary Native American Literary and Political Mobilization*. Edited by Bo Scholer. Aarhus, Denmark: SEKLOS, 1984: 40–56.

Rubenstein, Roberta. *Boundaries of the Self: Gender, Culture, Fiction*. Urbana: Univ. of Illinois Press, 1987.

Ryan, Michael. *Marxism and Deconstruction: A Critical Articulation*. Baltimore: The Johns Hopkins Univ. Press, 1982.

Said, Edward. "Opponents, Audiences, Constituencies, and Community." *Critical Inquiry* 9 (1982): 1–26.

Schultz, Elizabeth. "Out of the Woods and into the World: A Study of Interracial Friendships between Women in American Novels." In *Conjuring: Black Women, Fiction, and Literary Tradition*. Edited by Marjorie Pryse and Hortense J. Spillers. Bloomington: Indiana Univ. Press, 1985: 67–85.

Seem, Mark D. "Interview: Felix Guattari." *Diacritics* 4 (1974): 38–41.

Selous, Trista. *The Other Woman: Feminism and Femininity in the Work of Marguerite Duras*. New Haven: Yale Univ. Press, 1988.

Sherzer, Dina. *Representation in Contemporary French Fiction.* Lincoln: Univ. of Nebraska Press, 1986.

Showalter, Elaine. "Critical Cross-Dressing: Male Feminists and the Woman of the Year." *Raritan* 3 (Fall 1983): 130–49.

———. "Feminist Criticism in the Wilderness." *Critical Inquiry* 8 (1981): 179–205.

———. "Towards a Feminist Poetics." In *Women Writing and Writing about Women.* Edited by Mary Jacobus. London: Croom Helm with Oxford University Women's Studies Committee, 1979: 22–41.

———. "Women's Time, Women's Space: Writing the History of Feminist Criticism." *Tulsa Studies in Women's Literature* 3 (1984): 29–44.

Silko, Leslie Marmon. *Ceremony.* New York: Viking Press, 1977.

Simon, Jean-Marie. *Guatemala: Eternal Spring, Eternal Tyranny.* New York: W. W. Norton and Co., 1987.

Smith, Barbara. "Introduction" to *Home Girls: A Black Feminist Anthology.* Edited by Barbara Smith. New York: Kitchen Table Women of Color Press, 1983: xix-lvi.

———. "Notes for Yet Another Paper on Black Feminism, Or Will the Real Enemy Please Stand Up?" *Conditions: Five* (1979): 123–32.

Smith, Barbara Herrnstein. "Contingencies of Value." *Critical Inquiry* 10 (1983): 1–35.

———. *Contingencies of Value: Alternative Perspectives for Critical Theory.* Cambridge: Harvard Univ. Press, 1988.

Smith, Patricia Clark, and Paula Gunn Allen. "Earthly Relations, Carnal Knowledge: Southwestern American Indian Women Writers and Landscape." In *The Desert Is No Lady: Southwestern Landscapes in Women's Writing and Art.* Edited by Vera Norwood and Janice Monk. New Haven: Yale Univ. Press, 1987: 174–96.

Solomon, Barbara Probst. "Indochina Mon Amour." *New Republic,* Sept. 9, 1985: 26+.

Sommer, Doris. " 'Not Just a Personal Story': Women's Testimonies and the Plural Self." In *Life/Lines: Theorizing Women's Autobiography.* Edited by Bella Brodzki and Celeste Schenck. Ithaca: Cornell Univ. Press, 1988: 107–30.

Spillers, Hortense J. "Mama's Baby, Papa's Maybe: An American Grammar Book." *Diacritics* 17 (1987): 65–81.

———. "The Politics of Intimacy: A Discussion." In *Sturdy Black Bridges: Visions of Black Women in Literature.* Edited by Roseann P. Bell, Bettye J. Parker, and Beverly Guy-Sheftall. Garden City, N.Y.: Anchor/Doubleday, 1979: 87–106.

———. "Review Essay: 'Turning the Century': Notes on Women and Difference." *Tulsa Studies in Women's Literature* 3 (1984): 178–85.

Spivak, Gayatri C. "Asked to Speak as an 'Indian Feminist.' " Unpublished ms.

———. "Displacement and the Discourse of Women." In *Displacement: Derrida and After.* Edited by Mark Krupnic. Bloomington: Indiana Univ. Press, 1983: 169–95.

———. "French Feminism in an International Frame." In *Other Worlds: Essays in Cultural Politics.* New York: Methuen, 1987: 134–53.

———. *In Other Worlds: Essays in Cultural Politics [IOW].* New York: Methuen, 1987.

Strong, Frances Justina. Unpublished paper on Adrienne Rich and Helen Vendler. Presented at the Southeastern Women's Studies Association convention, February 1989.

Styron, William. *The Confessions of Nat Turner.* New York: Bantam, 1967.

Suleiman, Susan Rubin. "Nadja, Dora, Lol V. Stein: Women, Madness and Narrative." In *Discourse in Psychoanalysis and Literature.* Edited by Shlomith Rimmer-Kenan. London: Methuen, 1987: 124–51.

Todd, Janet. *Feminist Literary History.* New York: Routledge, 1988.

Todorov, Tzvetan. *The Conquest of America: The Question of the Other.* Trans. Richard Howard. New York: Harper & Row, 1984.

Tournier, Michel. "Faces of Marguerite Duras." Trans. Barbara Wright. *Vanity Fair,* July 1985: 64–67.

Valenzuela, Luisa. *Other Weapons.* Trans. Deborah Bonner. Hanover, N.H.: Ediciones del Norte, 1985.

Velie, Alan R. *Four American Indian Literary Masters: N. Scott Momaday, James Welch, Leslie Marmon Silko, and Gerald Vizenor.* Norman: Univ. of Oklahoma Press, 1982.

Vendler, Helen. *Part of Nature, Part of Us.* Cambridge: Harvard Univ. Press, 1980.

Wade-Gayles, Gloria. *No Crystal Stair: Visions of Race and Sex in Black Women's Fiction.* New York: Pilgrim Press, 1984.

Walker, Alice. *Living by the Word: Selected Writings, 1973–1987.* New York: Harcourt Brace Jovanovich, 1988.

———. *Meridian.* New York: Harcourt Brace Jovanovich, 1976.

Wallace, Michele. *Black Macho and the Myth of the Super Woman.* New York: Warner Books, 1980.

———. "Slaves of History." [Review of *Dessa Rose* and *Ar'n't I a Woman: Female Slaves in the Plantation South* by Deborah Gray White.] *Women's Review of Books* 4 (Oct. 1986): 1+.

Walters, Anna Lee. "American Indian Thought and Identity in American Fiction." In *Coyote Was Here: Essays on Contemporary Native American Literary and Political Mobilization.* Edited by Bo Scholer. Aarhus, Denmark: SEKLOS, 1984: 35–39.

Washington, Mary Helen, ed. and intro. *Midnight Birds: Stories of Contemporary Black Women Writers.* Garden City, N.Y.: Anchor/Doubleday, 1980.

Wicomb, Zoe. *You Can't Get Lost in Cape Town.* New York: Pantheon, 1987.

William Styron's Nat Turner: Ten Black Writers Respond. Edited by John Henrik Clarke. Boston: Beacon Press, 1968.

Williams, Sherley Anne. *Dessa Rose.* New York: William Morrow and Co., 1986.

———. "Meditations on History." In *Midnight Birds: Stories of Contemporary Black Women Writers.* Edited by Mary Helen Washington. Garden City, N.Y.: Anchor/Doubleday, 1980: 200–248.

———. *The Peacock Poems.* Middletown, Conn.: Wesleyan Univ. Press, 1975.

———. "Sherley Anne Williams." In *Black Women Writers at Work.* Edited by Claudia Tate. New York: Continuum, 1983: 205–13.

Willis, Sharon. *Marguerite Duras: Writing on the Body.* Urbana: Univ. of Illinois Press, 1987.

Willis, Susan. *Specifying: Black Women Writing the American Experience.* Madison: Univ. of Wisconsin Press, 1987.

WIRE. "In Guatemala the Poor Get Poorer." In *We Continue Forever: Sorrow and Strength of Guatemalan Women.* New York: Women's International Resource Exchange, 1983: 35.

Woolf, Virginia. *A Room of One's Own.* New York: Harcourt, Brace and World, 1929.

———. *Three Guineas.* New York: Harcourt, Brace and World, 1938.

Zagarell, Sandra A. "Conceptualizing Women's Literary History." *Tulsa Studies in Women's Literature* 5 (1986): 273–88.

Index

Index

Index

A NOTE ON THE AUTHOR

Elizabeth A. Meese is professor of English at the University of Alabama. She has a doctorate in English from Wayne State University. She has recently edited *The Difference Within: Feminism and Critical Theory* with Alice Parker, and her essays have appeared in *boundary 2, Frontiers, American Literature,* and *New Orleans Review.* She is also the author of *Crossing the Double-Cross: The Practice of Feminist Criticism.*